A JOURNEY WITH GHOSTS

Adventures in the supernatural heart of Britain and beyond

Nick Brazil

The Book Guild Ltd
Sussex, England

The Book Guild Ltd.
25 High Street,
Lewes, Sussex

First published 1999
Second printing 1999
© Nick Brazil, 1999

Set in Times
Typesetting by
SetSystems Ltd, Saffron Walden, Essex

Printed in Great Britain by
Antony Rowe Ltd, Chippenham, Wiltshire

A catalogue record for this book is
available from the British Library

ISBN 1 85776 317 3

Many people helped to make this book possible, not least all those brave and trusting souls who were kind enough to open up their hearts to me and recount their experiences. However, I am also deeply indebted to two people above all others whose support and enthusiasm ensured that I carried this task through to the very end. In fact, it is no exaggeration to say that without them, the book would never have been completed. So, without further ado I would like to dedicate this book to . . .

SYLVIA JAMES AND HILARY WILDING

I would like also like to thank Peter Underwood, Life President of The Ghost Club Society, Duncan Lucas (Greater Wigston Historical Society), Eleanor O'Keefe of The Incorporated Society for Psychical Research, Morris Garratt, my sister Priscilla Rosenberg, my aunt Erica MacDonald-Greene, Rita Spencer and my dear friend and companion Hilary Wilding, for all their invaluable expertise, time and encouragement.

CONTENTS

INTRODUCTION

The Question of Ghosts

'**Ghost** n. *The disembodied spirit of a dead person sup-posed to haunt the living as a pale or shadowy vision.*'
Collins English Dictionary

Very few people on this planet go through their lives without some form of unexplained experience or another. For many, it will be a single, fleeting glimpse of the unknown lasting a few seconds and leaving them wondering if they dreamed or imagined what they saw. For others, the experience will be more prolonged and the images more vivid. Many will be frightened by their experiences and many others will not talk about them, either through fear of ridicule or, more often, of what the telling might unleash. In fact, some of the more fascinating stories I have encountered whilst researching and writing this book remain untold for that very reason.

However, it is important to ask exactly what these people have experienced when encountering the unknown. Because an incident seems to have no rational explanation should not automatically mean that it is supernatural. For example, a family may live in a house where small, everyday items such as scissors, eggcups and plates disappear for no apparent reason. This in itself would certainly not constitute definitive evidence of a paranormal presence. Such disappearances are more likely be caused by an absent-minded family member than a poltergeist.

On the other hand, if these disappearances coincide with other strange occurrences such as sudden and extreme temper-ature swings or unexplained noises, then the chance that the particular house has a paranormal presence is consequently greater. Even so, the supposed ghost is more likely to be nothing more than an erratic boiler causing the sudden temperature changes and the floorboards to creak as they expand and retract. There are certainly precedents for such 'ghosts'. But if these incidents are also accompanied by sightings of strange figures, then we are beginning to be in an entirely different ball game. It is, I suppose, all a matter of degree.

So, does this mean that we should discount all paranormal incidents with a sceptical shrug of the shoulders? By no means. What we should do is approach the subject with a totally open mind unclouded by prejudice either for or against the existence of ghosts. Perhaps a good starting point is to ask if ghosts actually exist at all, and if they do, what are they? Behind these two seemingly straightforward questions lie centuries of controversy often clouded by charlatanism and wishful thinking.

Belief in ghosts has existed for as long as human beings. Ancient Egyptian pictures of ghosts appearing to humans have been found and there are documented stories of poltergeist hauntings in seventh-century Germany. *The Anglo-Saxon Chronicles*, written by monks, in the tenth and eleventh centuries makes frequent references to spectres, whilst many famous and celebrated people including George V, Queen Wilhelmina of Holland and John Wesley's father all claim to have seen or experienced ghosts. Those who believe in the supernatural would probably cite this as historical proof that ghosts are and always have been a part of our daily lives.

On the other hand, the sceptics would argue that anecdotal evidence certainly does not amount to proof positive of existence. They would also say that because someone is a member of royalty or a prominent clergyman does not make them any less prone to mistakenly believing they had seen a ghost than anybody else. So, George V's sighting of a spectral sailing ship in the South Atlantic in 1881 is no less likely to have been some trick of the weather because he was the future King of England than if he had been an ordinary rating. Ghosts, the unbelievers say, are all in the mind, a land of which we currently know only ten per cent. If the brain can will us to recover from terminal illnesses, then it can also conjure up phantoms.

I had two experiences that provide good examples of how powerful the mind can be in this respect. The first happened to me when I was staying in a very strange Balkan hotel whose only guests seemed to be aid workers and secret policemen. The intimidating presence of the latter gentlemen made for a very uneasy atmosphere and I went to bed fully clothed in case I had to leave in a hurry. Just as I was drifting off to sleep, I was awakened by a creature that I took to be a rat burrowing into my bedclothes. I remember actually seeing the rounded shape of its back as it ran down my stomach. I leapt out of my bed and searched it thoroughly but to no avail. So had I been haunted by a spectral rodent? No, real and frightening as this experience had been, I am sure that it was the product of my highly charged mental state rather than a ghost.

The second experience was no less real and also occurred at a time when I was half in and out of sleep. Suddenly, I became aware of a close and much loved relative standing next to my bed. She was looking into the distance and smiling sweetly. Seconds later, the figure moved rapidly backwards and disappeared to the sound of rushing wind. Although I knew this person would never hurt me, I felt my heart beating faster out of fear. After a minute or so calming down, I turned over and began drifting back into sleep. Then I awoke again to see two Victorian ballet dancers, one of whom I knew was my late grandmother in her youth. They were twirling around on the opposite side of the bed. Once again the vision only lasted seconds. Had this been a warning of imminent death with my grandmother coming to fetch her relative? The next day I was determined to find out and phoned to check up on the first relation. I was very relieved to discover that, although frail, she was in good health and spirits.

Some people might ask why I could be so certain that these two experiences were only ghosts of my mind; surely they could also be genuine paranormal events mistaken for dreams. My answer is that although there is a one per cent chance this is so, the weight of evidence points elsewhere. Firstly, on both occasions I was on the brink of sleep. Secondly, the two experiences both occurred when a great deal was happening in my personal life, putting my mind well into overdrive. Thirdly, I am prone to extremely vivid and surrealistic dreams, which is what I believe these two experiences were. On the other hand, the strange incidents that occurred to myself and my family related in 'The Ghost Next Door' (Chapter 3) were certainly not dreams or figments of our imaginations. The point I am making is that when dealing with the unexplained we have to be very careful to sift out those events that occur only in our minds. This is often not at all easy, as the next little incident shows.

It happened one morning when I was walking out of my flat to go to work. Framed in the picture window of a neighbouring house, I saw what I took to be the figure of a mediaeval nun standing there. Although I could not see her face, her white and black habit showed clearly against the darkness of the room. Curious, I walked forward to investigate the vision and discovered that my ghost nun was nothing more than a white anglepoise lamp standing on the window shelf. A slight rewriting of this scenario shows how easily my eyes and brain could have tricked me into thinking that I had actually seen a ghost. Suppose that before I took those few steps of discovery I had been distracted by a neighbour wishing me good morning. Let us also suppose that in the short time I was looking away, the occupant of the room 'haunted' by the nun decided to remove the lamp to place it elsewhere. When I turned back, the nun would have mysteriously vanished leaving me thinking that I had actually seen my first ghost. Indeed, most serious psychic researchers believe that 98 per cent of all paranormal experiences have a natural explanation similar to mine. However, I certainly do think that all the experiences related in this book are genuine and not vivid dreams or optical illusions. Nevertheless, my own three experiences show how wary you have to be when investigating the paranormal.

If the serious psychic investigator's task is not difficult enough already, he or she also has to contend with deliberate frauds. For example, in recent years, Harry Price's celebrated investigation into hauntings at Borley Rectory has been brought very much into question. In their book *The End of Borley Rectory*, Eric Dingwall, Kathleen Goldney and Trevor Hall accused Price of fraud: 'When analysed, the evidence for haunting and poltergeist activity for each and every period appears to diminish in force and finally to vanish away.'

Ultimately, only those directly involved know the truth behind the long series of paranormal incidents at the rectory and unfortunately they are all dead.

Both the Ghost Club and the Society for Psychical Research have been particularly active when it comes to separating genuine from fake hauntings. In his autobiography *No Common Task*, Life President of the Ghost Club Peter Underwood has these sound words of advice on the matter: 'One always has to be aware of the possibility of publicity-seeking by witnesses and other people concerned in reputedly haunted houses.'

There are also the many cases of mythical hauntings that gradually become 'fact' over years of retelling. A good example of this is the case of the Ring o'Bells public house at Middleton near Manchester. In this instance, a Civil War officer is said to haunt the pub and even has a favourite chair to sit in. Apparently, this spirit is of a Royalist who was mortally wounded after being involved in a desperate sword fight with local Parliamentarian forces. The more colourful versions of this story tell of the sword fight taking place in a secret passage below the pub. After dragging himself back to The Ring o' Bells, the unfortunate young man died on the floor. Ever since, it is said, he has haunted the hostelry where he expired.

This tale is not only very romantic and tragic but also totally bogus. Firstly, the Ring o' Bells was not built until 200 years after the English Civil War in which the soldier was allegedly killed. Secondly, the pub stands on a soft sandstone hill. Therefore, the construction of any secret passage would have had to be a major undertaking to prevent it from either breaking surface halfway down the hill or collapsing because of the unstable geology of the place. Needless to say, there is no historical evidence of either the tunnel or its construction. Nevertheless, this story is still being written up in ghost books as if it were a genuine paranormal incident.

Not all mythical ghosts are the result of wishful thinkers or pranksters. In one case, a ghost which was created as a serious paranormal exercise certainly took on a life of its own. In 1972, Frank Smyth, editor of *Man, Myth and Magic Magazine* decided to test people's unquestioning susceptibility where ghost stories are concerned. To do this, he made up a 'true' story about a wicked clergyman who used to prey on and murder sailors in London's Victorian docklands. According to an article in his magazine, the phantom clergyman was often seen in the area of Ratcliff Wharf. Despite being totally spurious, the story spawned at least eight books and many people came forward alleging that they had actually seen the ghost. If Frank Smyth had set out to prove the public's gullibility in the case of ghosts, then he succeeded beyond his wildest dreams.

Another serious experiment to 'manufacture' a ghost had even more dramatic results. In 1972, Dr A. R. G. Owen, a professor at Toronto University, decided to see if it was actually possible to create a ghost. The idea behind this was to discover whether ghosts were a true paranormal manifestation or simply 'hauntings' by part of the human brain. Dr Owen and his team of eight researchers invented a seventeenth-century English aristocrat called Philip with a great tragedy in his past. This was his failure to save the life of the gypsy girl he had loved. The most important requirement of this experiment was that everyone involved had to believe in Philip completely. After some difficulty, the group managed to 'raise' their ghost during a series of seances. The 'ghost' manifested itself by rapping noises and actually moving the table used during the seances. This was even filmed for a Toronto-based TV channel in 1974. Significantly, Philip ceased to exist when a spoilsport in the group told him that he had been a figment of their imagination. From that moment all manifestations ceased. Philip was re-created by the group at a later date presumably without the killjoy.

The Toronto experiment certainly proved that if a group of people are sufficiently single-minded they can create a ghost and move tables by telekinesis. This could provide the solution to some apparent hauntings, particularly in the case of poltergeists. However, it does not provide the definitive answer to all paranormal phenomena. For example, if hauntings are purely a creation of the human mind as this experiment seems to suggest, how is it that animals such as dogs and cats often react so strongly to such phenomena? There is also the question of what causes the drastic drop in temperature which often accompanies hauntings. Is it really possible that the human mind is sufficiently powerful to suck all the energy out of a localised area in this way? It is worth noting that the Toronto ghost was only 'raised' after months of concerted effort by a group of researchers who found it necessary to believe totally in Philip for the experiment to work. Even then, the manifestations were purely auditory and not visual. This is very different to the experiences related in this book, all of which occurred without warning to the individuals concerned. Also, far from being 'primed' believers as in the case of Dr Owen's group, many of these people were sceptics or total unbelievers before they encountered the supernatural for themselves.

Paranormal investigators should also treat photographic evidence of ghosts with great caution. Over the past hundred years or so, many 'ghost' photographs have surfaced. However, the majority of these are not genuine, but either hoaxes or the result of some optical illusion. The heyday for such photographs was in the Victorian era, when it was possible to create a 'ghost' on a negative simply by double-exposure. Ironically, advances in technology have rendered this trick impossible on most modern cameras. This is because virtually all of today's models will only permit the shutter to fire once for every frame of film. On the other hand, even modestly priced personal computers are capable of creating images of ghosts, devils or hobgoblins that are startlingly realistic yet totally bogus.

However, there are some examples of ghost photographs

that can not easily be explained in normal scientific or natural terms. One of the most famous of these is the ghost on the Tulip Staircase at The Queen's House, Greenwich. It shows what appears to be one or even two spectral figures running up a winding staircase. Indeed, if this picture *is* a fake, then the photographer picked the most difficult method to achieve his end. Firstly, he used a Zeiss Ikon Contina camera, which does not permit double-exposure. Secondly it was taken on Kodachrome X slide film, which has to be sent away to the manufacturers for processing, thus precluding the possibility of darkroom trickery. In his book *Nights In Haunted Houses*, Peter Underwood says that when the photograph was examined by experts from Kodak they found it to be genuine and not the result of a double exposure. Besides, there is the question of motivation, which is often overlooked by sceptics in their haste to rubbish evidence of the supernatural. For what reason would the retired Canadian clergyman who took the photograph perpetrate such a fraud and then lie about it? Money? Publicity? Hardly, since the ghostly figures on the photograph were only discovered by accident when the slides were being shown to friends. Even then, it was not published until some time after it had been examined by the experts. Also, I strongly suspect that if this photo were a hoax, The Reverend R. W. Hardy and his wife would have been unmasked or come clean long before now.

In his excellent book *In Search of Ghosts*, Ian Wilson has advanced an alternative solution. He suggests that an employee of the museum dressed in its white uniform coat actually ran up the stairs whilst the photograph was being exposed. The Hardys, who were of advanced years at that time, simply forgot about this incident by the time the film was returned from processing and thought they had a genuine ghost photograph.

Personally, I have a number reservations about this prognosis. Firstly, I think it unlikely they would *both* have forgotten or failed to notice a full grown man in white running up the stairs, especially since Mrs Hardy had been posted to ensure that nobody got in the way whilst her husband was photographing. Secondly, the quality and clarity of this hand held photograph taken under difficult conditions is certainly quite remarkable for someone who was supposedly so old and forgetful. Indeed, on a return visit the following year the Reverend Hardy was also able to show exactly how he took the shot. Surely, if he could remember that, he would also recall someone running into his field of vision. Thirdly, Ian Wilson disputes ghost hunter Peter Underwood's theory that the photograph is of a mediaeval monk. He points out, quite rightly that the staircase was built at least a hundred years 'after The Dissolution of the Monasteries had put the last monks out of business.' He also asserts that The Queen's House has no record of any ghosts. In this last matter, I believe he could well be mistaken. The late uncle of my best friend was actually the Chief Valet at The Queen's House for many years. He told him that he and other staff members saw and sensed the ghost of a young woman in period dress. With this witness now dead, his story is impossible to verify, but I have always thought the Hardy photograph to be that of a young woman wearing a ring, rather than a monk.

Finally, people often ask me whether I actually believe in ghosts. The answer to this is that I certainly do, otherwise I would not have wasted my own and a great many other people's time writing this book. Nevertheless, like everyone else involved in the subject I really have no idea exactly *what* they are. Telekinesis, imprints on the ether, trapped souls, spirits of the dead, crisis apparitions, products of the mind, the list of theories that various people have developed to explain ghosts and hauntings is indeed a long one. But nobody has yet been able to come up with a definite answer. It is this that makes the subject of the supernatural endlessly fascinating and frustrating.

Note: In some stories, actual names have been changed at the request of those involved. These have been marked with an asterisk.

1

The Start of The Journey

When one considers the long and often violent history of Britain and Ireland, it is hardly surprising that these islands are steeped in the supernatural. It is unlikely that there is a city, town or village in these countries that does not possess its own ghost. The common myth perpetrated by the media is that such ghosts only inhabit Tudor mansions or graveyards. Nothing could be further from the truth. Because a house is only a few years old does not mean it will not possess a paranormal presence.

A good example of this is the area of Essex that lies at the south-eastern tip of the United Kingdom. In recent years, it has been subject to intensive urbanisation, changing what was a collection of small rural communities 50 years ago into busy towns such as Basildon and Southend. Most people would have difficulty in believing that any supernatural presence lurked in the office blocks and filling stations of such places. However, there have been plenty of paranormal incidents in this area and if one looks at its history this is not surprising.

For example, in October 1018, Cnut bloodily and decisively defeated Edmund Ironside at Ashingdon, less than 10 miles from what is modern day Southend. Then at Rochford, a village on the outskirts of the town, there is a fine Tudor manor house where Anne Boleyn's family lived in the sixteenth century. Supernatural legends surround both locations. There is an ancient belief that grass would not grow on the 'bloodstained' field of Ashingdon and there have been sightings of Anne's ghost at Rochford Hall during many a Christmas.

When Anne met her tragic end, her family were also

dispossessed from their Essex property as a result. However, they were not the only ones to suffer Henry VIII's wrath, for the local monastery was also dissolved and the monks dispersed. Until the sixteenth century this area was the centre of religious power. It is this factor that seems to have left a spectral legacy as the following story illustrates ...

HOLY ORDERS

Jennie Lewis's Story

Every night Jennie Lewis would search her bedroom. Fearfully, the seven-year-old would peer under the bed and inside the wardrobe, but the strange men who crowded into her room night after night never showed themselves then. They would come later as she knew they would, just after she had switched off the light and slipped between the covers. Jennie would wait in the dark and, sure enough, four or five figures in hooded brown robes would come through the walls. Then they would walk around the room, their hands clasped in prayer. They never harmed her in any way but that did not stop her from being scared out of her wits, especially when one of them would peer down at her, his face obscured by the cowl over his head. Jennie had no idea what the strange figures were doing there she just wished they would go away and never come back.

On the face of it, a council estate in Southend-on-Sea in Essex is the last place one would expect to see phantom monks. However, if one delves beneath the urban sprawl and into the area's rich history, Jennie Lewis's experiences start to make more sense.

In the thirteenth century a rich landowner called Robert Son of Swein granted the French Order of Cluniac Monks some of his lands for a monastery at Prittlewell, which is situated not more than half a mile from modern day Southend. It was, he said: 'For the salvation of my soul and my wife and my father and my mother Beatrice and my grandmother and all those whose care it may be to maintain that place.'

Presumably, he believed that this way he purchased an easy way into paradise. Close to a safe anchorage and on the banks of a stream, Prittlewell Priory prospered. By the time of the Dissolution it had acquired 900 acres of surrounding land. Denton Avenue, where Jennie Lewis saw those monks in 1961, is a mile as the sheep strolls from the priory building.

'I didn't know anything about monks then,' she explained. 'I was too young and it was only years later that Mum told us Denton was built on the site of an old monastery.'

There is actually no historical evidence of any monastic buildings in that particular area. However, its closeness to the centre of such a powerful order would have meant the Cluniacs exerted both a strong influence and presence there. So, it is more than likely that Jennie Lewis had tuned in to the spectral imprint of a holy order that had been extinct for many hundreds of years.

When she was in her early teens, the family moved from Denton to a bungalow in Prittlewell. Unfortunately, if Jennie believed that the move put her paranormal experiences firmly behind her, she was mistaken. Shortly after moving in her father started to redecorate their new home. This meant that Jennie and her sister Glynis had to share the lounge as a temporary bedroom. Jennie was not happy with this arrangement, mainly because her sister's loud breathing kept her awake at night. However, when she complained to her mother Jennie discovered she was not the only member of the family to be disturbed by the laboured breathing. Her youngest sister Sian also said that she had heard it.

'It wasn't until I said I'd heard the breathing that everyone else admitted they had as well,' she recalled. 'That's also when things started to go missing, only to turn up later in obvious places such as on one of the beds.'

'It's not Glynis,' her mother said. 'I've also heard it and so has your brother. Besides, no girl or woman breathes as loud as that. I think this place is haunted.'

Jennie's mother had another unnerving reason for believing

3

this. One night, she was awakened by the sound of loud masculine breathing in the bed beside her. Thinking her husband might be unwell, she turned to see if she could help him but he was not there. It was then that she remembered he was away working a night shift.

The family have been gone from that bungalow for many years now and have never been able to find a satisfactory answer to those incidents. It may have been the ghost was a former owner who objected to the family's presence and the changes being made to its home. On the other hand, it could also have been connected with the Cluniacs, since the house was situated only half a mile from Prittlewell Priory. This was even closer to the centre of monastic power than the house at Denton.

There are many other ghosts who haunt the Southend area. Whilst some are imprints of the ancient past, like Jennie Lewis's monks, others are echoes from the more recent events of the Second World War or are linked to traumatic watersheds in people's lives. In the case of Carol Voice, who has lived in nearby Shoeburyness and Thorpe Bay for many years, her continuing experiences contain both these latter elements.

I first met Carol through a mutual acquaintance who also worked for BT. The subject of my book had come up in conversation and he suggested that she was someone who had a number of interesting experiences to relate. Not knowing quite what to expect, we met at her neat modern house on a windswept evening in early spring. Carol is a tall blonde woman in her early fifties who has a direct and honest way of speaking to people.

'Are you a medium?' she asked.

'No, I'm not,' I replied. 'Does that worry you?'

'No I just wondered,' she said.

I then explained that, although I did not consider myself psychically sensitive, this did not prevent me from having an active interest in the paranormal. At this point Carol seemed to relax and, leaning back in her favourite armchair she began

4

to recount her many stories into my cassette recorder. They begin in post war London when she was a young girl and was first alerted to the supernatural world:

AN OPEN DOOR

Carol Voice's First Story

All Carol Jacobs knew about her father's financial problems, was that the family had to move out of their lovely house into a horrible basement flat. Like most 11-year-old girls, she only had the vaguest idea of the pressures and problems that were besetting her parents. Nor was there much incentive for her to find out. When she tried to question them about it, her mother would rush off in floods of tears whilst her father would scold her as if it was all her fault. As it happened, Carol's father had gone bankrupt, losing everything, including the family home.

They only stayed at that first dingy flat for a short time before he found a larger, airier place in Tottenham. It was true that the place needed quite a bit of work doing to it. For a start, there was no electricity in the place, only gas, but Mr Jacobs did not mind. Feeling guilty about landing his family in such reduced circumstances, he regarded the new flat as the first step back up the ladder to better fortune. Unfortunately, Carol did not see it quite that way and at first, refused to stay in the flat.

'You'll go where you're put, my girl,' retorted her irate father. After all, he knew better than most how difficult it was to find suitable accommodation in the London of the 1950s.

Eventually, Carol had to accept her lot, but that did not mean she was happy – far from it. For she knew that there was something very bad about their new home and was determined to find out what it was. At first, she tried asking all the neighbours what was wrong with the place, but they either did not know or, if they did, would not say. Mr and Mrs Jacobs were infuriated by this apparent display of ill manners. They simply could not understand what had come over their daughter. In fact, what nobody yet realised was that Carol's intuition was telling her that there definitely *was* something very wrong with the flat. Most children have a highly tuned sense of psychic awareness which will very quickly identify any paranormal presence in a house. In Carol's case, these powers are exceptional and have stayed with her right into adulthood.

The room she feared most in the whole flat was her own bedroom. Situated at the back of the building, it was always as cold as a fridge and permeated with a presence whose hostility to her verged on the evil. Every night, Carol would go to sleep with the newly installed electric lights blazing. Her parents' bedroom was next to hers, but they moved out after only two nights. It was only years later that Carol's mother explained why. Firstly, her father, who ironically was an ardent unbeliever in the supernatural, felt an invisible force move his bed. Secondly, Mrs Jacobs saw the figure of an old man rush aggressively at her before vanishing. Neither parent said anything to her at the time, but Carol already knew the flat was haunted because she had also seen a ghost. One evening when brushing her hair, she was startled to see the reflection of an old man in the mirror. Although it only lasted seconds, Carol definitely saw him walk behind her. However, when she turned to see who the intruder was, there was nobody else in the room. On another occasion, both Carol and her father watched in disbelief as a large glass ashtray took off from a table and smashed on the floor.

'I was absolutely terrified of the whole flat, particularly the back part,' Carol recalled. 'So was my dad for that matter, especially after that ashtray incident.'

However, Carol would have to wait a number of years before she found an explanation for the unhappy presence in the flat. It was one of the neighbours who finally told her about its tragic past. Before the Jacobs moved in, an old and reclusive couple had lived there for many years. They were hardly ever seen outside the flat except on rare expeditions to buy a few groceries. In all the time they lived there, nobody ever recalled seeing any visitors knocking on their door. So, when the old couple finally died, it was some weeks before the authorities, alerted by neighbours, forced their way into the flat to discover their decomposed bodies. It was obvious that their unhappy spirits trapped between the worlds of the living and the dead, regarded the Jacobs family as unwanted intruders and sought to drive them from their private domain in the only way they knew how.

This was the first of many occasions that Carol's psychic awareness would alert her to something being amiss. Another incident occurred many years later when she was taken by a friend to see some converted flats near the town of Grange in the north of England. After travelling through spectacularly rugged scenery, they came upon the old Victorian mansion that had been made into the luxurious apartments. Her friend really thought that Carol would love to live there and was dismayed to see her friend in obvious distress as soon as they stepped inside the cavernous entrance hall.

'What on earth's wrong, Carol?' her friend asked.

'I don't know,' she gasped queasily. 'But this place is making feel sick. Let's go, please.'

Later, she discovered that the old building had actually been a mental hospital many years previously.

Then there was the time when her then husband, local businessman Peter Voice, decided to move to a larger house. He had found an attractive modern home surrounded by a beautifully kept garden in the Essex village of Hockley. However, when he took Carol to see the place, he was surprised and angered by her refusal to enter the house.

'What on earth is it *this* time, Carol?' he asked in exasperation.

'I don't know, Peter, but there's something terrible about this place,' she replied. 'Let's go, please!'

Carol was as worried as her husband about her reaction to the house, which would have made a beautiful home for them. So, she decided to find out why she had been so adversely affected by the place. Her first port of call was the estate agent, but they simply stonewalled her. Eventually, she spoke to a farmer who owned the neighbouring fields and it was then that she discovered the truth.

Like the flat in Tottenham many years previously, the story involved death and tragedy, but it also had the potent elements of sex and violence. Apparently the former owner of the house returned home unexpectedly to find his wife in bed with a local builder. In a terrible fit of jealous rage, he shot them both to death where they lay.

However, of all the paranormal experiences she has had in her life, those that occurred between 1970 and 1982 were the most unpleasant and unforgettable. At the time she and Peter lived on a private development near Southend called The Butterys. The succession of bizarre incidents began shortly after they moved in and culminated 12 years later in an event so terrifying that Carol still has difficulty in coming to terms with it.

At first the manifestations took the form of everyday objects such as a baby's dummy or brush disappearing from one part of the house only to turn up somewhere entirely different a day or so later. Then, various appliances began to mysteriously 'fix' themselves after breaking down. For example, her tumble-dryer broke down one day with a full load of washing on board. After 20 minutes trying to restart it, Carol reluctantly decided to call upon the expensive services of an electrical repairer. However, before she finished dialling the number, the dryer whirred back into life.

'My dad was a great handyman,' she recalled. 'So I think it was probably him just being helpful, you know.'

This was not the only way her dead father seemed to make himself useful. When her second son Stuart was about three, he began telling his mother that Grandpa had been reading him a story. At the time, Carol just put it down to a little boy's imagination. Then he said that a man with glasses kept visiting him in his cot. From the description, Carol took that to be her late father-in-law, but still felt it was all in her son's mind. However, events in subsequent years would make her think differently about whether her son's visitors were in the mind or not.

It was about this time that both Carol and her stepdaughter Denise began seeing the fleeting figure of a man flitting down the ground-floor hall. At first, they simply took it to be a reflection from outside and hung a thick curtain over the window by the front door, but the figure still appeared. Then, one night a friend of Denise who had come to babysit Stuart paused to tidy up in front of the hall mirror. While brushing her hair she was shocked to see the figure of a man pass directly behind her. Nobody else besides the two girls and the baby had been in the house at the time. Denise's friend never babysat for Carol or set foot inside the house ever again.

However, it was not just in the Voices' house that figures had begun to appear. One of her neighbours came to see her in state of great agitation one day. After Carol calmed her down with a cup of tea, the woman explained that she kept seeing a man in a white shirt walking up her stairs when she was the only one in the house. All Carol was able to do was commiserate with her neighbour and, explaining that she was not alone, told the distraught woman of her own experiences. Eventually the persistent hauntings became too much for the neighbour and she was forced to move away from The Butterys completely. Not for the first time Carol wondered if they were all being targeted by a spectral force who wanted them to leave.

Carol also learned that locally the area had a reputation. The Butterys took its name from a dairy farm that had occupied the land for many hundreds of years. Apparently, when the farm was sold for building land, a group of gypsies who were squatting there had been evicted. Their leaving had not been quiet and they were said to have laid a curse on the place. It may have been an old wives' tale, but Carol could not dispel the feeling that there was something very wrong indeed with The Butterys. It was not only the phantom figures that were disturbing the place, tragedy also seemed to be stalking their close.

In total, six of its residents suffered untimely bereavements over a period of about five years. Strokes, heart attacks and road accidents deprived them all of close and loved members of their families. Sadly, Carol was also touched by this cold hand of tragedy. Having already lost her first son, who died in hospital when he was a few weeks old, she began to experience difficulties in her marriage which would ultimately end in divorce.

'We were all right until we moved to The Butterys,' she recalled. 'Then the whole marriage just went up the wall.'

To add to Carol's growing unease, Denise had also started talking in her sleep. Night after night Carol would be woken to the sound of her stepdaughter shouting unintelligibly. When she entered the girl's bedroom, she would find her sitting upright in bed shouting in fluent German. Whenever she was asked about it the next day, Denise would have no recollection of any nightmares or unusual dreams. Their doctor was not a great deal of help either, diagnosing stress at school. What about the German speaking? Carol would ask him. To which he replied that he was not a linguist.

On another occasion, the ghost in Carol's house took on a more definite form than the shadowy figure in the hall. She woke up to see a young man in a powder blue uniform with three yellow lapel stripes in her bedroom. As he looked towards her, his face was lit by a dazzling smile and topped by a shock of beautiful golden hair. He was so real that she could have reached out and touched him if he had not vanished first. All these factors now convinced Carol that the house was haunted, but her husband Peter would have none of it.

'You're both crazy,' he said. 'There's nothing wrong with this house, or the rest of The Butterys for that matter!'

Then, as is the way with such things, an incident happened that would change Peter's attitude radically. Returning home one night, Carol found her husband sitting at the lounge table, the set of accounts he had been working on barely touched. One look at his face told Carol that something was very wrong.

'What's the matter with you?' she asked.

'There's been someone else in the room,' he replied. 'They've been around the corner there, smoking.'

'Don't be silly,' she said. 'There's nobody else in here but you. It must be your cigars.'

'I know the difference between cigar and cigarette smoke,'

10

he said emphatically. 'And someone else has been in here smoking fags.'

After that unsettling experience, Peter Voice decided to find out more about the history of The Butterys. He spoke to a friend on the local council and together they went into the background of the area.

'They found out that an enemy plane had crashed on the land where our house was built in the last war, killing a lot of Germans,' Carol recalled.

If this were so, it would go a long way to explaining the reason for the many bizarre incidents. Unfortunately, true-life mysteries are rarely quite as cut and dried as that. Although a number of Allied and German aircraft crashed in the Southend area between 1940 and 1945, when I checked the very detailed records of aerial activity and bombardment over the area during World War Two, I could find only one mention of The Butterys. This referred to a 250-pound bomb which landed there at five o'clock one morning in March 1944 but with no recorded casualties or fatalities to either humans or livestock.

Carol remembered that her husband said the plane was a transport. The only possible reason a German transport would have been flying over south east Essex would be to drop paratroops behind enemy lines or because it was lost. It is certainly possible that this happened and the whole incident was considered so sensitive all records were either hidden of destroyed. There are precedents for this. When hundreds of US servicemen were killed off Slapton Sands in Devon whilst practising for the D-Day landings, the truth was officially suppressed until the 1980s.

Then there was the case of the East Anglian historian who tried to investigate an abortive German commando raid on the Suffolk coast, only to find that all official documentation had mysteriously vanished. It is also possible that Peter's friend at the council had mistaken the incident of the bomb as a plane crash. Whatever the truth, it does not nullify Carol's many bizarre experiences in any way, but merely intensifies the mystery surrounding them.

In the meantime, she had a further experience that made her even more fearful about the house for it was an incident that seemed to defy all natural laws and logic. Always a light sleeper, she was in the habit of staying up until everyone else had gone to bed to catch up on some undisturbed reading or watch the late film on television. One night, when she had stayed up later than usual to finish off a chapter of her book, a deadly blossom of flame suddenly erupted in a corner of the lounge. For a moment or two, Carol was transfixed by fear, then she ran to the kitchen for a saucepan of water and woke Denise for help. After dowsing the flames, there was a large charred area on the wall and carpet, but no apparent reason for the sudden blaze. However, one thing was certain: if Carol had not stayed up that night the whole family could have perished in the mysterious blaze, adding yet another statistic to the Butterys' inventory of tragedy.

The long series of disturbances and tragedies finally culminated in that frightening occurrence which still worries Carol today. On a sunny afternoon in late May 1982 she returned home sticky and exhausted from the heat. Dumping the shopping on the kitchen table, she went through to the spacious L-shaped lounge, switched on the television and fell into her favourite armchair. All she wanted at that moment was a few minutes total relaxation before fetching ten-year-old Stuart from school. As a totally forgettable serial appeared on the screen she began to unwind.

After a short while, she became aware of a strange and unwelcome sensation. It was as if her feet had been plunged into a deep freeze. She looked down and was horrified to see a dense white mist had engulfed her feet and was rolling up her legs. For a few seconds, she stared with shocked fascination as she watched the mist travel up her body. When it reached her stomach, she made a break for the door.

Once in the kitchen, she leaned shakily on the table, feeling totally drained by the experience. What she needed more than anything at that moment was a cigarette to calm her nerves. The trouble was, her packet was back in the lounge with the mysterious white mist. Carol was simply not ready to face whatever was in there so she tried reaching for the cigarettes through the serving hatch with her eyes tightly closed. After flailing around and knocking some ornaments onto the carpet, she gave up that idea. There was no way round it, if she wanted a cigarette she would have to go back in there and fetch it.

'Pull yourself together, Carol!' she told herself. 'There's nothing there, you imagined it!'

As if to confirm her thoughts, the television droned on, spilling its trite story into the empty room. Eventually, she summoned enough courage to walk back in there and, sure enough, the mist had gone. In its place was the figure of an elderly man sitting in her chair, his hands resting on the arms.

Although he was angled away from her so she could not see his face, Carol recognised him immediately. It was her father, who had died six years before. Even though she remained in the lounge for a few seconds before fleeing the house, his apparition left an indelible impression on her memory. What struck her most was his solidity; he was so real, not like a ghost at all. Sitting there in his white shirt and blue jumper, he looked as if he had just popped in from the afterlife to catch up on a bit of telly.

It was probably this, coupled with the shock of seeing him, that caused her to run screaming in fear to one of her neighbours. Once there, she poured out her story.

'No, that's impossible, Carol,' the woman said, laughing uneasily.

'I'm telling you I saw him as plainly as you sitting there, Rose!' Carol replied.

'Well, supposing you *did* see him,' Rose said reluctantly, 'why be frightened? Surely he wouldn't come back to hurt his only daughter.'

'Of course not. It was just such a shock with all that horrible mist. Anyway, I don't know why he should come back now.'

The incident worried Carol so much that she decided to seek help. There were a number of relatives on the maternal side of her family who were mediums. However, because of

Mr Jacobs' hostility to spiritualism they had tended to lose contact over the years.

'He hated spiritualists and mediums,' Carol recalled. 'He didn't believe in them and would say that the only spirit was the one in a bottle.'

Eventually, and not without a certain amount of trepidation, she contacted a cousin who was a spiritualist and asked for help. She need not have worried, for the woman was both kind and understanding about her relative's plight. She took Carol to a house in Hornchurch, Essex where they met group of women who were all mediums. After hearing the story about her father, the mediums expressed the belief that Mr Jacobs still could not fully accept the fact that he was dead. Because of this, he had not yet been able to leave the living world for the Other Side, as they put it.

'Would you like us to help him break free at last?' they asked Carol. She most emphatically did.

'Very well, then do exactly as we say.'

Sitting in a circle around Carol, the psychics all laid hands on her. For a few moments nothing happened, then she felt something akin to an electric current pass into her body from the women's hands. The next moment, one of the mediums was flung across the room and into a chair and began speaking in a voice that was very familiar to Carol:

'Leave my daughter alone and get out of the bloody house!' her father repeated angrily.

It was a frightening incident yet not without irony. For here was the spirit of a dead man being raised by the very people he had always written off as eccentric fraudsters. Nevertheless, those mediums in Hornchurch seemed to do the trick and Carol has not seen or sensed her father since. Shortly after this incident, Carol left The Butterys, moving into a smaller house in nearby Shoeburyness. She was not sorry to see the last of a house where she had experienced so much psychic disturbance and tragedy. However, the house still returns to haunt her dreams. 'Even after all these years I still have nightmares about that place,' she confided with a shudder.

14

'You know, I dream that I'm back living there and that's just a horrible feeling.'

Fortunately, the house where she now lives has a more friendly and welcoming atmosphere. However, Carol still has psychic experiences there but of a generally less threatening nature than before.

At the time of her move, Carol's mother used to visit her regularly. The old lady was racked by a fatal disease that would soon kill her. She found her daughter's home a comforting refuge from the pain and fear she felt. Carol loved her mother dearly and sympathised with her distress. She was happy to see her and put up with some of her annoying little habits. One of these was the way she used to bang about in her daughter's kitchen when she became agitated.

'My mum was a terrible worrier,' Carol recalled with a smile. 'And she'd bang the china tea and sugar jars against the tiles on my kitchen wall. I'd have to keep telling her about it or she would have smashed them.'

During several visits just before she died, old Mrs Jacobs heard another woman calling to her. '*Doris, Doris, Doris!*' the dismembered voice would say, repeatedly using her Christian name.

'I thought it was very strange, since she was so deaf you really had to shout for her to hear you,' Carol said. 'But I think it may have been her dead mother calling her, sort of preparing her for death.'

Not long after the funeral, Carol began to sense her mother's presence in the house. Unfortunately, it was not a comforting feeling since the old lady seemed to be characteristically agitated. She often heard her mother calling her name as if she wished to speak to her daughter about something very important. Sometimes it was like the time it prompted Carol to discover a potentially lethal growth in its very early stages. On other occasions, she would hear the china jars in the kitchen banging against the tiles. It seems that some habits are hard to break, even in death.

Because her mother's continued unhappiness was causing her distress, Carol again sought the help of a medium.

15

'She's very upset because she has not accepted the fact that she has passed on from this life,' the psychic explained. 'But don't worry, they'll come and fetch her soon. Although nobody else will hear anything, you'll know.'

Sure enough, one afternoon Carol was sitting in her neat living room when she heard a tremendous commotion upstairs. It was as if two cats were chasing a bird from one room to another. She looked down at her old dog, who had always reacted to her mother's spiritual presence. If there had been cats upstairs, she would have been awake and barking, but she lay unmoving in a peaceful state of near slumber. A little later, the disturbance ceased. Carol shivered involuntarily for she knew that the medium was right and they had finally come to fetch her mother.

Carol still has other spectral visitors, some of whom are not at all welcome. Appearing without warning, they take the form of poorly tuned TV signals. Sitting in her lounge watching television or reading in bed, she will become aware of the indistinct figures standing in the room as if they are waiting patiently for her. She believes they are spirits who sense her psychic awareness and hope to use it as an entrance into the living world.

Numerous mediums agree and have warned her that she must learn to 'shut off', particularly at night when her psychic defences are low. Failure to do this could make her vulnerable to all comers from the supernatural world, including evil forces. The defence she has developed is both simple and effective for she quietly recites the Lord's Prayer.

'I never wanted this gift,' she said. 'But it seems that I'm stuck with it and will be an open door to the paranormal world for the rest of my life.'

Postscript: Since writing this experience, Carol has told me of a further paranormal experience. In May 1995, I visited her to say goodbye and thank her for sharing her experiences with me. It was a sad time for Carol because her old dog Amber had died not more than 24 hours before.

'You should have been here last night,' she said. 'The banging in the kitchen started and there were a lot of other things as well.'

Carol then explained in more detail. While she had been watching the television, she heard the china tea and sugar jars bang repeatedly against the kitchen wall. This was followed by the sound of someone moving restlessly about the bedrooms upstairs. Carol knew at once that her mother, who was also very close to the dog, had come back in her old state of agitation. Then she saw the ectoplasm.

One patch appeared and grew into a solid white mass by the French windows leading to the garden, whilst another spread over one area of the settee. During her life, Amber frequented both these areas, either waiting to be let into the garden or to sleep on the settee. It seems that the old dog had come to say farewell and Carol's mum had come to fetch her.

OUT OF HIS TIME

Carol Voice's Second Story

It was closing time again at the White Horse in Thorpe Bay and Carol Voice was not sorry. She enjoyed the conviviality of working in the pub, but there was no denying it could be very exhausting. She was pleased to be 'minding' the pub for only two weeks whilst the regular landlord and his wife were on holiday. She did not think she would be able to stand the late nights and long hours over a prolonged periods.

While the diehard regulars lingered over their final drinks, Carol tilled up and joined them on the other side of the bar. It was then that she saw a grey-haired man in a beautifully cut suit standing by one of the doors on the far side of the bar. As she watched, he walked right past her and then disappeared.

'What's the matter, Carol?' one of the customers asked jovially. 'Seen a ghost?'

It was not a joke that she felt like sharing and she said nothing until the next morning. Then she spoke to John, a

17

member of the staff who had worked at the pub for a number of years. After describing the incident to him, he looked thoughtful.

'You're not the first to have seen that bloke, Carol,' he explained. 'We've also had trainees who've had similar experiences.'

'Who is he, then?' she asked.

'He used to be a manager here, now he's in the graveyard next door,' John replied succinctly. 'You saw him stand at the door of his old office and walk across the bar exactly as he did every day of his working life. You see, he was very much a creature of habit.'

Like all the ghosts that Carol has seen, the late manager of the White Horse was not a bit ephemeral, but as solid as anyone of living blood and flesh. However, something about him told her that he was not 'in his own time', as she put it.

On Meeting the Dead

Lying 20 miles as the crow flies to the north-east of Southend, the ancient town of Colchester has been continuously inhabited for 2,000 years. As its name suggests, it began as a Roman settlement in the reign of Emperor Constantine. In AD 61 it narrowly escaped total extinction when Boudicca's forces massacred large numbers of the Roman inhabitants. There are no records of any spectral legacy of this slaughter, but there are plenty of other haunted areas in this part of Essex, and with good reason. In his book *The A–Z of British Ghosts*, Peter Underwood identifies seven locations in the county, including Borley Rectory, reputedly the most haunted house in England before it was burned to the ground.

Although this next experience happened in the Colchester area, the spectral presence it involved was really a visitor from another part of Britain. It is a story that involves Jessie Heard, someone who has had a long history of both seeing and communicating with the dead. Appropriately, my introduction to her was somewhat unusual. One evening in the autumn of

1994 I had a phone call that started with the following question: 'Hello, have you heard any good ghost stories lately?'

'Er yes,' I replied, somewhat taken off my guard. 'Can I ask who's calling?'

'I'm Jessie Heard and I have some experiences that might interest you,' the caller told me.

Like so many people who have had genuine and interesting supernatural experiences, Jessie was inclined to play them down. It was as if she could not believe anything she had experienced could possibly be of interest to the wider world. Needless to say she was quite wrong, as her stories illustrate.

However, before she told me of her experiences, a very strange coincidence occurred. Jessie was phoning in response to an article in the company 'house newspaper' *BT Today* explaining about my book. The article ended by asking any readers who had had paranormal experiences to contact me.

Jessie, who had worked for the company for many years prior to privatisation, was phoning me in response to that request. During this initial conversation it emerged that she had worked for my uncle in Amersham. There are many thousands of people who read *BT Today* every month and the only one who responded to that article had worked for the Brazil family firm in the 1940s. I wonder what odds a bookmaker would give against that happening – 10,000 to 1 perhaps?

We will meet up with her, like others in this book, time after time during our journey. In the meantime, here is the first of her numerous experiences.

THE BLACK BOOK

Jessie Heard's Story

Although Jessie Heard always knew that she possessed a high level of psychic awareness, she had never become involved in spiritualism. So, when in the summer of 1978 she accepted a friend's invitation to visit the Colchester Spiritualist Church, it was out of sheer curiosity. What, she wondered, actually happened at such places? Did people really receive messages from dead relatives or was it all little more than simple wish fulfilment? Jessie decided that it was high time to find out.

If she had come away from the spiritualist gathering totally unconvinced, it would have proved to be a thoroughly worthwhile visit for another very happy reason. For it was there that she met the Membership Secretary, who would shortly become her future husband.

She had been a widow for 14 years, since her first husband had died from a fatal liver infection contracted whilst patrolling with the British armed forces in the South China Seas. In all that time, she had not felt the strong mutual attraction she now experienced on meeting this spiritualist called Sidney. Shortly after that meeting they began to see each other on a regular basis. It was during this early stage of their relationship that Sid received the sad news of his elder brother John's sudden death in Malvern.

'You don't have to go to the funeral, of course, but I'd be delighted if you would come along and keep me company on the journey,' Sid said. Jessie readily agreed.

Although the journey and mournful event passed without incident, there would soon be a strange sequel for Jessie Heard. About a week after the funeral, she began to have a strong mental image of a very tall man with silver hair.

'At that stage, having only just met Sid, I knew very little about any of his family,' Jessie explained. 'But when I told him of the tall man in my thoughts he confirmed that the description closely matched that of his recently deceased brother John.'

She also began to hear a very persistent voice intruding on her inner thoughts.

'*I'm Sid's brother John,*' it would say. '*And I'm trying to contact him but he isn't receiving me.*'

Initially, Jessie just rubbed her eyes and pushed the voice and image to the back of her mind. The mixture of happy and sad emotions involved in first meeting Sid then seeing him bereaved must have put her imagination into overdrive, she concluded. But when the voice refused to go away she asked Sid about it.

'You'd better ask John what he wants,' Sid said. Then, after a short hesitation added: 'I'm afraid I can't receive him, so would you be prepared to act as our messenger?'

Having agreed to act as the spiritual go-between, Jessie tried to make contact with John. He came back to her immediately with the following request: *'Please don't let Edith my wife throw away my small black notebook. It has details of the family history in it that I want Sid to have. It's in the right-hand drawer of my desk.'*

However, there was one snag to this particular request. Edith hunted through every drawer of her husband's desk in his study, but no black book came to light. Reluctantly, Jessie and Sid concluded that the whole business must have been in her mind, after all.

With no children to carry on his business, Edith decided that John's printing company in Malvern had to be sold. So, several weeks later, she went to perform the sad but necessary task of cleaning out her late husband's office. As she searched through John's desk for any personal papers, she pulled open the right-hand drawer, only to discover the black notebook he had been so keen for Sid to have.

When Jessie and Sid looked through it, they realised why John wished to prevent it being thrown away. The book was a veritable mine of historical information about the family, enabling them to trace relatives back to grandfathers and great grandfathers.

After that, John and Jessie became firm friends, with the dead brother speaking to Sid via her thoughts on numerous occasions. By this time Jessie had also become a spiritualist. Both she and Sid would regularly travel from their home in Colchester to clairvoyants' evenings at a church in Clacton.

'We used to start off and John used to "come in",' Jessie explained. He would say *"Hello, I'll have a ride down with you. Say hello to Sid for me will you because he simply doesn't receive me".'*

21

After this happened a number of times, Jessie became worried that it was all a figment of her imagination.

'How do I know it's you, John, and not some rubbish in my head?' she asked on one occasion.

'*Right, Jessie,*' the dead man replied. '*Every time you don't believe it's me, you'll see a pheasant.*'

A few days later, on a long summer's evening, this incident had an unsettling sequel. As they set out on their regular journey to the Clacton spiritualist church, John greeted them in the usual way. On this occasion Jessie was feeling a little out of sorts and she told John that she was fed up with being his messenger. 'Say hello to Sid yourself if you want to, ' she told the spirit tartly.

Immediately after she said that, four pheasants flew in front of the car, nearly causing it to swerve off the road.

'After that, I always said "Hello, John" and passed on his messages,' she laughed.

In 1987, tragedy again scarred Jessie's life when her daughter-in-law died of leukaemia at the tragically early age of 38. Nevertheless, Jessie still feels she is watching over her earthly family even though she has passed from this life.

'I don't see her, but I hear her quite plainly when she comes through to talk about her children,' Jessie explained.

Like many clairvoyant people, Jessie Heard's psychic gifts are not something she has sought. To paraphrase the Bard, they have been thrust upon her.

'I don't question it any more because to me, the book was proof enough,' she said, then added: 'I can't do it to order or get up on a platform and neither would I want to. It sort of just happens at random.'

Further Up the Thames

From Colchester and south-east Essex our journey in search of the supernatural takes us on a journey that invaders, kings and commoners have all made over the centuries. It is a voyage up the Thames Estuary towards London. On the way, we will pass the ruin of what used to be a fine Norman castle.

In its heyday, Hadleigh Castle near Southend not only held a commanding position overlooking the Thames Estuary, but was also the home of three of Henry VIII's wives. Indeed, it was probably easier and a great deal more comfortable for the owners to travel by royal barge downriver from London than journey along the rutted tracks that passed for roads in Tudor times. Alas, like its royal incumbents, this impressive Norman castle has had its time and is now just a picturesque shell of ruined walls.

On hot summer days you can stand in its grounds and watch the container ships glide through the polluted haze towards London. Their journey will take them through a very different landscape to that of 500 years ago. Now it is a no man's land of refineries, cement works and factories. About 12 miles upriver from Hadleigh the nondescript town of Gravesend will slide by on their port bow.

It was here that Rod Williams spent his youth watching waves of German bombers fly over to blitz London whilst the fighters from the RAF and Luftwaffe engaged in deadly combat. At that time, ill health meant that his only involvement in the Second World War would be as a bystander. However, had he been fitter, Rod might well have been called up and would never have experienced the strange incident in the next story.

A VISIT FROM ST ELMO

Rod Williams' Story

Rod Williams's one encounter with the paranormal came and went like a thief in the night during the bleak winter of 1944 when victory over the Germans was still on a knife edge. Rod, who was 17 at the time, was living with his parents in the town of Gravesend on the Thames Estuary.

For three years he had suffered from tuberculosis, preventing him from either working or being called up to see active service. Although he now regards the illness as a hidden blessing, saving him from running the risk of death or injury in action, at the time he found it very frustrating. Positioned at the edge of the docklands and only a few miles from the centre of London, Rod was all too aware of the progress of the war. At first it was the waves of bombers, then the dogfights and finally the frightening and silent menace of the V1s and V2s.

To relieve his frustration and boredom, Rod took refuge in the written word, becoming an avid reader. Devouring books on virtually any subject, he was a regular visitor to the local libraries. However, there was one subject that fascinated him more than any other and that was the supernatural. He seized on any library books that had a paranormal theme, whether they were fact or fiction.

One night, he had been reading a particularly interesting book on the supernatural when he awoke at about one in the morning. Looking to his left and right, he realised that something very strange was happening. Surrounding his body was an aura of electric blue light. There was no feeling or sensation, just this eerie outline like St Elmo's fire. Suddenly, the brass light switch on the landing just outside his door clicked on. As the comforting yellow glow of the bulb flooded into his room, the blue aura surrounding his body vanished.

Fifty years have passed since that incident and Rod is no nearer an answer to his strangely electrifying experience.

Spectral Happenings in the Garden of England

Travel ten miles to the south-west of Gravesend and you will arrive at the Kentish town of Chatham. Situated at the mouth of the River Medway, it became famous as the main dockyard of the Royal Navy. For many hundreds of years men of war were built here to defend the country against a succession of foes, including the French, Dutch, Spanish and Germans. Now the dockyard is gone, leaving only the ghosts and memories of the past.

As well as having a great seafaring history, this part of Kent often played reluctant host to invaders such as Caesar and the armies of Hengist and Horsa. So it is hardly surprising that legends of ancient ghosts such as phantom legions should abound in this part of Britain. However, the next two ghost stories, which occurred in the Chatham area, had nothing to do with ancient warriors but were strictly family affairs.

John Wade, who told me the first story, has been a personal friend for some years now. We first met when I had the voluntary job of seeking out news stories for *BT Today*, the house newspaper. It was John's job to assess whether my stories were of sufficient interest for publication and, if so, write them up for the paper. John has had an interesting and varied career in journalism, with photography and vintage cameras his speciality. Not only has he published a number of books on the subject, but he was also editor of *Photography* magazine for a while. Now he runs his own journalism and creative writing company with his wife Barbara in Hertford-shire. However, any thoughts of journalism or running his own company were very far from his mind when the following incident occurred.

APPLE PIE ORDER

John Wade's Story

'Now, Mum, are you quite sure that this is the place?' John asked, trying hard to keep the exasperation from creeping into his voice.

'Yes dear,' his mother answered calmly. 'Although it has changed quite a bit since Grandma and Granddad lived there.'

'Well, that's hardly surprising, is it?' John said. 'That goes back quite a few years.'

'It's not that long ago, John!' his grandmother protested from the back seat. 'And it's definitely the place where Mum and Dad lived.'

'Let's go and talk to the owners, shall we?' his mother said, opening her door.

It was 1964 and 18-year-old John Wade had only recently

passed his driving test. For a treat, he had taken his mother and grandmother on a trip to their native Kent. Although the novelty of driving had not yet worn off, he was finding this hunt for the 'ancestral home' round the highways and byways of the Garden of England more than a little trying. As his mother knocked on the door of the pretty little cottage near Chatham, he devoutly hoped that this was the end of the search.

As luck would have it, the cottage proved to be the house where Mrs Wade had spent many a happy day in her childhood staying with her grandparents. The owners of the house were delighted to discover this and invited the party in for tea.

However, John's most abiding memory of the visit was not the discussions about the many improvements the new owners had made to the cottage, but the fact that they were the proud owners of a colour television set. At that time, it must have been one of the first in Kent if not the whole of England. It was certainly the first one he had ever seen.

So while John sat glued to the set, his mother and grandmother were shown around. Finally, the time came to go and Mrs Wade said farewell, with the promise that she would send some photographs of the cottage in its original condition. A week or so later, she had unearthed some black and white photographs of the old place. Sadly though, there were no pictures of her grandparents. A few days later, John's mother received a letter from the owners. As she read it at the breakfast table, she gave a gasp of surprise and disbelief.

'But that's impossible!' Mrs Wade said.

'What is it, Mum?' John asked with concern.

'Those nice people at Grandma and Granddad's cottage have described them to a tee!'

'Well, they must have been in one of the photos that you sent.'

'No, don't you remember me saying what a pity it was that we had absolutely no pictures of the old couple?'

'Yes, but you must have described them,' John persisted. 'Otherwise, how else would they know?'

Without another word, she handed her son the letter. Sure

enough, there were many details about the old couple, such as the way his great-grandfather had a white beard and tied his trousers with string. Or how his wife wore a long white apron down to her ankles. A little later on, John's mother phoned the woman and asked how she had known so many details about her grandparents.

'Well, you're going to find this a little hard to believe,' the woman replied. 'But they often come and sit in the kitchen with us. And your grandmother has given me a delicious recipe for apple pie.'

Spectral Smells

Like many smells, that of home baked apple pie is not only appetising and welcoming but also very evocative. Indeed, aromas seem to be one of the most powerful triggers of our emotions and memories. For example, the mere hint of a certain perfume can bring back vivid images of some long forgotten affair. On the other hand, a particular smell can also conjure up pleasant or unpleasant memories of a visit to a distant country.

Because this olfactory sense is so closely linked to our emotions is probably the reason why many hauntings are also accompanied by a particular smell. It seems that the dead will often carry an aroma closely linked with them into the spirit world. In some cases, these will be pleasant smells such as that of tobacco ('A Smell of Tobacco' Chapter 3) or a particular after shave ('The Wokingham Disturbance' Chapter 2). In others, the odours will be far from pleasant. This was certainly the case of a vicar's wife I know. Shortly after she and her husband moved into an old Welsh vicarage, she became acutely aware of the stench of putrefaction in one of the rooms. It was so powerful that they eventually moved out of the house. Subsequent investigation revealed that the dead bodies of a previous resident and his wife had actually lain in the building for some days before being discovered.

The smell that accompanied the haunting in the next story was not only unsettling and unpleasant but also remains unexplained. John and Barbara are also good friends of mine, but have asked that their real names are not given for personal reasons.

A SCENT OF MILDEW

*John and Barbara Allen's Story

Situated a few miles from Dover, the estate was a large one, owned by the same family since Norman times. As with many other estates in southern England, the family's ancestors had been given the land by a victorious William the Conqueror in gratitude for their part in the defeat of Harold. Over the years successive generations had added to the estate until it covered many acres, with numerous fine features like the lodge house, built at the main entrance. However, by the 1960s both great wealth and large estates were definitely out of fashion, falling victim to increasingly harsh tax regimes. The big estate near Dover was no exception and the family finally bowed to the inevitable. To pay off death duties and various other taxes, it was sold for building land.

Within a very short time, all that remained of the estate was a memory as the verdant parkland was covered by acres of houses. Not even the lodge house survived and it was demolished to make way for a large bungalow. The house changed hands a number of times before being bought in 1989 by the present owners, Kevin and Sandra Peterson. Close to their business and in a semi-rural setting, the property seemed ideal for them and they settled in very quickly.

Not long after they moved in, the couple noticed that their two pet boxer dogs began to behave strangely in the front room of the bungalow. They would stare intently at a particular area of this room and then bark as if there was an intruder. On occasions, their heads would also move, as if they were following someone across the room. Sandra also noticed that the area of the room which disturbed the dogs would suddenly start to smell of mildew. Then, just as suddenly, the odour would disappear. Nothing the Petersons tried would shift the smell and nothing would calm the dogs.

After some years both dogs died and were replaced by two bulldogs. However, they also behaved in exactly same way as their predecessors had when in the front room. The Petersons are very down to earth people and had always given stories of ghosts very short shrift. But a further incident in the same room finally convinced them that their home was probably haunted. One night, when they were sitting in there, Sandra's electric sewing machine whirred into life on its own before stopping a few moments later.

Like many successful business people, the Petersons had a seemingly inexhaustible supply of creative energy. When not building up their business, they poured this energy into improving the bungalow. Shortly after moving in, they decided to add an extra floor, and by the summer of 1990 the work was virtually finished. In the August, they invited Kevin's brother-in-law John and his wife Barbara down to spend the weekend and see the improvements.

The other couple always got on extremely well with the Petersons, so they welcomed this opportunity to visit for a couple of days. Because the new floor was not quite ready for habitation, the guests had to sleep in the lounge that was adjacent to the front room. When the time came to turn in, Barbara walked over and switched off the lights. As she returned to the settee where she was sleeping, the lights came back on again. Irritated rather than scared, she went back and switched them off a second time.

Much later that night, John, who was sleeping on a mattress on the floor, was awakened by a flickering sensation. Opening his eyes, he realised that this was caused by the lights flicking on and off. It was as if someone was playing around with the switch. After a while, the lights finally went out and mercifully stayed that way. The following morning, even before John mentioned anything, Barbara told him that she had also been awakened by the flickering lights.

The ghost had one last trick for the Petersons and their guests that weekend. Later in the morning, Sandra, John and

Barbara were all sitting in the front room, which was the focus of all the activity. Suddenly, a strange scraping sound drew their attention to a telephone socket on the wall. As they watched, it twisted through an angle of 45 degrees..

At the time of writing, the house continues to be the home of a paranormal presence. Both dogs still sense it in the front room and the smell of mildew comes and goes, having resisted all attempts at total banishment. In late 1994, there was also another bizarre incident. Sandra had placed a wall mounted cornucopia of flowers in the front room. The following morning she discovered it on the floor, with the flowers scattered across the carpet. Rather than risk the same thing happening again, she hung it in another room, only to have exactly the same thing occur in there.

Neither couple have any real idea why the house is subject to these inexplicable incidents. Kevin suspects that it may be connected with the lodge house, which provided the materials for the bungalow. On the other hand, the building work they embarked on soon after buying the property may have upset a supernatural presence that had existed there. Whatever the cause, they await the next paranormal incident with interest.

Gentle Angels of Death

Many hospitals in the British Isles are haunted. On numerous occasions shadowy figures have been glimpsed in deserted operating theatres or flitting through wards in the still, dark hours before dawn. Terminally ill patients have often spoken of mysterious yet kindly visitors who come to comfort them shortly before they die. Perhaps the most famous was the case of the Grey Lady, which occurred at a London hospital in the mid to late 1950s.

Dressed in the grey uniform of nurse from the turn of the century, she visited and comforted a number of patients who all died very soon afterwards. Paul Turner, a doctor at the hospital, was so impressed by the written reports of the nurses involved that he published an article about the six best documented cases in *The Journal of the Society for Psychical Research*.

I was told of a similar case by a nurse working in the geriatric ward of a Manchester hospital. One of her patients, an old woman, spoke of a 'beautiful lady' who came and held her hand for most of the previous night. She mentioned particularly how her visitor had made her feel calm and peaceful.

'I knew it could not be another member of staff,' the nurse told me, 'because none of us would have had that amount of time to spend with one patient.'

On the following night the old woman passed away peacefully in her sleep. The nurse, a very well-balanced person, certainly believes that this was a case of a spectral visitor preparing someone for the end of their earthly life.

Children dying of incurable diseases have also spoken of little boys and girls who visit them and ask: *'When are you coming to play with me?'*

Like the Grey Lady, these spectral playmates are only seen by those they have come to prepare for death. Other brief sightings of dead patients or members of staff have been reported from hospitals and nursing homes the length and breadth of the British Isles. Indeed, it would be strange if such buildings, where life and death dramas are everyday occurrences, did not have their fair share of paranormal activity.

The following incident happened in an old hospital at Maidstone which is situated only a few miles from the location of the previous two stories. It is closed now, but staff who worked there will tell you that the place certainly had a 'reputation'. For them, this may have been just hearsay, but for Janet Hickie what happened at that Kent hospital was as real as it was frightening.

THE FACE AT THE WINDOW

Janet Hickie's Story

In September 1973, Janet Hickie went south from her native Manchester to train as a nurse at one of the UK's top hospitals. Situated at Maidstone, the Kent County Ophthalmic and Aural Hospital had a fine reputation in its field. But, away from her large family in the friendly north for the first time in her life, this was cold comfort to Janet.

Like many a trainee nurse before her, she was homesick. In fact, if it was not for her burning desire to become a qualified midwife, she would have packed her bags and gone home after the first week at the hospital.

However, while autumn turned into winter, the pain of separation dulled as she became immersed in the training. Living in the home for the hospital's nurses was also an antidote for loneliness, with plenty of girls her own age to mix with and talk to. Her room was reasonably comfortable if a little sparse. Janet soon addressed this latter problem by decorating the walls with some of her favourite posters.

For the first month or so nothing out of the ordinary occurred. Then she began to have an uneasy feeling about the room. At first, she put it down to the fact that it overlooked a cemetery, but it was not long before she realised this had nothing to do with it.

'I had always felt strange in the room,' she explained. 'And I soon had the feeling that I was not always on my own in there.'

One cold and wet November night, she returned to her room exhausted after a long day training and working in the wards. All she wanted to do was to climb into bed, read for a while and then fall asleep. With a slight shudder, she drew the curtains to blot out the eerie sight of the mist-shrouded graveyard. Then she changed into her pyjamas and slid in between the sheets with her favourite book.

Minutes later, she was woken up by the dull thud of her

book falling onto the floor. Janet turned off the bedside light and drifted back to sleep. She was aware of nothing else until she suddenly awoke for no apparent reason some hours later. The room was very quiet and cold. Feeling strange, Janet turned over and looked towards the window. There, a disembodied head, the colour and consistency of egg white, hovered looking at her. Odd though it might seem, she was more curious than frightened as the manifestation drifted upwards then came slowly down to float about 2 feet from her face. At that point, she was overcome by a terrible fear.

'Go away!' she screamed, burying her head under the covers. A little later, she looked out fearfully, but the apparition had vanished.

In December of that year, Janet returned to complete her training in a Manchester hospital. Whilst she was there, she met a fellow nurse who had also worked at the same Maidstone hospital.

'It wasn't a bad place once you got used to it,' the other nurse said as they had coffee together one day.

'I suppose not,' Janet replied uncertainly.

'You don't sound very sure,' the other girl said. 'Didn't you like the other nurses then?'

'Oh no, I didn't mean that,' Janet said. 'They were fine. It's just that, well, I had this weird experience one night in my room.'

'Oh, what was that?'

Feeling a little foolish, Janet related her encounter with the ghostly head of a man with long straggling hair.

'Well, it may surprise you to hear that I was also troubled by a ghost when I was there,' her companion announced. 'I didn't actually see anything, but it kept turning the taps on and off. It nearly drove me mad at the time, I can tell you!'

'Which room were you in then?' Janet asked

'Thirty-five, I'll remember that as long as I live,' she replied.

'So will I,' Janet agreed. 'Because that was my room as well!'

After hospitals and pubs, vicarages seem to be the favourite places for hauntings. Perhaps this is because they are often the focus of many years' intense spiritual introspection as well as strongly conflicting emotions. Some Victorian vicars, for example were quite tyrannical and unchristian when it came to their families. This often caused intense feelings of frustration and even hatred amongst children and wives. A daughter forbidden to see a certain 'unsuitable' boy in her teens could harbour a secret grievance about it into the barren spinsterhood of old age. On the other hand, a son might never recover emotionally from his father's wrath at discovering his affair with a servant or village girl. The fact that such extreme emotions were often suppressed out of fear may well have imprinted them on the fabric of many such buildings. This is apparently the case of the next encounter, which occurred in the neighbouring county of Sussex:

THE GHOST AT THE VICARAGE

*Irene Derby's Story

If I were a ghost, one of the last living people I would want to upset would be Irene Derby. Even in her eighties, she is a formidable and strong-willed woman with what can only be described as a hard-nosed approach to the supernatural.

'I tell them they can't hurt me because I'm alive and they're dead,' she said during our interview.

This was to serve her very well when she and her family moved into a haunted vicarage in the first autumn of the Second World War. It was a beautiful old Georgian house in a small Sussex village and certainly did not look in any way forbiding when the Derby family first set eyes on it. However, they were soon alerted that something was amiss about the place by one of the builders who had been decorating the house in preparation for their arrival.

'I wouldn't sleep in this place for all the tea in China,' he said, packing away his tools and paints.

Indeed, the vicarage did have a local reputation for being haunted, as a headline in the local newspaper indicated. 'Ghost At Twyneham Rectory!' it screamed, and reported in detail the hauntings which had taken place. Apparently, the ghost was that of a vicar's daughter who had lived there in the nineteenth century.

'They said that she used to walk about the place saying "*a tisket, a tasket, a little yellow basket.*" I found that all a little fanciful,' Mrs Derby commented. 'But the place was certainly haunted.'

The ghost of Twyneham Rectory manifested itself on the first few nights of their stay. Mr and Mrs Derby would be lying in bed when their eiderdown would be ripped off and dumped on the floor by an unseen force. No sooner had they replaced it than it would be dragged off again. After this had happened on the third night running, Mr Derby lost his temper:

'Damn and blast this bloody ghost!' he exclaimed as he stepped onto the cold floor to retrieve the eiderdown yet again. Irene can only conclude that such language was a huge shock to the Victorian vicar's daughter. After that outburst the eiderdown was never pulled off the bed again.

A short while after the eiderdown incident, Irene's student brother came to stay with a friend. She put them up in a bedroom on the floor above her own room. 'He was a big strong lad and, like me, quite unafraid of ghosts,' Irene recalled.

However, the next morning, he came down to breakfast looking tired and rather bleary-eyed.

'You look terrible,' Irene told him. 'Didn't you sleep well?'

'I certainly didn't,' he answered. 'I don't know what's wrong with this house but I've never felt so restless in my life!'

Although Irene Derby suspected this may have been the work of the ghost, she still did not tell her brother. Instead, she told him he had eaten too much supper. If that satisfied him, it was a different matter with his friend.

'I'm very sorry,' the friend said, 'I simply can not sleep in that room because something was trying to drive me out all night.'

'Well, you have two choices, I'm afraid,' Irene said. 'You either sleep in that room or you'll just have to go home.'

In the event, the friend decided to return home rather than endure another night at the mercy of the vicarage's ghost.

'He really felt it as strongly as that,' Mrs Derby said to me recently.

After that, the ghost still manifested itself in a hostile but more subtle fashion. The bedroom where her brother and his student friend spent such a disturbed night seemed to be the focus of the paranormal activity. One day when Irene went in there to close the windows, she felt the ghost's hostile presence especially strongly.

'Look, I'm alive and these are *my* windows,' she said firmly, and the oppressively hostile atmosphere abated. On another occasion she gave the ghost short shrift when it made its mischievous presence known.

'I'm alive and you're dead, so scram!' Irene said bluntly, and that seemed to cure the problem.

'I suppose we were there about eight months in all and gradually the ghost's presence subsided,' she recalled.

Irene, who now lives in Cornwall, has had no other paranormal experiences. However, the events at the Sussex vicarage on the brink of the greatest war in history remain indelibly stamped on her memory.

2

Hauntings in The Home Counties

The next encounter also involved members of the nursing profession and happened in a training home some 50 miles to the west of Maidstone, in Windsor, Berkshire. It is an area that is no stranger to paranormal activity. For example, Herne the Hunter is said to haunt Windsor Great Park in full cry with horse and hounds. In the mid 1930s, there were also some well-authenticated sightings of the phantom figure of a man in black cloak and broad brimmed hat. On at least one occasion this figure was seen to walk through a herd of deer without disturbing them. Then there are the ghosts of no less than three monarchs who tread unhappily through the halls and corridors of Windsor Castle. Elizabeth I, Henry VIII and George III have all been seen or heard at various times within its massive walls. In Eton, on the opposite side of the Thames to Windsor, the church and vicarage of St John The Evangelist was subject to a series of frightening and well documented paranormal incidents over a number of years in the 1970s (*Nights in Haunted Houses*, published by *Headline* in 1993.).

Penelope Spafford, whose first supernatural experience is related in the next story, is a friend of many years' standing. Pea, as her friends call her, is tall, vivacious and articulate. She is also very psychic, with an extremely accurate recall of her many experiences, including this early one. It actually occurred in a large house situated in the small village of Clewer on the edge of Windsor. Background research has now revealed that the building where she had her experience had a long history of paranormal occurrences, as we shall see.

A VERY BUSY GHOST

Pea Spafford's Windsor Story

In the 1960s, if you wanted to take up a career looking after young children, the Princess Christian Nursery Nurse Training College was probably the best available. Set in its own secluded grounds, it was based in a Victorian house at Clewer on the edge of Windsor in Berkshire. Eighteen-year-old Penelope (Pea) Spafford had always loved children and was very pleased to gain a place at the college.

'I knew the place had a ghost called Emily,' Pea recalled, 'but when I went there I did not let it bother me. For that matter, I did not even think of it.'

However, not long after she started at the college, the ghost manifested itself in some very tangible ways. The first incident happened late one night when Pea was finding it very difficult to sleep because of Erica, another nurse's hacking cough.

The dreadful rasping sound was really beginning to irritate Pea. Of course, she knew that poor Erica could not help it, but the intermittent coughing was keeping her awake until the early hours every night. As a trainee nursery nurse with a heavy work schedule, the lack of sleep was beginning to affect her studies. On this particular night, she was about to fetch Erica a soothing drink when she heard brisk footsteps echoing down the corridor of the old house.

Thank goodness, thought Pea as they went past her door, *someone on night duty's brought her a drink at last!*

The footsteps paused outside Erica's room, then there was a tapping on her door. Shortly afterwards the coughing ceased for the rest of the night.

'I'm glad someone brought something for your cough last night because it was really driving me mad,' Pea said to Erica the next day.

'Nobody came to see me last night,' the other girl replied.

'Oh come on!' Pea protested. 'I heard somebody come to your room at about three and knock on your door.'

38

'I'm telling you that nobody came to my room last night,' Erica said emphatically.

Pea Spafford said no more to her fellow student, deciding to pursue the matter with the night staff instead. She was positive she had heard the footsteps and wanted to find out who was responsible. However, when she asked the girls who had been on duty the previous night, they all denied visiting Erica's room.

Even after the incident of the footsteps, she did not immediately connect it with Emily. She simply put it down as one of life's little mysteries. But after she did her stint on night duty a few days later, she began to think more deeply about the ghost.

Because the college was very conscious of obeying the fire regulations, one of the golden rules that everyone on duty had to observe was to shut the five large sash windows that ran down the corridor of 'Blue Boy' Wing, where Pea and Erica slept. This was to ensure that any fire had as little oxygen to feed it as possible. So, at eleven o'clock on her first duty night, Pea made certain that all the windows were shut tight. However, when she returned at a quarter to six the following morning, she was dismayed to find all five windows wide open. After making the same discovery on the following two days, she concluded that one of the other students had been opening the windows to relieve the stuffiness of the atmosphere. That was all very well, but it was against the rules, so she decided to speak to the others and put a stop to the practice.

'Look, I know it gets a bit stuffy in Blue Boy, but please don't open the corridor windows at night, it's a fire hazard and strictly against the rules,' Pea said.

She was answered by blank stares from the other girls and total denials that any of them had touched the windows.

This Emily is a very busy ghost, Pea thought to herself.

How right she was!

As an additional precaution against any fire spreading, swing doors had also been placed at regular intervals down the corridors. This way the passage of the fire could be slowed as much as possible without impeding the escape of any students.

Whilst she was on night duty, Pea was walking down the same corridor of Blue Boy when each set of these doors began to swing backwards and forwards just before she reached them. It was as if somebody was walking in front of her, except that she was completely alone.

The final most unnerving incident occurred when she least expected it. One drowsy, summer's afternoon Pea heard hysterical screams for help coming from the top floor of the building. Running up the stairs, she found one of the other girls standing in the corridor sobbing in fear, her face deathly white.

'Pea, for God's sake help me,' the girl cried. 'There's somebody, some *thing* in Annabel's bed!'

Pea peered fearfully into the room but it was still and empty. After calming down, the terrified girl told Pea what had happened. She had gone to her room on the top floor to have some rest after a spell of night duty. About an hour later she was awakened by the sound of heavy and regular breathing. Thinking it was Annabel, her room mate, she turned to greet her. However, Annabel was not on her bed, but in her place was a deep indentation, as if an invisible being was lying there.

'Nobody seemed to know who Emily was,' Pea recalled. 'Although somebody did see a figure in a crinoline walking down the stairs once, I can't say I ever actually saw her. But, I did see the way those doors moved and just knew she was walking in front of me. I didn't imagine those footsteps, any more than that poor girl imagined the presence in her room.

'Yes, you could say Emily was a very tangible ghost!'

Strange Events in Surrey

About 20 miles to the south of Windsor, just outside the cathedral city of Guildford, there is a hilly area of woodlands and ancient villages. It is still very rural here in spite of the intensive urbanisation that has occurred in the rest of Surrey. Helping to reinforce this 'county' image, there are a number of gracious country houses standing at the end of long drives in the midst of verdant parklands. An excellent example of this is Clandon Park, the home of the Onslow family.

Perhaps not as famous as Blenheim or Beaulieu, Clandon is nevertheless a fine example of mid-eighteenth century architecture. Built in the Palladian style by the Venetian architect Giacomo Leoni, it has a magnificent marble hall and beautiful gardens. Only the Georgians could make an oblong box of bricks and mortar look as noble and beautiful as this. However, that was not the impression Jessie Heard had of the place when she and her husband Sid visited it in the 1980s. To her, the place looked entirely wrong, as if something was missing:

THE CLANDON TIME WARP

Jessie Heard's Clandon Experience

Since she was a very young girl, Jessie Heard has always possessed an acute psychic awareness. This makes her a member of a very lucky but small minority of the population who do not lose this gift to the many material distractions that crowd in on our adult life. As a result, she has experienced a number of vivid paranormal experiences. What happened to her at Clandon Park one summer's day in the early 1980s was a very good example.

Sid and Jessie visited Clandon on that warm day not simply to view a stately home but also to try and trace a grey area of her family's history. In her youth, Jessie's mother was befriended by a member of the Onslow family whom Jessie felt could actually have been a relative. She hoped that this visit might provide a clue to this mystery. However, what she actually found at the old house was a series of spectral contacts with an earlier age.

Her first inkling that something strange was happening occurred when her husband Sid tried to photograph her in front of the house. Jessie would have none of it, since for some inexplicable reason she felt that something was not right about the front of the house.

After buying a programme they entered the house and went down for a meal at the restaurant situated in the basement. As Jessie sat there, the clatter of plates and hum of conversation died away to silence as she found herself in the cellar as it must have been a century before. Gone were all the tables with their crockery and menus. In their place was an ill-lit and cavernous room festooned with cobwebs. Suddenly a maid ran across the far end of the cellar and disappeared through a door, to re-emerge a minute later with a bottle of wine. Jessie empathised with the girl, who was obviously as frightened as Jessie was to be in such a dark and cold place. People often sense they are being watched by an invisible spectral presence. Perhaps this frightened servant girl also had this feeling, unaware that her invisible watcher was a ghost from the future.

A little later, Jessie walked around the outside of the mansion and again was overwhelmed by the feeling that the building had been changed. Looking up at the stable block, she was annoyed to see that the unusual clock which had graced it for so many years had vanished. Then she paused and asked herself a simple question: What clock? I've never visited this place in my life before, so how on earth could I know if one ever existed on the stable block?

Eventually, Jessie concluded that she had been mistaken. Nevertheless, the feeling of unease persisted. Quite why she had such strong feelings about the appearance of this house continued to baffle her.

Walking down to a grotto in the gardens, she looked at her reflection in the water and realised that her dress had changed. In place of her modern clothes, she wore a long, muslin sprigged dress with flounces. Feelings of a happy, part remembered childhood when she ran and played in the spacious gardens swept over her. As soon as they arrived the sensations vanished, depositing her back in the twentieth century.

She and Sid walked back into the house to make a full tour of the many spacious and lavishly furnished rooms. On entering the library, Jessie was to experience yet another shock.

There were a number of family photographs pinned to a fire screen. One of them was a photograph of three girls from the Onslow family. Looking closely, Jessie found herself staring at a mirror image of her mother. As they walked through the rest of the house, they came upon an empty room right at the top of the building. In it stood the old stable clock that had been removed many years before Jessie was even born.

A Hotbed of Paranormal Activity

Probably not more than 20 miles by road from Clandon are the towns of Farnham and Aldershot. Whilst there is some beautiful countryside in the surrounding area, it is being progressively squeezed out by housing development. Farnham itself is still a lovely town, with a high street that runs up a hill. At the top of this is the ancient Farnham Castle, which has allegedly been the site of many hauntings over the years. One of its most persistent ghosts is a monk, who has regularly been seen in the area of the Great Hall.

Then there is Bramshill House, near the neighbouring town of Hartley Wintney, which has, according to Peter Underwood, Life President of the Ghost Club, the reputation of being the most haunted house in Hampshire. In this Jacobean mansion, one ghost is that of a young bride who died under bizarre and tragic circumstances on her wedding night. Once again, she has been seen on numerous occasions, sometimes by large groups of people. Mr Underwood with his colleagues and some friends have conducted extensive investigations at both locations, which he relates in his book *Nights in Haunted Houses*.

However, if is not simply ancient houses that are subject to paranormal activity in this area. A garden centre at Bagshot has been haunted by a ghost the owners call Fred. This particular presence's stock-in-trade is to hide various items such as plants or flowerpots around the premises. In the town of Fleet, almost next door to Bagshot, an elderly couple had a much more sinister experience in their modern bungalow when they were plagued by unseen hands that kept touching them.

As our next story shows, the Foremans had an equally bad experience when they moved into an old house in Fleet in the 1970s.

A BAD REPUTATION

Dave Foreman's Story

It was a typical Victorian house, large, cold and rather gloomy, but, for newly-weds Dave and Sandy Foreman it seemed the ideal starting point. They felt it would be a good place to stay whilst they saved up to buy their first home. Situated on the Reading Road in Fleet, Hampshire, it had been made into flats and the Foremans occupied a living room downstairs as well as a bedroom and bathroom on the first floor. Being a dab hand at DIY, Dave set about brightening the place up with paint and wallpaper. It did not take long before the flat began to look much warmer and more inviting.

Everything was perfectly normal in the place for the first month or so, then both Dave and Sandy began hearing strange rasping sounds like someone rubbing gravel through their hands. Being a very practical man, Dave will always look for a logical and scientific explanation for something unusual. In the case of the rasping sounds he put it down to the aches and pains of an old house. But, try as he might, no amount of probing with a torch would reveal the source of the sound and it continued intermittently without any obvious explanation for the 18 months they were in the house.

He had also begun to experience another very strange sensation. Often when going upstairs, he would have a tingling feeling and the hairs on the back of his neck would stand on end. At the same time, he would feel a sense of great unease bordering on fear. Particularly unsettling was the fact that the sensation would come and go quite without warning, One day everything would be normal, the next it most certainly was not. As for 'Boy', his golden retriever, he flatly refused to go near the bedroom. Instead, he would stand at the bottom of the stairs and growl, with his hackles rising.

Then another unnerving incident occurred that made the couple feel even more uneasy. In the bedroom there was a long, bevelled mirror. Dave remembers that it was so heavy he was hardly able to lift it. Perhaps that was why it had been left leaning rather than hanging on one of the walls. Early one evening the couple were sitting in the lounge when they were startled by a massive crash upstairs. Rushing up to the bedroom, they discovered the mirror lying shattered on the middle of the floor several feet from where it had been leaning against the wall. It was now three months since they had moved in and even the sceptical Dave began to wonder if there was something paranormal about the place. His doubts were increased, rather than allayed, by the next incident.

It was about five o'clock on a peaceful summer evening and he was sitting in the spacious living room. At one end, there was a typical Victorian fireplace with a decorative clock placed in the middle of its wide mantelpiece. Without warning, the clock slid about 3 feet along the mantelpiece, where it remained vibrating violently for about 30 seconds.

'Call it telekinesis, call it what you like, but I have no explanation for that clock moving,' he said.

However, the incident that proved to be the last straw did not occur until they had been in the old house for about a year. They were lying in bed; when Sandy let out the most awful scream.

'What the hell is it?' Dave asked, flicking on the light.

'Oh Dave, I felt someone climb into the bed beside me!' she replied shakily.

After that, the couple never slept in the bedroom again, preferring a mattress on the lounge floor instead. Five months later they shut the front door of the Victorian house for the last time and moved to an unhaunted home of their own.

For a while, Dave kept in touch with the people who moved in after them. Most members of that family experienced nothing, but the mother also began to see and hear things.

Later, when Dave told his aunt about the incidents, she nodded knowingly.

'You. should have told me before you moved into that house,' she said helpfully. 'It's always had a very bad reputation!'

Hauntings in the Home of the British Army

If you drive the 4 miles or so from Fleet into Aldershot, you can not avoid noticing that this is a town with a very long military association. A Dakota belonging to the Parachute Regiment stands guard at the entrance to what is known as Aldershot Military Town. It is here that the army is concentrated, with a stark garrison church standing in the midst of barracks and married quarters whose names echo the many personalities and events in the history of the British Army: Wellington, Batavia, Arnhem, Salamanca . . .

However, times change. The barrage balloon that regularly used to hover above the town whilst parachutists made practice jumps has now gone. Some of the land formerly the preserve of the military has been given over to civilian use such as superstores or prestige housing. The soldiers who used to crowd the pubs and shops of Aldershot are also much thinner on the ground these days. The Peace Dividend and budget cuts by successive governments have ensured that. Nevertheless, the spirits of their long dead colleagues have not departed from 'The Home of The British Army' without leaving their spectral imprint.

For example, the figure of a Civil War officer has been seen by security guards at Telecom House in recent years, whilst the lonely presences of young squaddies who died in fights or committed suicide have made themselves felt in various pubs and snooker halls in the town. As a native of Aldershot, Debbie Ashton knows all about its paranormal history. In fact, as her story shows, she has actually been part of it.

SALAMANCA SKYDIVERS

Debbie Ashton's Story

Against the sharp blue backdrop of the summer sky, specks fall out of a small aircraft like bird droppings. Rapidly the tumbling dots become tiny figures with trails of red, blue and green smoke streaking from their outstretched legs. Thousands of feet below, the audience gasp and point, wondering if the skydivers' parachutes will blossom into life before they hit the ground. Of course, they always do, in 999 cases out of a thousand anyway.

But in the other one per cent, the result is fatal for the parachutists. There are no second chances in skydiving.

Barry Robe was not simply a skydiver, he was a member of the British Army's elite team of parachutists known as the Red Devils. Based at Aldershot in Hampshire, this team of hand-picked paratroopers was in demand to appear at shows and military tattoos the world over. Barry loved everything about being a Red Devil, the lifestyle, the glamour and, above all, the danger. It is a perverse side of human nature that we often thrive on living close to what we fear most. This was certainly the case with Barry and his skydiving. Having seen two of his closest friends die when their parachutes failed to open, nobody could accuse him of not being aware of the risks.

In 1980, it looked as if Barry might settle down to a quieter, more domesticated life when he became engaged to 19-year-old Debbie Ashton. They moved to a rented house in Salamanca Park, an estate built mainly for servicemen near the centre of Aldershot. Since it was quite a large house for just two people, they also shared it with another lodger called Ian Marshall.

Whilst Debbie was happy living there with Barry, there was one small cloud on the horizon. On a number of occasions, both she and Ian, the lodger, heard steps on the stairs when there was nobody else in the house. Whilst this did not frighten them exactly, it was a little unnerving, particularly since they knew a soldier had hanged himself in the house about four years previously.

'I'm not sure why he committed suicide,' Debbie said, 'but I think it was probably the result of some marital unhappiness.'

As far as Barry was concerned, there was no ghost. To him, the world consisted of what he could see and feel. Hauntings always had a rational explanation and he thought the footsteps on the stairs were caused purely by the movement that occurs in any structure.

However, Debbie was not to be shaken from her belief that the house in Salamanca Park was haunted. This conviction was further strengthened by an incident that occurred one cold night in October 1980.

Ian was away for a few days so the couple had the house to themselves. After going to bed on the night in question, they were soon asleep. Whilst Debbie did not remember her dream, Barry found himself in a disturbing and vivid world that he would never forget. He was standing on the grass of the airfield the team often used for skydiving. Bright and sunny with absolutely no wind, it was a perfect day for a dive and the two men walking towards him were dressed to do just that. Then as they came closer, he realised that something was very wrong, for he recognised them as two friends who had been killed skydiving a couple of years earlier.

'How can you be here?' Barry asked. 'You're dead.'

'I know,' one of the men replied. 'But it's fine really, Barry.'

'Yeah,' the other said. 'Why don't you come and join us?'

The two men stretched out to pull him and Barry started to push away defensively.

'No, no!' he said.

'Oh come on, you old stick-in-the-mud!' they shouted, continuing to pull him, but Barry knew instinctively that if he went with them, there would be no return.

'No, no, go back! Go back!' he said urgently.

As is the way of dreams, the struggle seemed to go on for a very long time before Debbie shook him back to wakefulness.

'Oh, thanks, Deb, that was a horrible dream,' Barry said once he was fully conscious.

'I should think so,' she replied. 'You scared the life out of me!'

'What do you mean?' he asked. 'You weren't there.'

'Well, of course not, it was just a dream,' Debbie said. 'But you made it sound as if it were real.'

'That's how it seemed,' he said quietly and then told her about seeing his two dead friends.

After listening to this, Debbie described what had happened whilst he was inhabiting his nightmare.

Half an hour after going to bed, she was awakened by the sound of Barry talking in his sleep. This was a new side to her fiancé's character that she did not know existed, so Debbie sat and watched him. Judging by the agitated tone of his murmuring, it was a very bad nightmare.

'Barry, are you awake?' she asked. He did not answer but began pushing his hands upwards from his chest as if trying to rid himself of some invisible presence.

'No, no! Go back!' he said in an increasingly agitated tone.

This sleep-talking continued intermittently for ten minutes and then his whole body began to move down the bed as if someone was pulling at his legs.

'Now stop mucking about, Barry, you're scaring me!' Debbie said nervously, but Barry ignored her.

'I know, you've got one of your feet on the ground,' she said, jumping out of bed to see if this was correct. However, both his feet were off the floor as his prone body continued to move slowly down the bed. Thoroughly frightened, Debbie decided it was time to wake him up.

'I think we both need a cup of tea,' Debbie said quietly after she told him

'Yeah, let's both go,' Barry said.

As she opened the bedroom door, they saw his jacket lying just on the other side of the door.

'I thought you left this hanging up downstairs,' she said.

'I did,' he replied simply.

Carrying the jacket down with them, the couple made one

other unsettling discovery. A plant that sat in the lounge in a wicker holder and stand had been tipped over, spilling some of the earth onto the floor. Debbie and Barry were certain that neither of them had pushed it over, and, since they had no pet, no other living being could be blamed.

Not long after this, Debbie and Barry decided to go their separate ways. It was an amicable parting and they are friends to this day. Barry also gave up skydiving and moved to America, where he now lives. So who or what had been in the house with them that night? The spirit of the suicide? Barry's two dead friends? Alas, like many similar incidents, it remains a tantalising mystery.

From the autumn of 1994 to the summer of 1995, I worked in a BT office at Aldershot. I shall always be grateful for that period of my working life since it provided me with three experiences for this book. Not only were my friends and colleagues Debbie Ashton and Dave Foreman kind enough to share their paranormal experiences with me, but also Suzanne Shaw, whose story appears next.

Like Debbie, she had also spent most of her life in the Aldershot area and has a good knowledge of its occult reputation, which she believes extends far beyond mere hauntings into the realms of witchcraft and black magic. Fortunately, her experience, whilst unsettling, was no more sinister than a straightforward haunting:

THE SANDY HILL SPECTRE

Suzanne Shaw's Story

Outwardly, the suburb of Sandy Hill, lying between Farnham and Aldershot, is typical of many parts of southern England. What had once been the wild, sandy heathland from which it had taken its name is now a sprawl of council houses climbing towards the crest of a wooded hill still used by the army for training. However, there is something lying deep beneath the thin soil of Sandy Hill that sets it apart from many other similar estates, for it was built upon an unconsecrated burial ground. This factor has given it a local reputation as a place of paranormal activity, with residents seeing dismembered hands thrusting through solid walls and hearing strange sounds.

Suzanne Shaw moved into a flat in Lyall Place in Sandy Hill with her young family in 1985. At that time, she knew nothing of any paranormal activity in the area. Her concerns were much more down-to-earth, such as how to make ends meet with too many bills and not enough money. Fortunately, Suzanne was both gregarious and resourceful, so it did not take her much time to become friendly with her many neighbours. Two people she befriended were the Everards, a middle-aged West Indian couple who lived next door. Suzanne felt a particular admiration and sympathy for Mrs Everard, who suffered from a rare wasting illness caused by an imbalance of potassium and calcium in her body. In spite of the pain and her inability to walk more than a few yards at a time, she was always cheerful, never complaining or feeling sorry for herself.

The summer of 1985 was an especially close one and, because of this, Suzanne found she had difficulty sleeping upstairs, even with the window open. So, after waking up regularly at two or three in the morning, she tried sleeping on the sofa in the lounge to beat her insomnia.

However, on her first night downstairs, she found herself wide awake in the early hours, but this time it was not because of the heat. Although the room was warm, she was drenched in a cold sweat and felt a penetrating fear. Looking towards the front door, she saw a tall female figure. Its overall colour was a pale, translucent pink whilst the face was a mahogany hue similar to the skin of a black person. Suzanne closed her eyes, willing the figure to disappear, but when she opened her eyes again, it was still there. Then she hid under the bedclothes for several minutes before peeping out again. This time the figure had departed.

In the bright summer light the following morning, Suzanne

almost convinced herself that what she had seen had merely been a figment of her imagination. Logic told her that it was nothing more than an image created by a mind halfway between sleep and consciousness. But in her heart of hearts she knew she had been fully awake. Any further doubts about what she had seen were dispelled the following night when the figure reappeared. This time it was much closer, standing in the middle of the room not more than 6 feet from where she was lying on the sofa. Once again, Suzanne was drenched in sweat, but, although she felt a deep fear, the figure did not move towards her or attempt to harm her in any way. Once again, she closed her eyes and hid beneath the bedclothes until the apparition finally departed. Sue also departed and would never again risk sleeping in the lounge of the house at Lyall Place.

To help make ends meet, Suzanne worked part time taking orders from families on the estate for a mail order catalogue. By offering everything from cutlery to double beds 'on the knock' she was able to make a modest but steady income. With every visit to the shops a major expedition, Mrs Everard found ordering from the catalogue particularly useful. About a week after Suzanne had seen the apparition, she called in to show Mrs Everard the latest catalogue. While she was flicking through it over a cup of tea with Suzanne, an attractive pink dressing gown caught her eye.

'How do you think I'll look in it, Suzie?' she asked.

'I think it'll suit you just fine,' Suzanne replied. 'Besides, if you don't think it's right we can always return it.'

In the event, although Mrs Everard loved the gown, she did not have that much time to enjoy it. Six weeks later, she lost the fight against her painful illness and finally died.

'I can't help thinking that what I saw on those two nights was an omen,' Suzanne told me. 'Perhaps to prepare me for poor Mrs Everard's death.'

THE MYSTERY OF THE BASING GIANT

Alan Turton's Story

Two miles outside Basingstoke in Hampshire, there was once a magnificent mansion. As big and every bit as beautiful as Hampton Court, it also played host to members of English royalty and aristocracy. This was Basing House, home of the Marquis of Winchester, one of the richest men in England. Today, it is difficult to imagine the house in its former glory when the aristocratic owner accommodated the combined courts of Elizabeth I and the French King during one of the Queen's legendary tours.

Where there were once high walls with delicate windows and towers of intricate beauty there are now only grassy mounds and some incomplete sections of the original structure. All sign of the first owners and their opulent lifestyle has been swept away as if they had never existed. For Basing House, like many other great houses and castles throughout Britain, fell victim to the catastrophe of the English Civil War.

In 1645, a two-year siege of the house finally came to an end when Parliamentary forces breached the walls and stormed the place. The Marquess of Winchester, who had held the house for the King during this time, was found hiding in the bread ovens and taken into captivity. Inigo Jones, the famous architect, was contemptuously stripped of his clothes and left to shiver. Others were not so lucky and paid with their lives. Among these was a Cavalier officer whose body was found by Hugh Peters, Cromwell's chief army chaplain. The officer was never identified and only the bare facts of his discovery in the smouldering ruins of Basing were recorded in Peters' diaries. However, the chaplain did make one special note about the man and that was of his extraordinary height.

In 1940, an interesting discovery was made in the ruins of Basing House. A skeleton well over 6 feet in length was found in the garden of the house which now stands on the site. Analysis revealed that the remains were those of a man who had died about 300 years previously. The discovery might well have remained a matter of little interest except to archaeologists, were it not for a series of paranormal incidents that have occurred over the years.

I discovered Basing's supernatural history quite by chance when I phoned the curator, Alan Turton, in the winter of 1995. Alan and I have been friends for many years and I have always found his great knowledge of British history of considerable interest. Whether you need to know the truth behind the Ninth Legion's disappearance or why the Jacobites failed, Alan can provide an answer and a theory. However, his speciality has always been the seventeenth century with particular reference to the English Civil War. A leading light in the English Civil War Society, he is a familiar and imposing figure at their many re-enactments around the country. With his black beard, richly authentic clothes and walking stick, he looks every inch a Parliamentarian officer as the smoke and noise of battle drifts around him. When I phoned him, it was to find out if there were any records of Civil War courts martial. Unfortunately, he explained, few such records still existed. However, the information he then told me about Basing's ghosts more than compensated for my disappointment.

Although he has not personally experienced anything paranormal, he has learned of numerous incidents that have convinced him the ruins are haunted. His immediate predecessor, Dennis Skinner, told him that he had always sensed the presence of three ghosts at Basing, two girls and a very tall soldier. Indeed, the figure of a tall soldier with someone much smaller has been seen on numerous occasions. Recently, one visitor told Alan he had seen the soldier walking with a girl at an old canal bridge near the ruins. However, when he attempted to follow them they vanished.

Alan was also told of an unnerving incident that happened to a local man when he was a 14-year-old boy. In the early 1960s the teenager, who was from the village of Basing, was given permission by the owners of the ruins to dig for relics there. He and his friends chose a spot near to the site of an old tunnel and the bread ovens of the house. At lunchtime his companions, who were older than him, retired to the local pub. Because he was under age, the boy stayed at the site and continued to dig. Whether this activity caused some psychic disturbance is difficult to say, but the next moment the terrified boy saw two dark forms emerge from the ovens before disappearing. Although he is now in his late forties and lives in the area, the man has never returned to the site since that traumatic experience.

It seems that the bread ovens are the focus of some manifestations on the site. Alan remembers talking to one visitor whose wife was physically unable to go near them because of the nausea she felt. The raising of the siege was indeed a bloody affair and it is possible that something unspeakable happened in that area. It is also worth bearing in mind that the inhabitants suffered a smallpox outbreak during those two terrible years.

Then there are the sensory hauntings. These occur in the area of the curator's office at the house and take the form of a sharp temperature drop accompanied by the smell of perfume. On other occasions, Alan's secretary has heard the sound of footsteps when she has been the only person in the building.

'Unlike some people, I am not sensitive to the atmosphere of places or buildings,' Alan concluded. 'But Basing certainly has a definite feel about it and even I can sense that.'

Southampton is probably most famous historically as a port for the fabulous ocean liners that used to dock there before and after the Second World War. However, all that has passed now and the docks, whilst still in business, are a shadow of their former selves. Nowadays, containers of goods for import and export have replaced the film stars and bejewelled dowagers who used to board the ships.

These days, people from all over the UK and the world are still drawn to the city, but it is the excellent university rather than the port which attracts them. The influx of students has meant that the character of some parts of the city has changed. For example, in the Onslow area of Southampton, which is close to the university, many of the fine Edwardian houses are now flats and bedsits for the students. It was in just such a building that the next series of paranormal incidents occurred.

THE WHITE MIST

Cathy Hartt's Experience

Sometimes strange incidents happen in our lives that leave us baffled for many years. Then a chance word or meeting will provide the solution to such a mystery. This was certainly true in Cathy Hartt's case. She was a 22-year-old student at the time, down from Manchester to study at Southampton University. By a happy coincidence, an old schoolfriend of hers called Christine was also at the university, so it was natural that they would arrange to share a house in Buller Road, Onslow. Another friend from the north called Peter Lee, who was studying building engineering, also had a room there.

Although they had always been good friends during their schooldays, Cathy always felt there was something very strange about Christine and her family. This was mainly due to their interest in the occult, which went way beyond the casual curiosity that most people have in the paranormal. Cathy vividly remembers one of their Ouija sessions in Manchester when they raised a particularly persistent spirit. The presence told them that she was a girl living in seventeenth-century England. This was fine as far as it went, but became very unnerving when the spirit refused to 'leave'.

'Christine was always very psychic,' Cathy recalled recently. 'And it was because she kept trying to involve me more deeply in such things that I lost touch with her, I'm afraid.'

The presence of such a psychically active person in the Southampton house could well explain the strange incidents which happened there in the summer of 1972. Cathy remembers waking up on a hot, still evening, to see the curtains rippling as if they were being deliberately shaken by somebody. She then became aware of another presence in the room. It took the form of a white mist that seemed to fill the whole living space. Cathy also sensed that it was in some strange way a cognitive spirit without actually being part of her world in any way.

'Then I made a conscious decision to go back to sleep,' Cathy told me. 'Not because I was actually frightened but that I didn't feel comfortable or at ease about this experience.'

It may seem strange that somebody is able to do this when confronted with a paranormal incident. However, sleep is often the body's best defence against shocks of this nature. The next day, when Cathy remembered the incident, she simply told herself that she had been dreaming. Nevertheless, she knew that this was simply untrue and that she had been wide awake. Deep down, she was convinced that something else had been in her bedroom the night before.

Some years later, when she had qualified as a midwife and was working in Manchester, she met Peter Lee again. It did not take long for them to start talking about the old times at Southampton.

'You know, I always felt that house in Buller Road was really weird,' he said, sipping his pint.

'Me too,' Cathy said. 'Did I ever tell you about that experience I had there?'

'You had an experience as well?' Peter said, sitting up straight. 'So did I, two of them actually. What was yours?'

At first, Cathy felt a little stupid relating her experience of the milky mist. It sounded almost inconsequential Then she saw that, far from disbelieving her, Peter was nodding in thoughtful agreement.

'That's exactly what happened to me,' he said quietly. 'A carbon copy. Did you ever think that might have had something to do with Chris?'

'I must admit that had crossed my mind,' she replied. 'Why do you ask?'

'Well, it's just that the other incident sort of involved her,' Peter said, and then he told her what had happened.

He had been sitting upstairs in his bedroom studying at the time when he heard the front doorbell ring. After it rang a second time, he went to the top of the stairs to see who was there. At that moment the door flew open and Christine walked across the hall and into her room. The next day, when Peter asked her why she had not returned his greeting, she was adamant that she had not been in the house at that time.

'Why should she lie about a thing like that?' Cathy asked.

'I don't think she did,' Peter replied. 'I don't think she was there in any normal sense.'

Cathy now thinks that the strange atmosphere at the house, coupled with Peter's and her experiences, were connected with some occult activities their flatmate was involved in. Perhaps there was some spectral presence that had been trapped there after a Ouija session, or worse. Whatever the truth, Cathy Hartt is now certain that her experience on that close summer's night was not a dream.

Windsor Castle and Eton are now only separated from the industrial sprawl of Slough by a thin strip of green belt and the M4 motorway. Meanwhile Ascot, site of the world-famous racecourse, rubs shoulders with the characterless new town of Bracknell with its hostile town centre architecture and soulless office blocks. It is a wonder that any remaining ghosts have not fled in disgust years ago. However, the first rule of supernatural occurrences is that they happen in the most unlikely places. For example, a council flat or modern house is as likely to be plagued by a poltergeist as a country manor. This point is well illustrated by the McKay family's experiences in the next story.

THE WOKINGHAM DISTURBANCE

Phyllis McKay's Story.

Nobody could ever accuse Phyllis McKay of having an easy life. Not only is she confined to a wheelchair, but she is also a widow, her husband having died of cancer some years ago. Today, she lives in a modest ground-floor flat in the Berkshire town of Wokingham.

Fortunately, her daughter Liz is a neighbour and she also has the companionship of a dog, cat and pet parrot. Like many people who have suffered more than one cruel blow in their lives, she refuses to allow this to blight her outlook. In short, Phyllis is a cheerful, friendly and matter-of-fact person, taking whatever fate deals out in her stride, even if this happens to be a poltergeist.

The first inkling that there might be something strange about her flat came one evening in August 1993 when she and John, her lodger, were washing up after supper. Phyllis had just put a cup away and was reaching for another when it flew out of the cupboard and smashed on the floor.

'That's unusual for you to be breaking the crockery, Mum,' John observed.

'It wasn't me, I never touched it,' she replied.

If that was all that ever happened in the flat, the flying cup might simply have been put down as one of life's little mysteries and forgotten. Instead, it was the start of a series of unexplained incidents that are still occurring at the time of writing. The next happening was late on a cold December night in the same year. Because the flat had only one bedroom, John, a mature student in his thirties, slept in the lounge. Mrs McKay had been a keen bird-fancier for many years so John shared the front room with some Turks, a parrot and a cockatiel.

On this particular night, both Phyllis and John were woken by a tremendous commotion in the lounge. It was as if a fox had been let loose in there. All the birds were very upset, frantically flying around their cages twittering in fear. Moreover, the flat was uncomfortably hot and airless.

'Something seems to have spooked the birds, Mum!' John called through to her as he tried to calm them down. Then the temperature plummeted, making the flat cold and clammy. After a minute or two, it returned to normal, leaving a couple of feathers floating to the floor as the only reminder of the experience.

John was more a son to Phyllis than anything, doing her shopping and gardening as well as cooking their meals, so it was a dreadful shock when he suffered a fatal heart attack in February 1994. At the time, the whole family, Liz, her boyfriend and daughter were watching a sports programme on television at Phyllis's flat. John had gone through to the bathroom where he suddenly collapsed. Although the ambulance arrived within minutes, the attack proved unsurvivable. Its severity can be gauged from the fact that John actually died twice that night, firstly in the ambulance to be revived by the crew, then in hospital a couple of hours later.

Everyone felt John's loss very deeply, but none more so than Lisa, the daughter of Liz's boyfriend Dave. She had regarded him as a much loved uncle and treasured every small item he had ever given her when he was alive. One of these was a favourite mug which Lisa used every time she visited Mrs McKay. A few weeks after John had died, the little girl ran into the sitting room crying. It seemed that she had just put the mug in the crockery cupboard when it took flight of its own accord and smashed on the floor. A short while after that, when Dave was doing the washing up a saucer broke under similar circumstances.

Apart from the flying crockery, which might or might not have had anything to do with John, the family were also conscious of other little reminders of their dead friend. Phyllis began to feel she was not alone in the kitchen and when Dave stood at the fishpond in the garden he always felt that John was standing behind him. Often, there was also the distinctive smell of Insignia, John's favourite aftershave, in the flat.

For a while the crockery stopped flying and the flat seemed

peaceful. Then, in early December 1994, inanimate objects started to fly about the kitchen again. Firstly it was a child's bat and bird's perch toppling off the top of the fridge. Then a tray suddenly flew out of a cupboard under the sink. It could possibly be argued that on the vibration of the fridge caused the first two objects to fall, but the tin tray was stored securely away. Besides, this was not all that happened.

On the evening of Friday, 9 December 1994, Liz, Dave and Liz's daughter Natalie had visited Mrs McKay. As they were leaving, there was a terrible crash in the kitchen. When she went through to see what happened, Mrs McKay found the tray in the middle of the floor. Hearing her pet cat Lara crying at the back door, she went to let her in. It was then that she saw the spare key oscillating violently. After unlocking the door, she held on to the key then gently let go. Instead of just hanging there, it began to swing backwards and forwards again. Although Lara normally slept in the kitchen, she bolted down her supper and then ran for the lounge, her fur standing on end. Then again on the Sunday night, the cat refused to enter the kitchen to sleep.

'Perhaps John's lonely,' Mrs McKay said, 'and this is his way of protesting at being left out.'

Although the cat seemed to bear out the theory that animals are traditionally more attuned to the supernatural than humans, John's old dog, who is now looked after by Phyllis, took absolutely no notice of the disturbances.

There was also another aspect to the disturbances that affected the McKay family. For Liz also had two strange experiences that she could not explain. Firstly, in November 1994 there was the case of the burning cigarette. One Saturday morning, she got up as usual and made breakfast for the family. After eating it whilst watching television, she went back into the bedroom to discover a freshly lit cigarette in the ashtray by the bed. Who had lit it? Since John used to live with Liz and was also a heavy smoker, she suspects it may have been his way of letting her know he was still around.

Then there was the incident of the spectral smoke column. In the autumn of 1993, Liz distinctly remembers waking up late one night to see a swirling column of black smoke in the corner of her room. After what seemed an age but was probably only a few seconds, it vanished after moving across the room. On checking the area where she had seen it, Liz could discover no sign nor smell of burning. She is at a loss to explain what it meant, thinking only that it was a visual omen warning her of the impending death of another friend and neighbour that occurred a few days later.

Like the Gallacher family's experiences in Glasgow and Reading ('A Ghost in the Family' Chapter 8), the McKays are a baffling tapestry of small events. Taken individually, they are seemingly brief and meaningless but, looked at as a whole form a pattern of disturbances that have affected the whole family. This raises the inevitable question, are some family groups more susceptible to paranormal activity than others? It is not one that can be readily answered either by the author or the family. All they wish is that there should be no further activity, and they are considering some form of exorcism to lay the unquiet spirits affecting their homes finally to rest.

3

The Ghosts of The Thames Valley

Situated about 10 miles from Wokingham, Caversham lies just across the River Thames from Reading in Berkshire. But although they are near neighbours, the two places could not be more different. Whereas Reading is a sprawling and very noisy mixture of commerce and high-density living, Caversham is genteel, with leafy streets of large houses. Most of these were built at the turn of the century, but there is one part of the town that was built in the 1960s. This area is known as Caversham Park Village and is the unlikely setting for the next story.

THE HAUNTING OF NEIL M.

*Neil M.'s Story

The little boy awoke with an intense feeling of dread and violation. Outside the bedroom window of the neat new house a storm was grabbing at the trees silhouetted by the street lights. This was enough to frighten any child, but it was what was inside the room that terrified the little boy.

The 6-year-old, who was called Neil, had just moved into the house in Caversham Park near Reading with his parents. Nothing happened for the first three months. Then, without warning, he found he was being subjected to this hostile visitation.

'I was completely paralysed with fear,' Neil recalled recently. 'I knew there was something in the room with me, although I wasn't sure what it was. It was also icy-cold, as if my soul was being frozen.'

In a freezing sweat, he found that he was unable to move or speak. It was as if he was being held by some invisible force so that he could be observed. Eventually, with what seemed like a superhuman effort, he managed to move his head so that he could see the trees waving around in the wind. However, partially obscuring his view was a large black void in the shape of a human hovering between the curtains and the window.

'I don't know whether this is something I have transposed over the experience in the intervening years,' Neil told me, 'but it seemed to be like a highwayman with a cape and three cornered hat.'

Time had lost all meaning for Neil, so it could have been seconds, minutes or even hours before the sinister figure vanished and he was able to scream for his parents. It was only after a considerable time that they were able to calm the boy down for him to go back to sleep. For a year after this incident Neil did not experience a single undisturbed night. If his parents were not wakened by his hysterical screams it would be his sleepwalking. He has no recollection of it now, but his mother told him of the numerous occasions she found him sitting up in bed apparently answering questions put by an invisible stranger. 'She said that I seemed frightened and scared of this person,' Neil recalled.

Then, after finding him trying climb his bedroom wall one night, they decided it was time to take him to the doctor before any real harm befell their son.

'He recommended that I didn't eat cheese,' Neil said with a wry chuckle. ' And I was put on sleeping pills.'

After that, Neil continued to live in the house for a further four years without incident, but he is certain that what happened on the stormy night was not a dream. The freezing temperature is one of the sensations he remembers most vividly. 'It was like the numerous other experiences I've had,' he explained. 'The freezing temperature seems to sear through your body as though someone or something is saying: "I'm here". Like a trigger for me to realise there is some kind of paranormal presence.'

Neil, who is now in his thirties, works with problem children and is an interesting case from a paranormal point of view. Unlike most people, the high level of psychic awareness he possessed as a child has not been squeezed out by the demands of an increasingly materialistic world. This has meant that he has continued to have supernatural experiences well into his adult life. We will share these with him in subsequent stories as one of our regular companions on this 'Journey with Ghosts'.

Although I have known Martin Smith for over 20 years, I must admit that he was the very last person I expected to have had any sort of paranormal experience. So, when I visited him and his wife Ruth for supper, I did not take my cassette recorder along. I was to regret that omission. It had been some years since we had last met and so there was a great deal of catching up to do. When I came to the subject of my book, he listened with great interest then said: 'Would you like to hear about my ghostly experience?'

I replied that I most certainly would and he told me the following story.

SEARLE'S FARM

Martin Smith's Experience

Between the south-western part of Reading and the M4 motorway there is a strange wasteland of disused gravel pits dotted with small copses of trees and isolated groups of houses. Most of the pits have now been re-landscaped into lakes where people can go yachting or water skiing. They also provide a sheltered home for various forms of wildlife. Marooned in the midst of this area is a fine old Tudor building known as Searle's Farm.

In the mid 1960s 19-year-old Martin Smith, who worked for a local haulage company, was looking for lodgings. One of the drivers who worked on contract for the same firm heard about this and approached Martin with a proposition.

'I hear you're looking for a place to stay,' the driver said.

'That's right,' Martin replied. 'Why, do you know of somewhere?'

'Yeah, the wife and I have got plenty of room at our house down at Pingewood. Interested?'

The room offered for lodgings turned out to be situated in Searle's Farm. Since it was not only very comfortable but also close to his work, Martin accepted the offer of lodgings there. However, when he arrived to move in a couple of days later, he discovered that the room was not quite ready for him.

'That's all right, my dear,' the wife said. 'We can put you up in one of the other rooms for a few days.'

With that, she led him through a maze of stairs and landings to a large bedroom on the opposite side of the house. As far as Martin was concerned, one room was much the same as another and he felt equally at home there. This was fortunate, because on his first night he had a strange and vivid dream.

It was as if he were an unseen observer in this room. As he watched, a youngish woman dressed in flowing white clothes appeared by the window. She did not look at Martin but stared outwards at the countryside. Although it was dark in the rest of the room, she was illuminated by a soft white light.

The next morning, he was greeted with expectant looks by the various members of the driver's family.

'Did you sleep all right?' the driver asked.

'Fine, thanks,' Martin replied, tucking into his bacon and eggs.

'Nothing unusual then?' the driver prompted.

It was a strange question to ask and caused Martin to pause and think.

'Well, actually, I did have rather a curious dream,' he said, then told them about the girl bathed in light. After he finished, the husband and wife exchanged glances then told Martin the real reason he had been put in the room.

66

In the 1800s, a young servant girl at the house discovered she was pregnant. Consumed by guilt and fear, she jumped from the window of that particular bedroom, killing herself and her unborn child. Since that tragedy, many guests who had slept in there had had a dream identical to Martin's.

'Putting me in there was a sort of initiation for their guests,' Martin recalled with a smile. 'The strange thing was, if you walked past that room there always seemed to be a light shining under the door, but when you opened it, the room would be in darkness.'

It was not just Martin who noticed this phenomenon, but also his future wife Ruth when she came to visit him.

Like most ancient buildings, Searle's Farm would very occasionally yield one of its many secrets. The dream manifestation of the unfortunate servant girl was one of them, the secret room behind the fireplace was another. This might have remained undiscovered were it not for some alterations being carried out by the owners. Breaking through a wall by the large fireplace in the main living room, they came upon a tiny cell of a room with no windows. In its centre was a chair and table large enough only for a midget or a child. Placed on the table was an orange shrivelled and dry with age.

The sealing of objects and animals behind walls was a common practice of mediaeval householders ('The Mystic West' Chapter 4). By doing this, they hoped to ward off evil and illness. This may have been the purpose behind the room or it may have been a priest's hole. These were common during times of persecution, when being the 'wrong' type of Christian had you burned at the stake. Wealthy Catholics would provide secret rooms to hide their priests when the authorities came looking for them.

On the other hand, the room may have had another purpose. Perhaps it was a secret, guilty memorial to the tragic suicide whose spirit seems to be trapped at the farm for ever.

We do not have to travel very far at all for the next two experiences since they occurred at Purley-on-Thames, which is situated not more than a few minutes' boat ride upriver from Caversham. Like its larger neighbour, Purley has roots that go back many hundreds of years. Today, only a small part of this original village now survives in the form of a few timbered cottages. Grouped on Purley's western edge, they seem to huddle together around a much larger building known as the Coach House. Built in the eighteenth century, it was here that Pat Edwards had a very strange paranormal encounter indeed.

THE PHANTOM PHOTOGRAPHER

Pat Edwards' Story

Like many very old buildings, The Coach House at Purley-on-Thames has a number of legends surrounding it. Indeed, with its ivy-covered walls, tall windows and multitude of rooms, it is easy to believe that this is a property that harbours many stories and secrets.

For example, there is the secret chapel discovered by the owners a few years ago which is thought to have been for the benefit of the Catholic monks of nearby Mapledurham House, who would hide and worship there during times of religious persecution. Another legend concerns the ghost of a headless horseman who would be seen around the property, particularly where the old stables were situated.

Pat Edwards, who lived there in the mid-1960s, never saw the horseman and treated the story with the same amount of reservation she would have about any unconfirmed local ghost story. However, soon after she moved in with her family, she became aware of a bitter and tortured spirit in the old house.

Although she never saw anything, Pat became increasingly oppressed by the terrible presence that was weighing down on her like a suffocating burden. It seemed as if this presence objected to her family being in the house and this was its way of forcing them out. Something just had to be done, so one day Pat took the bull by the horns. Sitting down at the large table in the old kitchen, she addressed the unhappy spirit directly.

'Now look here,' she said in a quiet but stern voice, 'this behaviour really has to stop, you know. We are here to stay, and if you can't accept that, well, I'll just have to take steps to get rid of you.'

The implied threat that she would have the presence exorcised if it did not behave worked perfectly. From then on, the atmosphere not only lifted completely, but the ghost became a reformed character. For example, often when Pat was approaching a closed door with a tray in her hands, the ghost would obligingly open it. On another occasion, it ensured that there was change in the cup she kept for the milkman's money. She always made sure that she thanked the spirit for these little courtesies.

Although Marmaduke, as she christened the ghost, never appeared to Pat or her husband Tony, there were two occasions when it manifested itself in a fairly concrete form.

The first was when her three-year-old son Trevor asked who the old man he had seen in his room was. His mother knew that ghosts were often attracted to the children of the house and concluded that Trevor had encountered Marmaduke. So that the little boy would not be frightened, she gave a nonchalant answer and passed on to the question of what game they would play after breakfast. With more interesting matters claiming his attention, Trevor soon forgot about his visitor and never mentioned seeing him again.

The other incident happened some years later when Trevor and his sister Tracy were small children in the winter of 1967. Pat remembers looking through a film she had just picked up from being developed. In it were all the usual family photographs: her husband Tony in the beautiful garden, Trevor playing the fool as usual and his sister Tracy beaming towards the camera. However, there were also two photographs in the pack that she had no recollection of taking. What disturbed her about them was not only the fact that they appeared to have been shot at strange angles through an ephemeral mist, but also because there had been nobody around to take them at the time.

The first picture had been taken in the kitchen, and if you did not know the circumstances surrounding it, you would probably write it off as a mistaken exposure. In the foreground there is part of an empty carrycot lit by the February morning sun and rather out of focus. In the background, Pat can be seen working at the sink. Taken at an angle, it is unremarkable as a picture, except that no living being actually shot it.

'That picture would have to have been taken from the large ledge on the kitchen window,' Pat explained. 'But at that time, there was no room for anyone up there since I was babysitting my nephew and had placed his carrycot up there. Besides, I would have noticed someone perched up there with my camera, which was packed away in a cupboard at the time.'

Close examination of the photograph does reveal two interesting facts that seem to contradict the basic laws of photography and physics. Firstly, although the sun lighting the carrycot is directly behind the camera, the photographer has cast no shadow whatsoever. Secondly, although the carrycot is out of focus, this is due to it being too close to the lens. Since the camera was an Instamatic with a fixed-focus lens, this should have meant that the background was reasonably sharp, but it is not. In fact, the images in the background are slightly elongated and distorted, as if the camera had been moved whilst taking the photograph. If this had been the case, the carrycot would also have been similarly distorted but it was not.

The second photograph shows Tracy smiling towards her younger brother. In the background the lower part of her mother's body can be seen standing against a window. Although the photograph has a rather muddy appearance to it as if it is underexposed, both the foreground and background are reasonably sharp. Unlike the carrycot photograph, all movement has been successfully frozen. Indeed, it is quite well composed, which in itself is remarkable since there was nobody else in the house apart from the three people in the photo. There is also one other very interesting feature about this picture and that is a crescent of faint blue light emerging from the top of Tracy's head like an aura. Pat is quite convinced that, somehow, Marmaduke took the photographs.

'My late husband Tony was always sceptical about the supernatural,' she recalled with a smile. 'And on one occasion when we had a meeting of Mensa at the house I asked the assembled group if they would like to see my "ghost photographs". I could see from Tony's face that he was very dismayed by this suggestion. However, he need not have worried since our guests were all fascinated by them and wanted to know all about the ghost.'

The story of The Coach House ghost has a strange finale. Whilst she lived there, Pat became acquainted with an old lady called Mrs Rose who lived in a neighbouring cottage. However, Mrs Rose was never happy about visiting the house and finally refused to set foot in the grounds because she said that the headless horseman kept putting his horses in the old stables. The house ghost may not have been a problem for the Edwards family, but for at least one of Purley's older residents it was a different story.

THE MAN BEHIND HER

Betty Ingram's Experience

Tradition has it that the Scots are fey, which is another way of saying they are especially psychic. Perhaps this is something to do with the geology of their country or because their is a strong Celtic vein running through their culture – who knows? However, if the experiences related by many Scots for this book are anything to go by, then there is more than a little truth to this tradition.

My ex-mother-in-law Betty Ingram, who was born just outside Glasgow, has always known that she has a high level of psychic awareness. She believes that a spiritual world exists in parallel with that of the living. She also thinks that it is

71

usually invisible to most people because their minds are simply not open to such things. On occasions, this paranormal world does show itself, like the tear in a thick curtain allowing a brief glimpse of what is happening on the other side. Betty has had three experiences of this sort in her life

The first was when she was a youngster of ten or eleven. The family had gone to the resort town of Ayr for their annual holidays. Like most middle-class British families in the 1930s, they also took along their Box Brownie camera to record the event for posterity. Betty's father, Mr Brown, shot off a roll of film, mostly of his wife and daughter on the beach and at various beauty spots in the surrounding area. It was only after the holiday was finished and they had the film processed that Betty and her mother noticed there was something unusual about one of the photographs. It was a picture of Betty standing on the beach and smiling into the camera. When the picture was taken, she was on her own, the flat sand and sea stretching out behind her, but now, just above her head, was the image of a Red Indian.

'Oh yes,' said her mother, a lifelong spiritualist, 'that's your spirit guide.'

Unfortunately, the photograph was thrown out when Betty's mother moved south to be with her daughter. What to other people would have been a strange heirloom worth keeping, was just another snapshot to old Mrs Brown. After all, the spirit world was very much an everyday matter for her.

'You see, what everyone else would make a song and dance about, we just shrugged off as kids,' Betty explained to me recently. ' Mum would say "That's your spirit guide" and we'd just shrug. It was no big deal to us.'

Her next brush with the paranormal came some years later when she was a young newly-wed. At the time, she and her husband Ken were living in a fourth-floor flat in Glasgow. In those days, there were few lifts in such buildings, and Betty found herself making the irksome journey down to the dust-bins on the ground floor on a daily basis. To cut this down to a minimum, she would put all her rubbish in a box and sit it on one of the kitchen shelves to take down once a day. This was fine, but not the sort of thing a house-proud young wife would want visitors to discover, especially if they were two intrusive and straight-laced aunts.

'We went to see young Betty the other day and guess what? She keeps all her rubbish in a box!'

However, it was this very nightmare that almost occurred when the same aunts paid their first visit to Betty. They were coming for tea, that very Scottish social phenomenon which consists of much more than scones and cucumber sandwiches and is actually almost a full-blown fourth meal. Betty was in a panic checking and re-checking that all the silver was in place and that she had bought enough ham. In her haste, what she had forgotten was to put the rubbish box downstairs. Suddenly, a few minutes before the aunts arrived, it took flight from its spot in the kitchen and landed gently in front of the flustered newly-wed.

'There was no way it could have done that on its own,' she explained. 'I just think it was a dead relative helping me out. That would be just like them.'

After many years in southern Africa, Betty finally returned to the UK to live at Purley-on-Thames, just outside the Berkshire town of Reading. Now a widow, she joined the local Women's Institute to keep active and for the company. It was just after one of the weekly meetings of her local institute in the summer of 1993 that she had her most recent experience.

It was a sunny day, with a wind blowing through the tall beeches as she drove two of the other members home from the village hall. In the front seat was Mrs James*, a rather frail and retiring widow in her mid-seventies, and in the back was one of the younger married members. When they arrived at the old lady's house, the younger member escorted her to the door while Betty waited in the car. As the woman walked back to the car, Betty watched the old lady wave goodbye before slowly shutting the door. It was then that she noticed a very tall man in his thirties standing directly behind Mrs James. For a moment her attention was distracted, and when she looked back and the man was gone.

'Who's that man staying with Mrs James?' Betty asked her friend as she climbed back into the seat.

'What are you talking about?' the other woman asked, frowning. 'She lives on her own, there's nobody else in the house.'

'But I definitely saw a tall man standing behind her at the doorway,' Betty persisted.

'Oh my God,' her friend gasped. 'Do you think she's got a mugger?'

They drove back to the house and checked, but Mrs James was perfectly all right and completely on her own. After that, their drive home was particularly quiet and thoughtful. Betty has never discussed the apparition with the old lady since she is of a somewhat nervous disposition, but she would dearly like to know who the tall man was. She had a feeling that he was in the forces. Perhaps her husband or a long lost son had returned to keep an eye on her in her twilight years.

Researching and writing about the paranormal is often like assembling a strange jigsaw which only makes sense when the final piece is in place. This was certainly my experience in the case of the next story. As will be seen, it tells of a manifestation that occurred to at least three people over a period of 50 or 60 years. I had been told by two of them about their experiences but for some reason did not consider them quite strong enough to constitute a true-life ghost story. Then one day I was doing some research in Reading library when I came across a book that linked the three seemingly disparate events together and brought everything into sharp focus:

THE HAUNTED BRIDLE PATH

Gerry Tidbury's First Experience

Just across the Thames from Purley is an ancient bridle path that I know very well indeed. This is because I use it to travel

74

to work on my mountain bike. Running from the village of Whitchurch, where I live, to Caversham, near Reading, it passes through ravishingly beautiful farmland. I can not think of a better way to commute on a warm summer's morning when the only traffic I am likely to encounter are deer, pheasants and the odd tractor.

At the Caversham end this bridle path emerges onto a long, straight road called The Warren. With beechwoods on one side and views of the Thames on the other, it is beautiful in summer. However, on dark winter nights this part of the route takes on a much more sinister aspect. There are no street lights and the canopy of trees blocks out much of the moonlight, so it is like travelling down a long tunnel. It is certainly a road that should be avoided by the faint-hearted at such times, as I can testify, having walked its length on several midwinter evenings.

I neither saw nor sensed anything remotely abnormal on those occasions, but that has not been everybody's experience. During our interview, Neil M., who used to visit friends in The Warren, mentioned that he often saw indistinct shapes move across the road and vanish into thin air. He also said that the sounds of carriages and horses had often been heard in the vicinity of an old coach house in The Warren.

In his book *The Ghosts of Berkshire*, the late Angus Mac-Naughton also tells of a spectral encounter there a year or so before the Second World War. It happened to a veteran journalist, probably most sceptical of all professionals when it comes to the paranormal. However, this man was not just a reporter but Jim Pettengell, the Editor of *The Reading Standard* at that time.

As Jim was walking along the road one Christmas Day, he heard the distinctive sounds of a horse's hooves galloping behind him. Standing aside to let the horse through, he looked, but saw nothing as the equine phantom clattered past him and into the distance.

Twenty years later, in the 1960s, Gerry Tidbury and a friend were walking home to Pangbourne down the same stretch of the bridle path when they heard a horse cantering up behind them. Stepping onto the verge, they also had the sensation and sound of a horse galloping past yet again there was nothing there.

One could speculate for many months about who the phantom horseman or woman is and still be none the wiser. Perhaps it is the ghost of a highwayman who used the bridle road as an escape route. On the other hand, it could just as well be the imprint of someone who rode along there regularly. However, the accounts of the horse cantering past indicate a considerable level of urgency. So it is likely that the manifestation is linked to some traumatic event in the past, and once again we find the English Civil War casting its long shadow over our journey.

In 1643, the Royalist stronghold of Reading was under siege by the Parliamentarians. As the months passed, food and supplies began to run dangerously low. In a desperate attempt to relieve the town, King Charles sent a raiding party to try and force its way into the town, thereby breaking the siege. A fierce battle ensued on the Caversham Bridge just downstream from The Warren. The raid was unsuccessful and the Royalists were driven from the bridge, leaving a number of their men dead and injured. As in all routs, the vanquished side scattered and fled for their lives. So maybe the hooves are the echoes of some Royalist cavalryman trying desperately to outrun his vengeful pursuers.

The Haunted Village

Complete with an ancient church, two pubs and a manor house, the village of Whitchurch, close to Purley, possesses much of what is considered most charming about rural Britain, including a fair number of ghosts. I discovered this when I decided to put out an appeal in the village magazine for any of its residents to tell me of their paranormal experiences. I am very glad I did, because that request uncovered a wealth of fascinating stories. Since I also happened to live in Whitchurch, they all came from friends of many years' standing. In fact, I already knew of at least two haunted houses in the

76

village before starting my researches as I had lived in both of them. So it is probably appropriate that I should begin this part of the book with my own family's experiences in the haunted village.

THE GHOST NEXT DOOR

The Brazils' Story

Johannesburg in South Africa is not a city that is overendowed by very old buildings, so when my family and I moved back to England in 1976, it was not surprising that we chose an old house in an ancient Oxfordshire village. Called Whitchurch-on-Thames, it has origins that go back over a thousand years to the seventh century AD. In fact, Whitchurch is the derivation of Wit Cerc, the Saxon name for a chalk-stone church.

Our home, known as The Gatehouse, was about 120 years old. Converted in the 1960s, it had originally been the coal cellar and servants' quarters for the adjoining house. With its white walls and blue windows, it is a charming building which is quintessentially English in character. It will always have a very special place in my memory as probably the best family home we ever had.

From the downstairs lounge, there was a long passageway, at the end of which stairs led up to a long landing. Here, my daughter Amanda's bedroom led off to one side, with the bathroom directly opposite. At the end of the landing, there was a toilet and washbasin, with the main bedroom adjacent to it.

Although our memories of Whitchurch at that time were generally very good, my wife Diana noticed something strange about The Gatehouse almost immediately after we moved in.

'It was always very cold and spooky in the hallway and up the stairwell,' she recalled. 'The problem seemed to be mainly in an old cupboard at the foot of the stairs. The doors kept creaking open for no apparent reason.'

At first, Diana put this down to the uneven nature of the

cupboard's manufacture. However, her feeling of unease about that particular area of The Gatehouse not only remained but increased. If it was not the doors of the old cupboard opening without prompting, it was the floorboards creaking as if someone was walking along the landing.

On one occasion Diana's brother Chris, who often came to stay for weekends, was sleeping in my daughter's room when he awoke to see the figure of an old woman standing over him. His heart pounding with fear, he closed his eyes, willing the figure to disappear. However, when he opened them again, she was still there, obscuring his view of the mirror on the opposite wall. He closed his eyes once more, this time for some minutes. Mercifully, when he reopened them, the phantom had gone. Other guests had encounters with the lady too. Once, when my mother came to stay, she heard the distinctive swish of a dress and the sound of feet on the landing.

Like many ghosts, the phantom woman seemed to have a fascination for electric lights. For example, when Di was drying three-year-old Amanda after a bath, there was a strange incident with a bedside light. Because the bathroom was so small, she had to crouch down to do this, with her back edging onto the landing through the open door. This meant that my daughter could see straight through into her bedroom across the passage.

'Oh look, Mummy, my light's just gone on!' the little girl suddenly shouted out in pleasure.

Turning round, Diana saw that Amanda's night light, a jolly round orange figure with hat, had indeed gone on. It made her feel anything but jolly – scared was more like it. 'It wasn't as if the switch was half on or off,' Di explained. 'It wasn't dodgy at all.'

Then in 1978, there was an incident when I was in the house entirely on my own. My wife and daughter were both in South Africa at the time, visiting Di's parents. Every night I adhered to the same routine of switching the lights off as I went up to bed: first the lounge, then the hall, followed by the landing, until I reached our bedroom. On this particular night, I got to the washbasin to clean my teeth, turned round, and found all the lights in the house blazing away. Try as I might, I have never been able to find a rational explanation for this incident. Apart from a chill feeling down the nape of my neck when I stood in the hallway, that was my only paranormal experience whilst living in The Gatehouse. But this was not the case with Diana, who seemed to become the focus of the ghost's mischievous attentions.

On several occasions when she was vacuuming Amanda's room she would hear a child's voice calling her repeatedly. One day, it all became too much and, abandoning the Hoover in the middle of the floor, she ran out of the house, not daring to return until I came home from work. A few months after that, she saw the old lady for the first time.

'I remember that I had locked up last thing at night when you were already in bed,' she recalled. 'As I came up the stairs, putting the lights out, I turned round and saw an old woman standing at the bottom of the stairs. I never saw her face because she was looking down, but she had thinning hair and was big-breasted, wearing a powder-blue crossover dressing gown tied with a cord. She seemed about to lift her head when I ran up the stairs in fright.'

Matters finally came to a head when kitchen utensils such as knives and spoons took on a life of their own, jumping off tables. This was when Diana started addressing the spirit directly.

'Please go away, you're frightening me!' she would shout.

Then, coming down the hall one day, she was confronted by the sight of the old cupboard door opening on its own, and her temper finally snapped.

'Please go away, you're frightening me!' she screamed, slamming the cabinet door.

After that, matters eased. The doors stopped opening on their own and the lady was never seen again. But the creaking on the landing never ceased. Nor was Diana's unease about the hallway or Amanda's bedroom ever fully dispelled.

'The first year was the worst,' she said. 'But I think that as our personalities became ingrained in the house, it seemed to ease off. Perhaps it was the combination of the family atmosphere and my not wanting her that caused the haunting to finally cease. In fact, I think it would be highly unlikely for her still to be there.'

After interviewing my ex-wife, I spoke to Liz Batten, who lived in The Gatehouse with her late husband when it was first converted. She told me that they had never experienced anything remotely abnormal. The same was true of the Plumb family, who bought the property from us in the early 1980s.

As for myself, I recall having a strangely ambivalent attitude to it all at the time. Whilst I never really accepted the fact that the house was haunted, I did not dismiss the idea either. Perhaps I was afraid of ridicule, or perhaps my attention was taken up with more earthly matters at the time. I am ashamed to say I simply sat on the proverbial fence, failing to give Diana the support she probably needed at the time.

It was only when I started revisiting this story for this book that I became fully aware of how the hauntings had affected my daughter Amanda. For example, she recalls always being frightened of sleeping on her own in her room. In fact, I remember this very clearly, but I had always put it down to the fear under-fives tend to have of the dark. She also reminded me that neither our dog nor our cat would willingly go into her room. Once, when she tried to keep the cat in there with her for company, it fought, cried and scratched so much that she had to let it out.

Why this particular ghost chose to manifest itself to our family was probably due to three factors. Firstly, we had some major renovation work done before we moved in, as a result of which two ceilings collapsed. Building work on old properties often has the effect of stirring up resident spectres who regard any such changes as an intrusion into their private territory. Secondly, the ghost may have been attracted by a young family filling the house after it had been empty for some time. Thirdly, all of us have always possessed a high level of psychic awareness, which would have made us particularly receptive to any resident ghost's attentions. As to her identity, she was probably a housekeeper or servant in the large Victorian house that adjoined The Gatehouse.

Finally, there is an interesting postscript to this story. Twelve years after leaving our beloved Gatehouse, I found myself living in Whitchurch once more. This time, however, it was as a single man, Diana and I having separated two and a half years earlier. Call it chance, fate or whatever you like, but the property I moved into was actually the ground-floor flat adjoining my old home. If I looked out of my kitchen window, I could see into my old front yard.

Leading from my kitchen, there is a long, narrow storage area. It was here that I left the three tea chests I used for my move. I placed two of them against the access door connecting my flat with the main house. Since I had no occasion to use this particular door, it was kept bolted on both my side and the house side.

Early one evening in the autumn of 1993, I returned home from work to find that a light was on inside the otherwise dark flat. *That was careless*, I thought. However, in my heart of hearts I knew I had not left any lights on. Further investigation revealed that not only was the offending light in the storage area burning away, but two tea chests had been moved from in front of the access door to just inside the kitchen. My immediate reaction was to rationalise the whole matter and assume that workmen had gained access from the adjoining house via the connecting door. But how could they have done this when it was bolted on both sides?

Then, in the early summer of 1994, my son Peter came to stay with Harry, my daughter's highly loveable and intelligent miniature poodle. At about nine o' clock in the evening, Harry stood at the entrance to the kitchen and, staring intently at the opposite wall, began barking in a friendly and enquiring manner. About a month later, he gave a repeat performance. It was as if he had encountered a friendly stranger who was able to allay the normal hostility and fear that animals have of the supernatural.

Two other facts should be noted about these incidents. Firstly, the kitchen where Harry saw something is exactly next door to The Gatehouse's kitchen where the knives and spoons moved of their own accord. Secondly, the mobile tea chests were situated in a direct line with the hallway in The Gate-house which caused Diana so much unease. Perhaps the old lady from next door has decided to move in with me.

A SMELL OF TOBACCO

*Tim and Jill's Experience

In 1977, Tim and Jill moved into a pretty whitewashed cottage in Whitchurch. With a neat English garden and a splendid view of the village's old Manor House, it was everything they wished for in a home. In fact, it had rather more than they bargained for, because this cottage also had a ghost.

The couple discovered that they were sharing their home with a supernatural lodger not long after they arrived. They became aware of the pungent aroma of shag, that strong dark country tobacco much favoured by rural pipe smokers at the turn of the century. Where it came from was a complete mystery since neither of them smoked, and it was only notice-able in the sitting room. Neither of them was frightened or disturbed by the smell and it did not even bother those most psychically perceptive creatures, their two cats.

The smell came and went intermittently for a number of years, then one day a friend asked Jill if they enjoyed living in the cottage.

'Yes, very much,' Jill replied.

This prompted a further and rather curious question from her friend: 'But do you find anything *strange* about it?'

'Well, there is this strong smell of tobacco,' Jill said.

It was then that her friend told her about an incident that had occurred when her son was renting the cottage a few years earlier. On this particular occasion, his girlfriend had called in to see him. Since he was not in at the time, she let herself in with the door key he had lent her. As she walked into the sitting room she was surprised to see an old man with white hair and a dark suit standing in the room.

Two years after they moved in, Jill's mother came to stay to be nursed through her final illness. After she died, the smell of tobacco disappeared.

'I think the old gentleman was keeping an eye on the place,' Jill explained. 'You know, making sure we were looking after it. When Mum died, perhaps she told him the cottage was in good hands and he need not worry. We always found him to be a most benign and gentle presence.'

A FIGURE IN THE TWILIGHT

Bart and Eileen's Experience

A couple of doors down the High Street from Jill and Tim's home stands the oldest cottage in Whitchurch. Built in the fifteenth century of wattle and daub and reinforced by huge oak beams, Swanston Cottage is typical of the ancient England so beloved by the tourist industry. Bart and Eileen lived there for many years and, considering this and the age of the building, it is surprising that they had only one brief supernatural encounter.

It happened late one summer's evening when they were finishing off a regular hand of bridge with a friend. They were in the cottage's low-ceilinged lounge at the time. Because it was late, Bart decided to retire to bed. Minutes later Eileen looked up and glimpsed her husband moving across the room.

'Bart, I thought you were going to bed!' Eileen exclaimed.

However, Bart did not answer, because he *was* already in bed asleep. Whoever walked across the room that evening certainly was not him. Neither was it the only other two people in the house at the time for they were both seated playing bridge. So who was that mysterious, fleeting figure? Perhaps it was the spirit of former owner who, like the old man of Jill and Tim's cottage, had come to keep an eye on his earthly home.

A FRIGID VOID

Geoff and Merel Weir's Experience

When Geoff and Merel Weir moved down to Whitchurch from the Midlands in 1976, they chose a 200-year-old terraced house called Myrtle Cottage. Like many of the buildings in the village, it oozed old-world charm and had a great deal of space. The previous owner, an eccentric old lady, had done little to the place over the years so it also had 'great potential for improvement', to use the estate agents' parlance. With plenty of room and a large and secluded garden, it was an ideal property to bring up their young family. However, there was one small, albeit intangible, drawback to Myrtle Cottage which Merel encountered from the moment she set foot in the place. This was a powerful feeling of being watched.

'It is very difficult to explain that particular sensation,' Merel told me. 'But it was just as if someone was always there observing us. Of course, when you turned around, there was nobody there.'

After a couple of years the Weirs embarked upon some major renovations to the cottage during which they made a strange discovery. Whilst demolishing a wall in the kitchen area, the builders accidentally broke into a sealed and window-less room at the rear of the property.

'You would expect a space enclosed like that to be cold,' Merel said. 'However, the total lack of warmth in that area was quite unnatural. I can only describe it as a frigid void.'

All old houses, particularly haunted ones, possess secrets, many of which are dark and never discovered. Had it not been for those alterations, Myrtle Cottage might have kept this one indefinitely. As it was, after that eerie hidden place was uncovered, the feeling of being watched left the Weirs completely. Because of this, Merel and Geoff believe their renovations finally released a supernatural presence that may have been trapped in the house for centuries.

THE FLINT HOUSE

Pea Spafford's Second Story

Situated a short distance down the same road as The Gatehouse and Myrtle Cottage, is an unusual-looking building known as The Flint House. Originally constructed as a Victorian schoolhouse, it took its name from the flints which were used to dress the outside of the building. Set back from the road against a hill covered with beeches, it was a very attractive house in a lovely location. I always liked The Flint House and would have killed to own it. However, many of the people who lived or stayed there were of a different opinion. It was said that the old place had a 'strange' atmosphere or that there was something 'peculiar' about it.

In the early 1980s we became good friends with Pea Stinton (as she then was) and her husband Michael, who lived there. They had moved into The Flint House a couple of years previously and filled it with four noisy children from this and two previous marriages. Pea is a very talented artist and was able to decorate the place with just the right mixture of old furniture, paintings and oddities from antique shops. She also painted some beautiful murals in her daughters' rooms, depicting cheerfully rotund pigs in richly coloured rural settings. With a large garden, it was a paradise for the children to play and grow up in.

Pea had noticed the strange atmosphere from the moment they moved in. As if to confirm this feeling, objects then started to go missing, only to turn up in unexpected places weeks later. For example, on one occasion a very large and ornate picture frame vanished from the living room. Months later, it reappeared in one of the children's bedrooms. After satisfying themselves it was not one of the children playing pranks, she and Michael began to suspect that they might have a problem with a poltergeist. At the time, a teenaged relative had come to stay and was proving to be rather a handful. It was possible, they reasoned, that some spirit had become active as a result of this. What occurred in the autumn of 1982 might or might not have had a connection with this.

During its construction, the steep slope behind The Flint House had been cut into, leaving a bare chalk face. Either by design or accident, this has helped to lighten the house, particularly on cloudless days when the sunlight is reflected into the building's interior. On clear autumn nights the effect is the same, except that the rooms are bathed in a colder and more eerie glow.

It was on just such a night that Pea was awakened by someone ferreting around in the corner her bedroom. Opening her eyes, she saw a figure standing with its back to her by the bedroom washbasin. At first she thought it was her husband Michael and she asked him what on earth he was doing there. When there was no reply, she repeated the question, but still the figure ignored her. Putting her hand out, she felt Michael sleeping peacefully beside her. It was then that she began to feel a twinge of alarm. Sitting upright, she had a chance to study the figure in the silvery moonlight. Dressed in an indistinct, single garment, it had the appearance of being a deformed young adult rather than a child. Its most striking and memorable feature was a shock of wild and unkempt hair standing straight up from its head.

Apparently sensing that Pea was watching, the figure stopped its rustling and moved furtively towards the door.

'I saw this little wild figure creeping away quite fast, hugging the passage wall,' she recalled recently. 'So immediately after watching it, I went to check on the children and, sure enough, they were all asleep.'

Little of note happened over the next couple of months, then, late one night, Pea's ten-year-old daughter Candida had a bad fright. As she walked along the landing to the lavatory, something in the stairwell caught her eye. Looking down, she saw a little creature with wild hair staring up at her. Immediately, she ran into her mother's room and woke her.

'Mum, Mum, Mum! There's somebody at the bottom of the stairs,' she said urgently, shaking her mother.

After calming her down, Pea made Candida explain what

she saw. The description was a carbon copy of her night visitor. Mother and daughter then returned to the stairwell, but the creature had gone.

'Obviously I had not told any of the children about my experience because I did not want to scare them,' Pea explained, 'so she couldn't have known what I saw. But Candida's description matched mine perfectly.'

Although Candida still refuses to discuss the incident, one of her childhood friends recalled how shaken and frightened she was the next day.

'She told us about the thing she saw,' Justin White told me recently. 'And I'll always remember how terrified she seemed at the time.'

Two years later, a friend of the Stintons called Phil Seymour visited them for dinner on a soft summer's evening. Phil, who is also a mutual friend, is always very good company and this occasion was no exception, with everyone enjoying an entertaining and pleasant night. Even though he had had little to drink, Phil wisely decided to stay. It was well after midnight when everyone retired to bed. For some reason, Phil left the door of his room wide open. Not more than an hour later, he awoke to hear the front door slam shut and the sound of someone walking through the house. The footsteps came up the stairs, along the landing and stopped at the entrance to his room. Phil looked expectantly, but there was absolutely nobody there.

'I have no idea who it might have been,' Phil told me. 'But it was definitely an adult. No, I wasn't asleep.'

Neither Phil nor Pea have ever found a satisfactory answer to the mysterious incidents at The Flint House. Nowadays, when I pass the house I always feel that it does have an unusual air about it. Standing etched against the white of the chalk with its arched windows and flint stones, it is as if The Flint House knows it is concealing many strange secrets.

Postscript: Wherever possible, I have investigated the background of the paranormal incidents that appear in this book.

This is because I have always believed that hauntings occur for a reason. In the case of The Flint House, which was a school in Victorian times, I felt that the ghost Pea and her daughter saw may well have been a child who died there.

To help me in this research, Pea lent me a fascinating book published by the Oxfordshire Record Society. Called *Village Education in Nineteenth Century Oxfordshire*, it is the school attendance diary in published and edited form. These diaries were written up by the head teacher of the school and make fascinating if, at times, rather melancholy reading:

> *April 11th 1879. Rec'd a doctor's certificate for Fred'k Shaw who is suffering from a diseased brain.*

> *April 17th 1879. Funeral of Fred'k Shaw.*

> *October 12th 1885. William Newman away with Scarlet Fever.*

> *October 22nd 1885. Rec'd information that Ida Hazell was dead. She had been suffering from Scarlet Fever.*

In the 11 years between the summer of 1879 and the spring of 1890, five children from the Whitchurch School died either from disease or accident. However, none of these pupils appear to have actually died at The Flint House. So, whilst this book gave me an interesting insight into school and village life at the turn of the century, it failed to provide me with any real clues as to the identity of the strange, wild creature who haunted the house. It may well have been any one of the deceased children listed in the book, there again, it may not.

At a recent arts and crafts exhibition in Whitchurch, I met the current owner of The Flint House. After introducing myself, I explained my interest in her home. To my relief, she reacted with great interest rather than horror.

'You know, it's a funny thing,' she said. 'Some friends of ours always teased us about The Flint House being haunted, but we never really took it seriously.'

Had she or any of her family actually seen or sensed anything? I asked.

'No, but I'm not at all sensitive to such things,' she replied. Then, after a pause, added: 'Although I have often *thought* I've seen figures passing by the window. You know, from the corner of my eye. But we do have a number of cats about the place, so it could be them.'

Possibly, but they could also be the spirits of the Victorian children who died prematurely from disease or accident. Perhaps they return to play spectral games of hopscotch or tag on the site of their old playground. If so, their presence is quite harmless if a little sad.

THE DOCTOR

Pea Spafford's Third Story

As Penelope savoured her coffee, she felt totally at peace. From her vantage point on the balcony, she had a magnificent vista of the steep cliffs tumbling into an impossibly blue sea. From the cobbled village below, the sounds were an occasional dog's bark and the bell summoning the black-clad women and men in suits to church.

Sunday breakfast with her family *al fresco* on the balcony of their villa was just one of the many delights of living in southern Italy. It seemed that here, every day was like Sunday, relaxed and totally devoid of stress. This laid-back Latin culture could not have been further removed from that of her native England, but that suited Pea and her family just fine. Pea, her children and husband Michael had lived in Italy for three years and already she could not imagine staying anywhere else. For no better reason than habit, she checked her watch as she munched a croissant. It was ten past nine.

Suddenly, her peaceful reverie was blotted out by a dark mental cloud. She felt as if something evil and alien had invaded her mind.

My God, she thought in total panic, *something awful's happened in England! I've just got to get back!*

'Hell, what's happened to you?' Michael asked her, his face creased with concern. 'Your pupils are all dilated and black. Are you all right?'

'No I'm not, Michael,' she replied. 'We've got to get back to England. Something's happened to Dad, I just know it! We've got to go home today!'

'With due respect, Pea, you can't just climb on a flight to England because of a bad feeling now can you?' Michael said with mild exasperation. 'Besides, if anything has happened, we'll hear soon enough.'

Reluctantly, she agreed and, after an uneventful day, began to feel slightly better and more relaxed. However, the sense of foreboding of that morning had not gone away but lurked in the back of her mind like some beast waiting to strike. Pea simply could not shake off the certainty that something dreadful had happened to her father.

At lunchtime the following day, Pea realised that her intuitive sense of dread was more than just an illogical feeling. One of their oldest Italian friends, a local hotelier, arrived in a state of great anxiety.

'Penelope! Penelope! Quick, *telefono*! Your mother in England!' he said excitedly. 'Come quickly!'

This is it, she thought as they went down to the hotel, which possessed one of the few telephones in the village. Although it was 1978, Italy was still telephonically in the dark ages and it took some time before Pea was able to speak to her mother in Oxfordshire.

'Pea darling, I've had the most awful trouble trying to get you. I'm afraid I have some very bad news,' her mother said, her voice crackly and distant.

'Yes I know what your news is, Mum,' Pea replied. 'It's Dad, he's died, hasn't he?'

'That's right, but how did you know?' her mother asked.

'It happened at ten past nine yesterday morning, didn't it?' Pea said.

'Well, that's nearly right,' Mrs Spafford said. 'He actually died at ten past eight.'

In fact Pea was correct, because Italy is one hour ahead of British time. This meant that her feeling of foreboding occurred at exactly the time her father was dying of a silent coronary.

'He had just woken up that morning and *bang!* he died,' Pea recalled. 'It was just the most dreadful shock.'

There was no question now, they had to return to England. Twenty-four hours later, they were comforting Pea's bereaved mother in Whitchurch, where she and her husband, a local doctor, had lived for many years. It had been a long, harrowing day. Pea and Michael felt physically and mentally exhausted. While Pea and her mother talked quietly in the kitchen of Whiteways, the family home, Michael went into the lounge with a large gin and tonic. Twenty minutes later, he came back into the kitchen, his face deathly white.

'He's there! Your father's in the lounge,' he said unsteadily.

The two women laughed in disbelief. To hear Michael, the arch sceptic about the paranormal, talk like this was a shock in itself, but he would not be shaken from his story.

Apparently, whilst he had been relaxing in the living room, he saw Dr Spafford's favourite chair suddenly jerk backwards, the cushions flattening with a *Whumpf* as if somebody had suddenly sat down heavily in it. However, the chair was empty and nobody else was in the room at the time.

For the next six weeks, the late Dr Spafford was with them in the house both night and day. When the family were sitting in the drawing room at night, they would hear doors opening and closing in the bedrooms, followed by the sound of restless footsteps on the stairs. Pea's children would often hear footsteps go past their bedroom and enter their dead grandfather's dressing room next door. Then on one occasion, they all heard the sound of somebody riffling through a paperback in his deserted surgery adjoining the house.

'Oh God, he's looking for his joke book,' Pea's mother said with a nervous laugh. After the joke book was left out, the activity in the surgery ceased. However, the same could not be said for the rest of the house, where the restless footsteps and manifestations continued. For example, Pea's brother Peter also had an unnerving experience in the lounge when he saw the handle of a door to the garden move of it's own accord. It was as if Dr Spafford had still not come to terms with his sudden death.

Of all the incidents that occurred during that difficult period, there are two that stand out in Pea's mind above all others. Both incidents happened when they were sleeping in her parents' old bedroom. The first was when she and Michael were awakened by two strong and familiar smells they always associated with her father.

'Can you smell that, Michael?' Pea whispered.

'Yes, it's your dad's pipe smoke and aftershave,' he replied.

The second incident, which was much more unnerving, happened a few days after Dr Spafford had died. It took the form of a dream in which Pea was following her father down the main stairs in the house. At the bottom, he turned and gave his daughter a look of terrible emptiness. His startling blue eyes that had always been so full of sparkle and humour were now devoid of all life. As soon as she awoke, she started to tell Michael about the dream and get it off her chest. However, before she could begin, he stopped her.

'Hang on, let me tell you about my dream first,' he said. What he described next was a dead ringer of his wife's nightmare, right down to the frightening look and the lifeless eyes.

Many years later, Pea still has difficulty in accepting and understanding those identical dreams. She thinks that one possibility is that they were a spiritual watershed when her father finally realised he had died. When he next came to her some nights after the dreams, his presence seemed much calmer and philosophical.

At the time, Pea's mother was in a state of great unhappiness and remorse not uncommon in people who have recently been bereaved. As she lay on her bed listening to her mother crying in the other room, she became aware of her father standing very close to her.

'Darling Pea, stop her grieving like this,' he said in a gentle and compassionate voice. 'It's not her fault and now that I'm here it's all clear and I can see where I went wrong.'

Pea did as her father requested and went in to comfort her mother. As a result of that experience, she felt able to help her mother through the difficult period of bereavement much more effectively than would otherwise have been the case.

Pea has only definitely felt her father's presence twice since those traumatic weeks following his death. On both occasions, they were at dinner parties when she sensed him observing and enjoying the conviviality of his earthly family. He no longer seemed restless and disorientated, but totally calm and at peace.

Chrissie McBurnie, whose story appears next, is one of those interesting paradoxes, an agnostic who not only believes in ghosts but feels they are due to spiritual survival after death. This conviction is due partly to her experiences in Whitchurch, but also because of an incident when she was 14. At that time she was living with her parents in Crawley. Every morning she would take her two dogs for a walk before going to school.

On a misty autumn morning in 1982, she was walking down a path that ran along the main railway line. Suddenly, both dogs ran off in fright, and about 30 yards in front she saw the figure of a man. Although he had a solid enough appearance, Chrissie was struck by the fact that his features were lost in a whitish-grey appearance, as if he was made of wax. She also could not see his eyes, or any other detail of his face except for his nose. After looking in her direction for some seconds, he turned and walked towards the railway line.

Thinking it strange that he should pick such a dangerous spot to cross the line, she carried on walking to the point where the man had been standing. However, when she arrived there, she realised he must have walked straight though the chain link security fencing. There was also no sign of him on the track or in the woods beyond. Then as her dogs gingerly returned, their hackles raised, she realised the figure had not been mortal.

Like most people, Chrissie probably did not think she would see more than one ghost in her life. What happened when she moved into an ancient estate cottage would prove how wrong one can be about such things.

THE HARDWICK HAUNTING

Chrissie McBurnie's Experience

About halfway between the Mapledurham and Whitchurch locks on the Thames, there is a magnificent Tudor mansion. Flanked on three sides by beechwoods, it has a splendid view of the river across a sweep of lawn. This is Hardwick House, a property with a long and fascinating history. The original house was built by the Normans in 1078, just 12 years after the Battle of Hastings. Over the centuries, successive owners added to the property, making it the large manor it is today. In the sixteenth century, Queen Elizabeth stayed there. To honour their Queen, the owners had the ceiling of her bedroom decorated by Dutch craftsmen. With intricate patterns of leaves and cupids fashioned out of plaster, it is a permanent tribute not only to the Virgin Queen but also the great artistry of those anonymous artisans.

At the turn of the century, the Hardwick estate was purchased by the Rose family. They added many features to the house and grounds, including some magnificent Turkish baths. Sir Charles Rose also became friendly with a local author called Kenneth Grahame. If anyone has ever wondered where Grahame gained his inspiration when writing *The Wind in the Willows*, they need look no further than Hardwick and its surrounding area. Sir Charles, a very keen motorist, was the real-life character on which Grahame based Toad and the house was Toad Hall. It was through its cellars that the Wild Wooders came to take possession of the place whilst Toad languished in jail. With such an eventful history, one would have expected Hardwick to have a ghost, as indeed it has. However, the only identifiable haunting on the estate occurred, not in the main house, but in an old cottage nearby called The Bothy.

Standing in the shadow of Hardwick House, it has served as a home for people employed on the estate for at least 300 years. The fact that it was haunted apparently only became known in the 1980s when a family called the Hollises lived there. They noticed that a large picture in their son Neil's bedroom would often vanish completely, only to reappear some hours later. Who was behind this activity remained a mystery until they left the cottage in 1992. The next occupants were Chrissie McBurnie and her partner, Terry. It was during their stay over the next four years that the paranormal activity reached its peak.

Originally from Crawley, Chrissie had come to work on the estate as a milkmaid. A fresh-faced 28-year-old, she has a passion for outdoor work, particularly hedging. Because of this, she found working for Sir Julian Rose, a leading local organic farmer, especially rewarding.

Psychically perceptive people often sense a good or bad atmosphere about a haunted house as soon as they set foot across the front door. In the case of Chris and Terry, this did not happen when they first moved into The Bothy. However, it was not long before they realised they were not alone in the place.

It was Terry who first discovered this. At the time, he was working on a night shift which meant that he regularly returned to The Bothy between one and two in the morning.

At one thirty every morning he would hear the sound of footsteps, three strides across the floor of the attic.

'At first we thought it might be an owl,' Chrissie said. 'But we soon dismissed that idea, because these were definitely footsteps that occurred at exactly the same time every night.'

They also thought the sounds might be the old clock on the roof of the house. However, they soon dismissed that idea, too.

'The sound of the clock mechanism was totally different to

those footsteps and happened at different times,' Chrissie explained. 'It would whirr and click as it chimed on the hour, whilst the footsteps only occurred regularly at one thirty every morning. You could set your watch by them.'

The strange thing was, there was actually no floor where the footsteps 'walked', just felt insulation. Nevertheless, they still believed there must be some rational explanation for the footsteps, and tended to push the subject to the back of their minds. Then they made a discovery which seemed to up the supernatural ante considerably. Whilst clearing out a cupboard under the steep stairs, Terry found two old photographs covered in dust. One was of three servant girls in uniform sitting at an outside table. Nobody could identify who the girls were, but it was thought the photograph may have been taken in the 1920s or before. The other was of a man in his twenties standing proudly over a baby lying on a table in its christening shawl. On the back of this photograph were the words 'Alan Edward aged three months'.

'That's a nice old picture,' Chrissie remarked, and gave it pride of place on a window sill. After a few days, the couple noticed that the picture had vanished.

'Where's the old photograph gone?' Chrissie asked.

'I don't know,' Terry replied. 'I thought you'd moved it.'

'No, I haven't touched it,' Chrissie said.

'Well, nor have I.'

A week later, the photograph reappeared in its old position on the window sill. However, something else was now missing from the cottage. The three footsteps that had paced the attic with such monotonous regularity every night had now stopped.

For some reason, Chrissie moved the photograph to the middle of three shelves they had just fixed next to the fireplace. She felt it looked more at home there amongst their collection of books and videos. To keep it company, she placed it next to her favourite ornament. This was a china elephant with a delicately curled trunk.

The following morning, she came downstairs to find the middle shelf ripped out of the wall, its contents scattered across the floor. By rights, the china elephant should have been smashed to pieces. Instead, it had been carefully placed on top of a log in the wood basket which sat next to the fire. The figurine was in perfect condition and had not even suffered a chip or a small crack. But there was no trace of the old photograph. Once again it had completely disappeared.

'We looked everywhere for that picture,' Chrissie recalled. 'Under both the carpet and the wood basket, but it had simply vanished.'

As well as the footsteps, Chrissie had gradually become aware of a supernatural presence in the cottage. Because it seemed benign she did not feel threatened in any way. In fact, she even tried talking to the ghost on several occasions, but without any success. Somehow, this made the incident with the shelf even more disturbing. It seemed such a worrying departure from the ghost's normally passive nature. Chris and Terry began to wonder if they actually had a poltergeist on their hands.

However, they need not have worried for that was the only time during their stay that the ghost caused any damage. Meanwhile, the photograph was still missing. It was winter at the time and the need to heat the cottage necessitated many trips to the woodshed. Every time they carried the wood basket out to fill it, the couple looked to see if the photograph had somehow fallen behind the basket, but it was not there. Then, three days later, when they lifted the basket up, there was the photograph. It had returned as mysteriously as it had vanished.

'After that, I trapped the picture under a paperweight, then put it in a frame,' Chrissie said. That seemed to do the trick, for it never vanished again and the footsteps also stopped.

Like the Hollises' vanishing picture, the reason for the shelf incident must remain a matter for conjecture. Chrissie McBurnie's theory is that it was the ghost's way of making a point.

Perhaps the ghost was one of the two people in the picture and objected to it being moved. That is also only a theory, of course, since nobody on the estate, including Sir Julian's mother, Lady Rose, could shed any light on their identity.

Whoever those people were in the photograph, they apparently had a strong link with the ghost in The Bothy.

When she left The Bothy, Chrissie inserted a short note in the frame of the maids' photograph. It was a general request to all future residents of the cottage: 'To avoid upsetting the ghost, please do not move these pictures. We were happy here, Christine and Terry.'

Once again the two photographs reside under the stairs at The Bothy quietly gathering dust. It seems that the house's ghost is happy with that, for it is a long time since he was last heard walking in the small hours.

Shadows of War and Lawlessness

Travel over the toll bridge from Whitchurch, and you find yourself in Pangbourne, a town with an equally long history. According to *The Anglo Saxon Chronicles*, King Alfred was called to the aid of the Eoldermen of Pangbourne when the Vikings sacked the place in 870. Over the next few weeks, several fierce battles ensued, culminating in a victory for the Saxons at the Battle of Ashdown, fought on the nearby Berkshire Downs.

Eight hundred years later, the Pangbourne area saw more slaughter and bloodshed when the opposing armies of King and Parliament swept across the countryside during the English Civil War. The armies of both sides had many unruly elements and the famous seventeenth-century diarist John Aubrey records how he witnessed the sacking of Aldermaston Court by Parliamentarian troops.

Meanwhile in Newbury, a group of troopers also from the Parliamentarian side shot an old crone whom they suspected of being a witch. Small wonder that sometimes the local populace would take the law into their own hands and lynch any soldier they found straying from the straight and narrow. This would appear to be the fate of the unfortunate individual in the next case.

THE YATTENDON TROOPER

Gerry Tidbury's Second Story

It was nearly six o'clock on a dark November night in 1980 and Gerry Tidbury was in a hurry to return to his father's TV shop in Pangbourne. He had been delivering a newly repaired television set in the nearby village of Yattendon and now he was eager to be home on such a cold and inhospitable night. As his van drove down the winding road, he entered an ancient wood, its gnarled trees appearing in the beams of the headlamps. Then, as he came out of a particularly sharp bend, he saw a man standing in the middle of the road. Gerry applied the brakes immediately, but there was no time for any evasive action. The last memory he had of the man before he hit him was his floppy black hat and buttoned tunic.

Screeching to a halt, he felt nauseous and his hands shook uncontrollably. He knew he had to go back to see how the man was, but was afraid of what he would find. Taking a deep breath, Gerry climbed out of the van and walked back to where the accident had occurred.

However, there was no sign of the man. Thinking that the impact had flung the body off the road, he searched the surrounding woodland but found nothing. The man he had hit and probably killed had simply vanished. Before returning to the shop, Gerry reported the accident to the local police station and the duty officer promised to keep him informed.

For the next two weeks Gerry said nothing to anyone about the accident. Every day, he scanned the newspapers expecting to read the dreaded words: 'Man's Body Found at Yattendon'.

Eventually, when nothing came to light, he mentioned what had happened to some friends in the local pub.

'Oh, so you've seen Henry,' one of them chuckled knowingly. It was then that Gerry discovered the truth behind his accident.

Berkshire was not a very safe place during the English Civil War. It was not so much the danger of being caught up in the fighting, but the looting, rape and robbery that came in its wake. Unlike their modern equivalents, sixteenth-century battles tended to be set-piece affairs with the opposing troops gathering days beforehand This gave the local population plenty of time to make themselves scarce before hostilities commenced. However, so many ill-fed troops gathering in an area meant that the many isolated villages, farms and hamlets were in constant danger of being attacked by bands of foraging troops. Sometimes they would simply be robbed of any food or livestock by these marauding bands. On other occasions they would suffer rape or murder at the hands of the soldiers.

On occasions, the villagers would have a chance to exact their own revenge. The legend goes that 'Henry' was a Parliamentary trooper who was caught on his own in some act of robbery or worse. The villagers of Yattendon must have been badly upset for they lynched him in the wood where Gerry saw the ghost.

Looking back, Gerry remembers the old fashioned look to the clothes. He also recalls that there was no sickening sound of flesh hitting metal at the time of the accident. However, it took him a long time to accept that the man he thought he hit on that night had actually been dead for many centuries.

Postscript: During the Civil War, a daring attempt was made to relieve the besieged Royalist stronghold of Basing House. Against all odds, a Royalist officer called Sir Henry Gage led a small force from Oxford with ammunition and supplies for Basing, 40 miles away. In the event, his force not only reached Basing with their much needed supplies, but it returned safely to Oxford a few nights later.

In peacetime, the normal route from Basing to Oxford would have been along the Thames as far as Pangbourne, then 20 miles across country to Basing. However, during the Civil War this road would have been thick with Parliamentarian patrols and therefore far too risky for Gage's party to use. Since records show that they went through Wallingford and Aldermaston, the most likely route the force would have taken was over the Berkshire Downs, passing through or very close to the village of Yattendon.

Gage's daring venture cost him the lives of 11 volunteers. It is quite possible that Henry the Civil War ghost was one of them and not some lynched miscreant.

The next experience is also thought to have a connection with the Civil War since it occurred in an area that was close to two major battles of that sad conflict. In the 1640s, Thatcham was a small village situated on the Bath to London road just outside Newbury in Berkshire. In peacetime this meant it had prospered as a coaching stop. However, the Civil War had hit business hard, with the only traffic being military, which, often as not, had no money to pay for lodgings.

Twice during the war the town had seen major troop movements through its streets as Parliamentary forces moved in to engage the King's forces at the first and second battles of Newbury. The occupants of the house where the Wilkins' experience occurred would have been witness to all this since the building was on the Bath Road. The next story might well be due to some violent incident during this turbulent period of English history.

A LOST CHILD

The Wilkins Family Story

Time does not appear to be at a premium for ghosts. Often, they come and go throughout the centuries with no apparent or regular pattern. For example, a spectre that was seen regularly in the 1900s might not appear again until 50 or 60 years later. This was definitely the experience of the Wilkins family. In their case, the ghost was gone for nearly 30 years before making itself known to the least susceptible member of the family.

Their paranormal experiences began when they moved into

one of the oldest houses in the Berkshire town of Thatcham in the 1960s. Standing on the busy Bath Road, as it had done for the past 350 years, the large brick building served well both as a home and premises for the family bicycle shop. It was not long after moving in that certain family members became aware the place was haunted. This particular ghost was very much a sensory rather than a visual presence. While nobody in the family actually saw anything, they certainly *felt* the spirit of a playful little girl about the place on a regular basis.

For example, on many occasions Wyatt, the father of the family, felt a child climb into bed between himself and his wife. Assuming that one of his children had been frightened by a nightmare, he would turn to comfort them, only to discover that there was no child in the bed. Then there was the sensation that his 15-year-old daughter Sue had when walking about the house. She would feel two little arms wrap themselves playfully around her legs, as if a child was trying to involve her in a game. However, when she turned round, there was nobody to be seen. Like the rest of the family, she also had other unexplained experiences in certain parts of the house.

'I often smelt burning in my parents' bedroom,' she told me recently. 'I don't know why, but it was very strong and only in that particular room.'

Sue's younger sister Sarah also recalled feeling the spirit of a little girl on a very regular basis. For a period of weeks, she would wake up at about three in the morning with the unmistakable feeling that a young girl had entered her room and sat on her bed. Then, for no particular reason, the nocturnal visits would stop, only to resume a month or so later. Whilst she never experienced it herself, Sarah remembers her parents discussing the smell of burning coming and going in one of the upstairs rooms.

'At first I'd be a little anxious and then I'd think it's OK, it's just a friendly spirit,' she told me, adding, 'I don't know why, but I always thought it was a child, and so did Mum.'

Sadly, Mrs Wilkins is no longer alive, but all her sons and

daughters clearly recall her speaking of an identical experience to that of her husband Wyatt. She would feel a small child climb into bed with her, but when she turned to look, there would be nobody there. Strangely, the whole family had the strong impression the ghost was that of a little girl, despite the fact that they never actually saw her.

As is often the case with resident ghosts, most of the family soon came to accept the phantom child as part of the fabric of their daily lives. The exception was Sue's elder brother Nick. He never saw or felt anything and certainly did not believe there was anything remotely supernatural inhabiting the house at Thatcham.

Over the next 20 years, the family grew up and went their separate ways. Wyatt, now a widower, moved to Caversham, fairly near to where Sue, who was now married, lived. Meanwhile, Sarah went down to Cornwall, while Nick carried on the family business of selling and repairing bicycles with his father. Although the old house in Thatcham was no longer the Wilkins' home, it remained in the family, the ownership passing to Nick. He split it up into three separate flats and moved into the part that used to be his parents' bedroom.

One night just after he moved into the flat in the late autumn of 1994, he was lying in bed about to fall asleep when he felt somebody sit heavily on the bed. Thinking that he had an intruder, Nick jumped out and switched on the lights, only to find himself totally alone in the flat.

'I had my back to the door and I thought: 'My God, someone's come into the flat and sat on the bed without me knowing!' Nick told me recently. 'But when I had the courage to turn round, I could see that nobody was there. When I rang my sister to tell her about it she confirmed that this was exactly the same sensation she had experienced. I am a rational person but definitely felt someone sit on the bed, causing it to move, even though I was totally alone at the time.'

Then in January 1995, he had the sensation that something was in the bed and moving it, yet when he checked, the flat was totally empty. Interestingly, Nick's bedroom used to be his grandfather's sitting room, which was the focus of much of the paranormal activity. The fact that the only member of the family who never really believed in the ghost had now also experienced it amused and delighted both Sue and Sarah

'When Nick told me about his experience I was really pleased,' Sarah told me. 'My first reaction was "It's lovely to know it's still there." But then I thought: "Why shouldn't it be? Because twenty years or so is no time at all for a ghost".'

Nobody in the Wilkins family really has a clear idea who the little girl might have been. Perhaps she was killed as a result of some action in the Civil War or perhaps she was burned to death in a tragic domestic fire. Either way, it seems that her lonely spirit is still trying to find playmates amongst the living.

As things turned out, yet another story of phantom children surfaced in Thatcham whilst I was writing this book. In November 1995, I had a phone call from local historian Roy Tubbs to tell me of a local family who were experiencing a number of strange happenings in their house less than a quarter of a mile from the haunted cycle shop.

On Tuesday evening of 11 December 1995, I telephone Nick Coventry and conducted an initial interview. He gave me the following account of his family's experiences.

MORE LOST CHILDREN

The Coventry Family's Story

Hartley Way in Thatcham is a street of houses built in the 1960s. As is so often the case with sites of hauntings, it certainly does not look remarkable in any way. However, when Mick and Beverly Coventry moved into Number 20 with their three children in the summer of 1991, they certainly noticed one strange thing about the house. The back passage leading from the kitchen to the back door was always as cold as a deep-freeze. At first Mick thought this might be due to poor insulation, so he put tight-fitting draft excluders round the door and double-glazed the window. After all that expense and effort, he was dismayed to find that the area remained as cold as ever even during the hottest of summer days.

At the time, Mick's sister-in-law and her husband were living with them for a while. They were convinced that the house was haunted by an old couple whom they had both seen on two occasions. However, apart from the frigid area at the back of the house, the Coventry family had no inkling of anything supernatural until August 1995.

Then an area of wasteland behind their house was cleared in preparation for work on a new housing development. It was this work that seemed to spark off a chain of paranormal incidents in Mick and Beverly's house that are still continuing at the time of writing.

'It was when they flattened the ground that all the activity started in our house,' Mick explained to me.

Mick and his brother-in-law Jason, who lives with them, started seeing fleeting, shadowy figures of children in the kitchen. These manifestations have continued, as have certain strong smells. These odours are cheap perfume, shag tobacco and fish, which come and go at no set times. To date, their source has proved impossible to identify. The family have also experienced interference with electrical equipment. For example, one evening in early September, Beverly and Mick took their Jack Russell terrier out for a quick walk. Before leaving, they switched off the television in the lounge but left the light on. Not more than five minutes later, they returned to the house to find the television blaring away in the dark and empty lounge.

'Jason, why did you leave the telly on in the lounge if you weren't going to watch it?' Mick asked, with some annoyance.

'I didn't,' Jason answered, putting his head round the bedroom door. 'I've been up here all the time.'

'Well you must have!' Beverly said. 'Who else would have switched it on?'

'I thought it was you back from your walk,' Jason replied.

'No, we've just got in this minute,' Mick said.

Beverly and Mick looked at each other. They both knew Jason well enough to judge when he was telling the truth and when he was having a joke. It was quite clear that on this occasion he was genuine about being in his room the whole time they were out. This left the obvious question: Who *did* switch that light off and the television on? The in-laws who had previously lived in the house with them always said it was haunted. Now the Coventrys believed them.

Other incidents involving the electrics in the house followed this one. In spite of putting in a new electrical circuit, the landing light would blow with monotonous regularity. Then one evening in early October 1995 their music centre, which, like the television, was in the lounge, developed a mind of its own. Beverly, who was cooking in the kitchen at the time found she had to go in and switch it off repeatedly. Once again, the living room was completely empty at the time.

'It was strange,' Mick recalled, 'because the power switch on that music centre is one that you have to press in to start and not just touch it. This certainly wasn't a case of an oversensitive button.'

The next incident also occurred in October 1995 when Mick's sister and her husband came in to babysit for them. Once they had settled the children down in their beds, the couple sat down to watch television. After a while, their attention was drawn to the door handle as it suddenly moved downwards of its own accord. The door then opened and shut as if someone was entering the room. As it closed, the handle moved up and down again. The couple immediately checked the rest of the house, only to find it silent and empty except for the three boys who were fast asleep upstairs.

On another evening in the same month, Beverly looked up the stairs to see the figure of a small boy disappearing into the bathroom. At first she thought it was her husband since her three sons were all away that night.

'What are you doing upstairs, Mick?' she called out to her husband.

'I'm not upstairs, I'm down here in the living room,' Mick replied.

Beverly was baffled, there was nobody else in the house except herself and Mick. Yet she had seen the figure of a boy, who she now thought was her eldest son, walk into the bathroom. Running up the stairs, she checked both the bathroom and the bedrooms but they were all empty.

However, the most definite spectral sighting of all happened at about 6 p.m. on Wednesday 6 December 1995. Mick Coventry was in his bedroom at the time when he turned around to see a little girl standing in the doorway staring at him.

'She was aged between twelve and fourteen, had long hair and wore an old-fashioned pinafore dress,' Mick told me. 'Although she was looking straight at me, I couldn't see any detail of her face, only the outline. I will admit, it gave me a bit of a shock at the time.'

Hardly believing what he had seen, Mick looked away and then back at the door, but the little girl was still standing there. After about ten seconds, she slowly turned and walked out of sight towards Jason's room.

'I asked Jason if he had seen her but he told me he saw absolutely nothing,' Mick recalled. 'I should point out that all the lights were on at the time.'

Both Mick and Beverly were struck by a number of common factors about the hauntings. Firstly, they were all children, secondly, they always seemed to be walking to the back of the house, which faced onto the new housing development. It was also curious that none of their three boys had seen or sensed anything. This was also the case with their dog Jack, who seemed to sense nothing at all – with one exception.

Whilst I was interviewing Mick on the telephone he suddenly broke off with an exclamation of surprise. When I asked him what had happened he said that his front door knocker had banged twice and the dog had run growling into the lounge, his hackles raised.

In an effort to find out the reason for these manifestations, the Coventrys looked up some old maps in the Newbury library. However, apart from deducing that there had been an old pub in the immediate vicinity and possibly family accommodation for the workhouse, there were few clues as to who these ghostly children might have been when they were alive.

The next experience, which also occurred in Thatcham, is of special interest to me since I learned about it as the actual events unfolded. This came about because I was working with Jonathan Griffiths, who suffered and eventually overcame the attentions of the malign paranormal presence. It was February 1990 and we were both employed by a video production company in Reading at the time, me as a salesman and Jonathan as an editor. Having recently moved up from the Wales to work at the company, he and his young family had moved into a house in Thatcham about 12 miles away. I remember that Jonathan was a keen motorcyclist and he would make the daily journey to and from Thatcham on a magnificent blue and silver machine that looked like something out of *Star Wars*.

One morning, I met him in the main editing suite and asked him, by way of conversation, if he had seen *The Amityville Horror* on television the previous night.

'No,' he replied quietly. 'I've already got an Amityville Horror in my own house.'

When I asked him what he meant, the following story unfolded:

THE POUND LANE POLTERGEIST

Jonathan Griffiths' Story

Pound Lane in Thatcham is a street of unremarkable detached and semi detached houses built in the late 1960s. Indeed, driving down this road recently, I was struck by its air of total normality. It seemed hard to believe that in a small street off this was where Jonathan Griffiths and his family had such a scary encounter with a poltergeist. They had not been in the house long when the manifestations started. At the time, Rachael, his wife, was busily planning their baby son Dale's christening without any thoughts of ghosts or 'unquiet spirits'. It was this that made the manifestations even more of a shock when they came. Ironically though, it was also the christening which indirectly provided the solution to their poltergeist problem.

The first sign of trouble that Jonathan noticed was the way his pet dog suddenly began behaving strangely and totally out of character. He became very hostile to Jonathan refusing to go near him. The animal also developed the habit of running up to closed doors in the house, and sniffing and digging at the carpet as if there was somebody or something on the other side. Then, Jonathan found one of the metal handles on the stand holding the baby's carrycot bent at a most peculiar angle.

After that, the disturbances became more and more disruptive. Anyone who has had a young family knows how much washing and ironing this involves. The Griffiths family was certainly no exception to this rule and Rachael was in the habit of putting a basket of washing on the lounge table last thing at night ready for ironing the next day. On a number of occasions, Jonathan would come down in the morning to find the basket on the floor with the washing flung all over the lounge.

'Most of the time I don't tell Rachael,' I remember him saying to me. 'It would only upset her.'

However, Rachael had already been badly disturbed by the ghost. During the daytime, when only she and the baby were at home, she would hear someone running about upstairs and banging the bedroom doors. This became so unnerving that she threatened to move out completely.

'What do you think I should do?' Jonathan asked me one day.

'Well Jonathan, I think there is only one course of action in a case like this,' I replied. 'You'll have to exorcise that poltergeist.'

Fortunately, the priest who was christening their baby proved sympathetic to this idea. A day or so later, one of her colleagues performed a simple ceremony of prayers bidding the unruly spirit to 'depart this place'. Initially it seemed as if the exorcism had the opposite effect when the house was filled with the intermittent and angry sound of doors banging for two days.This seemed to be 'the last kick of a dying horse' as the the house became a much calmer and quieter place.

However, it was never totally at peace with itself and the presence continued to manifest itself albeit on a much reduced scale.

The Bothy, Hardwick Estate, Whitchurch-on-Thames. See The Bothy.
© Nick Brazil 1998

Judge Jeffrey's lodging, Dorchester. See *The Dorset Hauntings*.
© Nick Brazil 1998

The Wessex Royale Hotel, Dorchester. See *The Dorset Hauntings*.
© Nick Brazil 1998

The Crown Hotel, Amersham. See *Guests at the Crown*.
© Nick Brazil 1998

oe Winnen's cottage at Wing, Bucks. See *A Haunting Dilemma*.
© Nick Brazil 1998

Flag marking the position of Richard III's H.Q. on Ambion Hill, Bosworth
Battlefield. On the flag can be seen the cross of St. George, Richard's own insignia –
a boar and the white rose of York. See *Richard's Pikeman*.
© Nick Brazil 1998

The Godley Hall pub, Hyde, Cheshire. See *The Haunted Restroom*.
© Nick Brazil 1998

The Queen's Head, Stockport, Cheshire. See *A Ghost at the Queen's Head*.
© Nick Brazil 1998

4

The Mystic West

Travelling west down the old coaching route from Thatcham takes you deeper into the mystical world of the ancient British kingdoms such as Wessex. Here the sense of occult mystery becomes even greater the further you go. For example, some years ago I remember the manager of The Bear in the Berkshire town of Hungerford telling me of a strange find made by builders when they were renovating the place. Breaking through an old wall, they discovered a witch's broom that had been hidden there hundreds of years previously. Unfortunately, when they tried to pick it up the ancient charm crumbled to dust in their hands. The most likely purpose of such a talisman would have been to ward off the unwelcome attentions of any local witch.

The use of such charms was not uncommon in mediaeval times as a similar incident at Great Missenden in Buckinghamshire illustrates. When an old Tudor farmhouse was being renovated, a mummified rat was discovered in one of the original fireplaces.

'It was obvious that it had been deliberately placed there, because it was in its own grave,' Frank Pearce, the owner, told me. 'This was like a mini sarcophagus about four feet under the surface of the floor.'

Frank arranged for the rat to be examined by experts at the Victoria and Albert Museum in London and it was they who identified it as a charm against the Plague.

'Apparently, there should also have been a cat buried under similar circumstances,' Frank said. 'But we think that went when the Georgians knocked out another fireplace to make a window.'

111

After the rat had been examined, Frank and the builders had a small ceremony, during which they re-interred it in the centuries old grave beneath the fireplace, where it remains to this day.

Not only has The Bear been a coaching inn and hotel since the twelfth century, it was also one that was favoured by at least two monarchs. Evidence of this can be seen upstairs in the oldest part of the hotel. Here, all the bedrooms have individual names and two of them are called Henry VIII's Room and Queen Elizabeth's Room, for these were the suites exclusively used by King and daughter whilst travelling in this area of their kingdom.

As one would expect of a hostelry with such a long and eventful history, The Bear is also haunted. The beamed reception area, with its comfortable chairs and old paintings, appears to be one of the main focuses of these manifestations. A member of staff told me how she would often hear footsteps there in the quiet of the early morning. They would come down the passage behind her but when she turned, nobody would be there. On numerous occasions, she and other staff have also smelled the pungent aroma of cigar smoke and an indefinable perfume whilst preparing breakfast in the empty dining room. 'There is also a story that two children were burned to death in room eight,' she said. 'I don't know how true this is, but I know from my own experience that no matter how hard you clean the mirror in that bedroom, it always seems to have smears like little fingerprints on it.'

Continue your journey down the Bath Road from Hungerford and you soon cross the border into Wiltshire, a county particularly well-endowed with ghost stories and occult legends. Take Littlecote House for example, a beautiful stately home haunted by an ugly secret. One night in 1575, a midwife called Mother Barnes was awakened by the sound of a coach drawing up outside her house in the nearby village of Shefford. Answering the insistent rapping on her door, she was confronted by a masked man who told her she had work to do. Blindfolded, she was taken to a large house. As she was led

112

up a sweeping staircase and into one of the bedchambers, she could only guess where she was.

Once she was in the bedroom, the blindfold was removed, but the mystery of where she was and who she was to attend only deepened. Lying on a bed was a masked woman in the final stages of labour. As Mother Barnes went about the task of delivering her baby, the masked man went and stood by a large, crackling fire. Within minutes a baby boy was born. However, no sooner had the umbilical cord been cut than the infant was snatched out of Mother Barnes' hands by the masked man. Instinctively both she and the mother knew that something evil was about to happen. In vain they pleaded with the man not to harm the child, but shrugging them off, he threw the baby on the fire as if it were just another log.

We can only guess what thoughts passed through the midwife's mind on the journey back to her cottage. Horror, guilt, and remorse certainly must have crowded in on her tortured brain, but also the question of who had been involved in the infanticide. It was a question that did not remain unanswered for long.

After agonising for a few days, Mother Barnes finally went to the authorities with her terrible story. With her she took a crucial piece of evidence. Whilst in the house, she had surreptitiously cut a piece of fabric from the curtains surrounding the bed. From this, the magistrates were able to identify the house as Littlecote and the finger of suspicion pointed at the owner, the cruel and wicked 'Wild' Darell. It was rumoured that he had perpetrated the dastardly act because the child was the result of an incestuous relationship with his sister.

They say the devil looks after his own and that certainly seemed to be the case with 'Wild' Darrell. When he came to court, he was tried and inexplicably acquitted of infanticide by Judge Popham, a relative. However, Darell was not to enjoy his freedom for long. Within a year he was killed when his horse suddenly threw him at a place on the Littlecote estate that is still known as Darell's Stile. The legend quickly grew that the horse had been startled by an apparition of the murdered baby, and from then on Littlecote was never free of ghosts. As for Judge Popham, he inherited Littlecote shortly after Darell's death, fuelling suspicions that this was the pay-off for a rigged trial. There are no records to show that the judge was ever bothered by the house's ghosts, but many other people have been.

It was said that 'Wild' Darell's phantom coach and four could be heard arriving at the front of the house when a death was imminent at Littlecote. Furthermore, it had gained the chilling reputation that no child born there would ever survive to adulthood. In her book *Ghosts and Legends of the Wiltshire Countryside*, Kathleen Wiltshire tells of several hauntings linked to Littlecote and the surrounding area.

There was the case of a guide who was badly shaken when he saw a woman in blue glide up the main stairs, and pass through a rope barrier before vanishing. On another occasion, Mr Sidney Martin was teaching his wife to drive on the Hungerford to Salisbury road near the house when they saw a beautiful woman on a white horse cross the road in front of them and then disappear. Were these manifestations the tragic spectral echo of Darell's abused sister perhaps? Possibly, but then not all the hauntings have been linked to the baby murder. During the Civil War, Cromwell's Parliamentarian troops were quartered at the house and Miss Wiltshire recounts how a curator definitely saw these troops.

Alan Turton also told me of an incident that happened when he was at Littlecote on one occasion. The English Civil War Society were at the stately home doing an historical re-enactment of both a battle and seventeenth-century life. A medium who was connected to the society mentioned that she had seen a group of phantom troops observing the proceedings.

'She said that they seemed very happy to see us there,' Alan recalled. 'But then they would be since we are also Parliamentarians.'

However, this was not the only intriguing spectral discovery made by the medium. She also told Alan and others of seeing a group of Roman soldiers marching diagonally across the area in front of the house. One thing that struck her was the fact that their feet seemed to have been 'cut off' by the ground. It was not until some years later that a Roman road was discovered in exactly the place where the medium paced out the direction the phantom soldiers marched. Furthermore, the lower level of the road would have accounted for the fact that their feet appeared to be below ground level.

A similar sighting of Roman soldiers occurred in the cellars of the Treasurer's house in York in 1953. Harry Martindale, an apprentice plumber, saw a group of about 20 Roman soldiers march through one wall across the cellar and through another wall. On that particular occasion Mr Martindale also heard the sound of trumpet and the indistinct murmuring of the soldiers. As in the case of the Littlecote sighting, the soldiers appeared to be cut off at the knees for some of the time they were marching on their spectral journey. Later, a Roman road was also discovered running diagonally across the cellar. Mr Martindale did not actually make his experience public until 21 years later.

A Roman villa has also been discovered and excavated in the grounds of Littlecote. Whilst the archaeological works were being carried out, those involved stayed in a caravan on the site. Late one night a man who was working on the project, looked out of his window to see the unmistakable helmeted figure of a Roman legionnaire

However, the occult history of Wiltshire goes back a good deal further than even the Romans. This is testified by the Neolithic stone circles and chalk carvings that litter the landscape of rolling fields and downs, their true purpose hidden for ever in the deep folds of prehistory. Easily the most atmospheric part of this magical area is Avebury with its huge ring of sarsens marching through the beautiful old village like an army of misshapen giants. Appropriately it was very close to here that *Neil M. found himself confronting supernatural evil in our next story.

A VENGEFUL PRESENCE

*Neil M.'s Wiltshire Experience

Neil M. is a slightly built man in his thirties who speaks of his many paranormal experiences with a mixture humour and down-to-earth logic. An atheist, he is at pains to point out that he does not feel they confirm the existence of life after death. By the same token, he is at a loss to explain what it was that caused such incidents, which have occurred to him throughout his life in various parts of the UK. The unnerving events that unfolded in a quiet Wiltshire village were typically alarming.

In April 1990, Neil moved away from Manchester for six months to work in a vegetarian restaurant at Avebury. For the first fortnight of his stay, the manager of the restaurant allowed him to live at a cottage he owned in a nearby village. Converted from the old village post office and general stores, the 300-year-old building had been made into three homes.

'The house was full of antiques,' Neil remembered. 'Which, in itself made me unwilling to live there and I never felt comfortable about the place. Anyhow, I moved in.'

It was not simply the presence of many valuable antiques that made Neil uneasy. He sensed that the whole atmosphere in the cottage was not good. This air of foreboding was confirmed on his first night when he awoke with the definite feeling that somebody or something was watching him. Half fearing there was a burglar, he checked the bedroom and the house thoroughly, but there was no other living presence in the house besides himself. The next day, he went through to the spare bedroom to make it ready for his friend Rene and two others who were visiting from Manchester for the week-end. Immediately he entered the room, he was assaulted by an intense feeling of cold.

'It went right through me and I knew from my previous experiences that this was the focus of the ghost haunting the cottage,' he recalled.

All day, as he busied himself preparing for his three guests,

116

he felt that he was being scrutinised by an invisible watcher. Whilst this was not a particularly threatening feeling, it was not a very pleasant one either. Remembering how psychically aware Rene was, he had already decided that she would not want to sleep in the spare room. Sure enough, when she was shown it, she shrank back in revulsion.

'I'm not sleeping in there, I'm not sleeping in there!' she said, her voice quivering with fear.

'It's OK, Rene, you don't have to,' Neil said soothingly.

From that moment on, there was a change for the worse in the cottage's atmosphere. Although neither of them actually discussed it at the time, they both felt a mixture of anger, resentment and hatred building up around the house. That night the spare room remained empty while they all crammed into Neil's room. As it happened, the night passed without incident, but the next morning was a different story.

When Neil and Rene went down to make tea for everyone, there seemed to be an unnatural stillness enveloping the cottage. Then the temperature dropped to freezing point and the lights began to flicker. As Neil climbed the stairs, balancing mugs of tea in his hands, he realised that Rene had not followed him. Going back down to her, he found her immobile and white with fear.

'What's up, Rene?' he asked, his voice loaded with concern.

'I don't know,' she replied. 'But whatever's in this house hates me!'

By this time, the evil atmosphere had built up to bursting point. As Rene set foot on the stairs, she knew that something was pursuing her. As she dashed past Neil for the bedroom, he felt a wind sweep after her up the stairs and into the spare room, slamming the door behind it. Simultaneously, a light bulb on the landing blew with a resounding pop. For the rest of their stay, everyone tiptoed around the house expecting a repeat performance by the entity, but nothing further occurred. The following evening, the friends returned to Manchester.

Once again, as the sole occupant of the house, Neil became a focus for the attentions of the presence. Returning from work the following day, he found that the cottage he had locked so securely in the morning now contained a pigeon staring at him quizzically. A bad atmosphere still remained in the cottage, but this time the rage had been replaced by vengeful mirth. It was as though the entity was trying to provoke a response from Neil, to frighten him.

Two days later, he resigned from his job at the restaurant and left the cottage. When he walked out of the front door with his bags, he sensed a huge release of tension, as if the presence was sighing with relief and satisfaction at having rid the cottage of its unwanted occupants.

This was by no means the first or the last of Neil M.'s paranormal experiences and, as we journey through Britain's spectral landscape, we shall encounter him on a number of other occasions.

Although the next manifestation occurred not more than 20 miles from Neil's frightening experience it was considerably more benign. It also involved someone whom we have already met in the case of 'The Black Book' and 'The Clandon Time Warp', for this was yet another of Jessie Heard's experiences.

THE DOWNTON CAT

Jessie Heard's Experience

In 1957, after an eventful two years which included some very unpleasant riots, Jessie Heard and her family left Hong Kong. As her husband's tour of duty there had now finished, they returned to England. Not unnaturally, one of the first visits Jessie made after docking at Southampton was to her mother in Wiltshire.

Like Jessie, her mother was a service wife and would normally have been living in one of the many married quarters dotted around the country in those days. However, on this occasion she had taken up residence at a large house called Meadow End in the village of Downton near Salisbury. Owned by a Mrs Pinkney, it was a stately home that she had converted into self-contained flats for financial reasons.

Jessie had always been very close to her mother so their reunion was a particularly joyful one. The two children hugged their grandmother for all they were worth while Jessie and her mother embraced.

'Come and see the flat, it's really lovely,' she said to Jessie as they walked through the grand entrance hall and into the main bedroom. Suddenly, an extremely large tabby cat stalked through the open door and disappeared under the bed.

'Where did that beautiful cat come from?' Jessie asked.

'Cat? Oh no, you must be mistaken, dear, we don't have any cats here,' her mother replied.

'But I just saw it!' Jessie exclaimed. 'He was a huge tabby and he ran under your bed.'

'Well, we'd better get him out,' her mother said.

'It's OK, I'll do it,' Jessie told her, and knelt down to coax the animal out, but all she found under there was an empty area of carpet. The large cat had vanished.

'What did I tell you, dear? There aren't any cats here,' her mother said.

Although Jessie did not pursue the matter any further, she knew the cat was real and not a figment of her imagination. So she decided to raise the matter with Mrs Pinkney at the earliest opportunity. This came a few days later when she met the old lady whilst walking in the grounds of the house. After listening carefully to Jessie's feline encounter she smiled wistfully.

'Yes, you've just described my old cat Prince,' Mrs Pinkney said. 'He died ten years ago and if you look to the left of the front door you will see his headstone under the rose bushes.'

Jessie believes that what she saw was Prince's spirit stalking the house where he had found so much love and happiness in his lifetime.

*

119

The people of Dorset know a thing or two about the supernatural, as well they might, for this county is as much the cradle of mysticism as is Cornwall to the south-west. Take Cerne Abbas, for example. It is exactly the type of village the tourists love, with thatched buildings made of honey-coloured stone, a thriving local shop, two excellent pubs and an ancient church complete with some wonderful abbey ruins. However, what Cerne Abbas is most famous for is not its quaintness but the huge chalk carving on the hill directly above the village. Known as the Giant, he is certainly a Neolithic fertility symbol of great magical importance. Besides the club he holds in his right hand, no doubt denoting his prowess as a hunter, he also sports a massive erect penis.

About 10 miles down the road from Cerne is Dorchester, the capital of the county. The name derives from the Latin *Dunovaria* and literally means 'fist fight'. This could be a reference to the amphitheatre which lies just outside the town. On the other hand, it could refer to the warlike local tribe called the Durotriges who built a massive fort on a hill, the remains of which now overlook modern Dorchester. It is highly likely that they carved out the Cerne Abbas Giant as a tribute to one of their many gods.

The Durotriges are long gone, as are their conquerors, the Romans. Mercifully, though, the gracious old town of Dorchester is largely intact, having survived the ravages of modern development. Its centre would still be recognisable to Thomas Hardy who immortalised it in his book *The Mayor of Casterbridge.* I can think of few places in Britain where so many of the ancient streets and buildings remain relatively unspoilt. One of the most famous of these is situated right in the centre of the town and has been a restaurant for as long as I can remember. It is, in my opinion, one of the finest examples of Tudor architecture in the whole of England and is known as Judge Jeffrey's Lodging.

I first went there with my parents when I was a ten year old schoolboy with a painfully short haircut, chapped legs and scratchy grey trousers. Forty years later, I had tea there again. This time my hair was thinner and my trousers longer for it was my fiftieth birthday. It was a chance visit but one which gave me a wonderful birthday present in the form of an interesting story for this book.

THE DORSET HAUNTINGS

The McLellan Family's Story
The Old Market House and The Wessex Royale

Pat McLellan and her son Stephen are a very good example of the way some people seem to attract or become sensitive to ghosts wherever they go. Although originally from London, the McLellan family had been running hotels in Dorset for many years.

'It's strange that every building we've had in Dorset has been haunted,' Pat's husband Ian explained. I was intrigued that he should have made such a comment since I understood that he had always felt the family's spectral experiences must have a natural explanation.

Their first haunted establishment was a restaurant called The Old Market House in Cerne Abbas. Most visitors would associate this ancient Wessex village with fertility rather than the supernatural. For it is here that the prehistoric inhabitants carved the huge figure of a man on a a chalk hillside. He can still be seen today in all his glory sporting a club and a 30-foot-long erect penis. The main stock in trade of The Old Market House was to serve the many tourists who came to view this incredible Cerne Abbas Giant. However, before it became a restaurant, the building was the premises of the village clockmaker and it is he whom Pat believes haunts the place.

On numerous occasions, she would hear footsteps when nobody else was about. Then someone kept knocking on doors, but when they were opened, there would be nobody there. What convinced her that it must have been the dead watchmaker was the fact that no clock would ever work properly inside the building. It certainly seems perverse that a clocksmith would make all the timepieces go wrong in his old shop. On the other hand, he might simply have been showing his disapproval of the building's change of use. It certainly would not be the first or last time that the dead have tried to resist change.

After leaving The Old Market House, the McLellans took over The Wessex Royale Hotel in the county town of Dorchester. Situated at the top of the High Street and with a splendid Georgian frontage, this hotel is just one of many fine historical buildings in Dorchester. As the new owners and their staff were soon to discover, it also possessed a number of ghosts including a Civil War Officer, a grey nun and a black cat.

The Nun, dressed in a grey habit, was first seen in 1940s by members of the Prideaux family who owned the hotel at that time. They said she appeared in the back part of the hotel. Then, 40 years later, an archeologist who came to work at a local 'dig' had several encounters with The Grey Nun as she became known.

On her first visit the archeologist walked all around the hotel before choosing one of the smaller rooms. Pat thought this strange since it was not the most comfortable accommodation for a long stay but the guest was adamant that this was the room she wanted. She returned for digs over several years and reported seeing the Grey Nun accompanied by a black cat on many occasions. Not everyone was so accommodating about the ghosts. In fact, a former owner of the hotel reportedly went after The Civil War soldier with a gun and dogs. Quite what he hoped to achieve by confronting a ghost in this way is anybody's guess.

Although Pat never saw this soldier she had a variety of other experiences which convinced her that the hotel was haunted by more than one ghost. On one occasion the indistinct figures of two men appeared in front of her. Believing the best form of defence is attack, Pat decided to confront them.

'I don't mind hearing you, she said. 'But I just don't want to see you because it frightens me. Just don't appear anymore'

This must have been the right approach because she never saw the figures again. However, the ghosts continued to make themselves felt in other ways.

'Often when I was tidying up the bedroom adjacent to the lounge, I'd hear footsteps walk across the carpet and onto the wood floor,' she recalled. ''I'd always think it was a member of the family in the lounge, but when I looked there would be nobody there.'

Then there was the strange incident in the Still Room, the area where tea, coffee and soup was prepared in the hotel. Late one night, Pat decided to make herself a cup of coffee. However when she entered the Still Room, she found the whole place rattling and vibrating as if a train was passing close by. Instinctively, she stepped backwards out of the door. Then, composing herself, she walked back into the room and spoke to the presence:

'It's alright, I just want to make myself a cup of coffee.'

Immediately the disturbance ceased. As quickly as possible Pat made her coffee and left the ghosts to their own devices.

Over the years, other members of staff as well as Pat encountered the hotel's ghosts, the most persistent of which seemed to be the black cat. Michael Stone who worked for the McLellan's at the hotel remembers catching glimpses of the animal running across a landing at the top of the stairs.

'I knew it wasn't the McLellan's own cat because this one was black, whilst theirs was white and fluffy.' he told me recently.

The phantom animal would also appear in places it had no business to be such as the kitchen leaving faint paw prints across the surface of the deep freeze.

'This area was strictly out of bounds for our cat,' Pat explained. This was no small matter in the hotel business where allowing any animal into an area where food was prepared could cost the owner their licence. Eventually, the McLellans moved from the Hotel to run a restaurant in an even older building down the High Street. Once again, the place was haunted but this time by a much more hostile presence. Considering the history of the place this was hardly surprising.

JUDGE JEFFREYS' LODGING

The figure appearing in front of Pat McLellan took her breath away with fear and surprise. It was like seeing an image developing on photographic paper. Firstly, there was only a grey outline. Then this was fleshed out with other features until standing in front of her was the figure of a middle aged bearded man in seventeenth-century dress. She knew that the figure was a ghost and, remembering the advice given on a radio programme, spoke firmly to it.

'I'm used to ghosts,' Pat said in what she hoped was a steady voice. 'We've bought the place and we're staying so you'll just have to get used to us.'

But the apparition did not leave. Instead, exhuding aggression and hostility, it swept past her across the timbered room, finally disappearing through a solid wooden door.

This incident occurred in November 1988 when the McLellans had just taken over Judge Jeffreys Lodging, a famous Tudor restaurant in the centre of Dorchester after leaving The Wessex Royale Hotel.

'The ghosts at The Wessex were definitely quite harmless.' Pat told me. 'But this Cavalier in the Lodging, he was different, he wouldn't listen to a word you said and was both aggressive and unhappy.'

During the ten years they owned J.J. as they called the restaurant, that particular ghost never accepted the McLellans' presence. On the contrary, he often made his displeasure known in a frightening and unpleasant way.

Pat was not alone in seeing this malevolent sixteenth-century figure. Michael Stone, who had worked for the McLellans at both the Judge Jeffreys and The Wessex Royale also had several encounters with him in the five years that he worked there.

'I first saw it about five months after I started,' he recalled to me recently. 'I went into the store room to get some stuff one night and as I came back through, there was this dark person there with a sort of cloak. I was so frightened I just froze on the spot. Then, as he came towards me I just ran through the room to the stairs.'

After that, the ghost would appear coming down an oak spiral staircase that led from the storeroom. Whilst he never actually harmed Michael, he would contemptuously flick his cloak at him.

With a history dating back over 400 years this building possesses all the necessary requirements for a haunted house. In fact, when one reads what went on here, it is not surprising that it is frequented by more than one ghost. In 1536, Henry VIII confiscated the building from the Abbots who were then dispossessed or executed. In 1588, it became the property of The Russell family who would own it for the next 130 years. During the English Civil War, it was used by the Parliamentarian troops based in the South West of England.

However, the most infamous period of the house's long history would come in the latter part of the seventeenth century. For it was in 1685 that the building became the lodging of Judge Jeffreys during the period of the dreadful Bloody Assize. The property had been confiscated from the Russell Family after Lord William Russell was executed for plotting to assassinate The King in the Rye House Plot. The man who relentlessly prosecuted him and the other plotters was none other than George Jeffreys.

King James liked the Judge's handiwork and, having appointed him Lord Chief Justice gave Jeffreys the task of presiding over the trial of another set of rebels in 1685. These were the followers of Monmouth, bastard son of Charles II and Pretender to the English throne. If he had not been such a disastrously weak and indecisive leader, Monmouth may well have toppled King James II. As it was, his adventure lead only to death and ignominy. Monmouth was finally executed and nearly 300 of his followers were tried in what became known as The Bloody Assize.

For the duration of the trials George Jeffreys was given Lodging in Lord Russell's confiscated house in the centre of Dorchester. From there it was a short distance to the Court building where he dispensed summary 'justice'.

Drinking copious drafts of alcohol to drown the pain of his gallstones, Jeffreys handed down harsh and dreadful judgements on the unfortunate West Country farmhands who had comprised Monmouth's Army. Two hundred and ninety-two defendants were found guilty. The majority were deported to work as slaves on the Caribbean plantations. Seventy-four were condemned to death, their heads displayed on the railings of St Peter's Church across the street from the Judge's Lodging.

Looking up at the leaded windows of the buildings, it is easy to imagine the ruthless Judge peering out at the heads of those he had condemned as he sought solace in bottle after bottle of claret. Harder to imagine is exactly what went through such a cruel man's tortured mind. With such a dark history, one would have thought the Judge might have left his spectral stamp on the building, but the paranormal is not as neat and convenient as that.

'Our ghost is not The Judge,' Pat's daughter-in-law told me. 'After all this is just one of many places he stayed at.'

'No I don't think it's the Judge,' Pat agreed. 'That would be too neat, but I do think he is the ghost of someone who lived here.'

Whilst that in itself would not prevent him haunting the building, it is worth noting that Jeffreys is always depicted as being clean shaven whilst the Lodging's ghost has a beard. Whoever it was, the manifestation proved both persistent and hostile over the years that the McLellans ran the restaurant.

The focus of the haunting is a very old staircase at the back of the restaurant. Pat, her son Stephen and other members of staff all saw the same figure on numerous occasions. On another occasion, an Irish waitress left the restaurant immediately after seeing the figure and never returned. The small laundry room and office half-way up the stairs is as far as either Stephen or Pat were really happy to go. The rooms above remain cold, totally empty and deserted except for their ghostly inhabitant. When I asked if I could visit the upper floors Pat readily agreed enquiring whether I was sensitive to the atmosphere of buildings.

'Because if you are, you will know immediately which room he is in,' she said.

'No, I have no feelings like that about any building,' I replied.

However, climbing up into the chill, midwinter gloom of those upper floors was a dramatic and atmospheric experience. I was very glad that I had my son Peter for company as I looked into one room after another. Lit only by the street lights streaming through the leaded windows they had a cold, damp feel to them. This, of course is normal in buildings that have been unoccupied for any length of time. However, The Lodging's seventeenth-century ghost had a much more marked effect on the temperature when he appeared. Michael Stone recalled that the atmosphere would become as cold as a fridge when he was present.

Whilst Pat often saw the ghost, she also felt him brush past her when she was working in the laundry. On two other occasions, she had even more frightening sensory encounters with the spectre. It happened in the Summer of 1995 when she was standing at the top of the stairs in the front of the restaurant. Suddenly, she felt a violent push in the small of her back. Had she not been able to grab the banisters, this would have resulted in a nasty fall down the stairs.

Then, late one Saturday night after the restaurant had closed, an incident occurred which actually drove her out of the building. This was when she collected the tablecloths and other linen to be cleaned in time for opening again on Monday morning. On this occasion she felt an entity spring on her back and weigh down like some evil shroud. No amount of rubbing and pushing would shift 'the damp, horrible cloak' as Pat described this presence. It was only when she eventually managed to stagger into the street that the weight left her.

'It was oppressive,' she recalled. 'As if he (the ghost) was on my back and I couldn't get him off. Oh it was horrible.'

127

Her son Stephen also experienced the supernatural when in the deserted restaurant late on wintry nights. Although he was the only person present, the upstairs doors would slam and he would hear the heavy tread of boots across the floorboards.

'When I told my father the next day he would say "That's just the building cooling down,"' Stephen said. 'But that wasn't the building cooling down, I'm convinced it was the ghosts banging and crashing around.'

As if this was not enough paranormal activity to contend with, Pat McLellan also met another of The Lodgings' ghosts. Fortunately however, this manifestation was a gentle and passive spirit. On several occasions she saw an old lady dressed in a jersey, long skirt and thick stockings climbing the stairs, presumably to go to the toilet. Judging by the way she pulled herself up, Pat realised the old woman must have been partially crippled, probably by arthritis. After this happened a few times, she became curious and checked the upstairs room that the old lady had entered. She found the room empty even though the old lady had not returned down the stairs which were the only way out. It was then that Pat realised the woman must be a ghost. So, during the next encounter, she decided to put her theory to the test.

'You're dead,' she said to the old lady. 'You're a ghost.'

Immediately, the figure vanished, never to reappear.

Some time later, she spoke to some regular customers who had been coming to J.J.'s for many years. From Pat's description of the old lady, they were able to identify her as the wife of a former owner who had run an antiques business at The Lodging before the Second World War.

I found out about these ghosts purely by accident for it is not something that the McLellans chose to trade on during the ten years they owned J.J.'s. Hilary, Peter and I had visited the restaurant to have tea on a bitterly cold January day. As I paid the bill I asked if the place was haunted and it was then that Pat told me of their experiences. Like everyone who finds they are rubbing shoulders with the supernatural, her attitude is one of total practicality. This was reflected in her comment about the very first time she saw the ghost:

'I thought "What am I going to do now? I can't really go and tell my husband we've got to sell the restaurant we've just bought because it's haunted!"'

The McLellans have now sold the restaurant leaving the identity of The Lodgings' seventeenth-century spectre still open to question. Assuming that it is not that of Judge Jeffreys then who is it? Pat referred to the ghost as that of a Cavalier because of the clothes it was wearing. There is a common misconception that the opposing sides in The English Civil War wore distinctively different dress and fashion styles. Many would say that the Royalists ('Cavaliers') sported fine clothes and wore their hair long. The Parliamentarians ('Roundheads') on the other hand were always drably dressed with pudding-basin haircuts. In fact, the two sides were difficult to tell apart with some of the finest dressers on Parliamentarian side.

Records show that the building was used by the Parliamentarians during The English Civil War so it is highly likely that the ghost is from that era. Its apparent hostility may well stem from the fact that the spectre is of some Parliamentarian officer whom, having died suddenly and violently still does not realise he is dead. Trapped in time, he sees many changes and people that he simply cannot comprehend. With all these strangely dressed 'interlopers' in the middle of military headquarters, no wonder he is reacting so strongly.

These days, the bulk of the traffic travelling west uses the M4 motorway, which links South Wales with London. As one would expect of an ancient Celtic country, Wales is a land thick with legends and stories of the supernatural. These include phantom legionnaires, dwarf miners and farmhouse poltergeists. However, although the next experience occurred in the Principality, it has nothing to do with its mystic past, but is firmly rooted in the present. Furthermore, it happened to someone who never believed in ghosts until he saw one himself. I had met *Richard Tait on a couple of occasions, but it was through a close mutual friend that I learned of his experience, which took place during the festive season.

A GHOST AT CHRISTMAS

*Richard Tait's Story

Working in the retail furniture business is demanding both in terms of time and sales targets. Staff manning those large stores offering kitchens, bedrooms and lounge suites have to work long hours, often for meagre remuneration. They never have a problem of what to do on a Saturday or Sunday because they are always at work on those days. Having been in the business for a number of years, Richard Tait knows this downside very well. So, when he was invited to spend Christmas in 1994 with a friend's family in South Wales, it was a very welcome albeit brief opportunity to escape from the Manchester store where he works.

Far from being a traditional white Christmas, this was a very wet one for Wales, with floods cutting many roads off and driving hundreds of people from their homes. Fortunately, this was not a problem in Neath, where Richard was enjoying the festivities. He knew the family well and they made him feel most welcome. However, there was another reason why he felt particularly appreciative of their hospitality for he knew they were all worried about a close relative who was dangerously ill at that time.

'It was very hard both on my friend Daryl and his mother,' he explained. 'Since they still missed her late husband terribly.'

Richard, who had been shown pictures of his friend's father on previous occasions, knew how hard it had hit Daryl. He had only been 14 at the time and his father was snatched from the family by a brain tumour whilst still only in his fifties. Nevertheless, everyone in the family worked hard to make it a good Christmas.

Shortly after the Queen's Speech ended, Richard noticed that the greyness of the wet day was finally brightening up a little. *Perhaps we'll have a bit of sun*, he thought as he looked towards the lounge window. At that moment, something in the corner of his eye caught his attention. Turning to look, he saw the figure of a man in his fifties standing between the window and the drinks cabinet. The man, who was completely motionless, seemed to be watching the family. Richard remembered that the figure was grey in texture with a slightly indistinct outline.

'It was as though he had been standing there some time,' he said. 'It didn't scare me, but I was disturbed, I suppose because it was something I couldn't account for.'

However, what unnerved him was the man's face, for it was unmistakably the same one he had seen in the photographs of Daryl's father. About ten seconds later, the figure simply vanished. Later, he told his friend of what he had seen who asked him not to tell his mother since he feared it would upset her too much.

Before seeing the ghost, Richard had been sceptical about the supernatural, believing, like many people, that such phenomena always had a rational explanation. Now he admits to having a much more open mind about the paranormal. Why he, rather than any members of the family, saw the ghost remains a mystery. Perhaps it did not wish to frighten the ones it loved. I certainly hope so, for it is a pleasant and comforting thought.

5

The Ghosts of The Chilterns

Towards the middle of England, there is a pleasant landscape of hilly woodlands known as The Chiltern Hills. Probably the most striking feature of this area is the long escarpment that runs from Oxfordshire in the west to the Bedfordshire border in the east. Tumbling down into the flat and fertile plain known as the Vale of Aylesbury, these hills are enhanced by the beechwoods and chalkstone fields that cover them. This is truly one of the most beautiful parts of Britain.

There is also a great deal of mysticism and supernatural lore locked into the landscape. For example, above the little village of Whyteleafe, there is the strange shape of what appears to be a cross surmounting a pyramid carved into the chalk hillside. Local legend has it that this was done by the early Christians to obscure a pagan fertility symbol. Directly behind this village there is a large area of woodland that is reputedly haunted. Whilst I am unable to say if this is largely truth or legend, I do know of one strange story that emerged from this area. It concerned an old friend of my father's who was a local garage owner. One night in the 1950s he was driving through the woods when a strange creature that seemed to be half man and half beast leapt across the road in front of his car. In spite of the ridicule from his friends, he stuck to his story until his dying day.

These were the same woods that were part of the estate owned by John Hampden, a brave and outspoken Parliamentarian who risked King Charles I's wrath by opposing an unfair tax. Eventually, the implacable opposition of Hampden and other Parliamentary colleagues like Cromwell and Ireton led the country into Civil War in the 1640s. It was a conflict that cost Hampden his life. He was mortally wounded at the Battle of Chalgrove fought in the shadow of his beloved Chiltern Hills. Like many ancient battle sites, Chalgrove has the reputation of having a strange and unsettling atmosphere. My cousin Theresa went further, always claiming that there was an unmistakable whiff of gunpowder in the area immediately surrounding the site of the battle.

There are numerous other ghost stories about this area, such as the phantom coach of Potter Row near Great Missenden and the ghost of Sir John de Plessis, thirteenth-century Lord of Missenden, who is said to ride across the hills on his favourite charger. Whilst these may simply be colourful legends, a number of close friends and relatives have experienced paranormal encounters in this area. For example, my family lived in a large white house called Mapleton in Potter Row, the hamlet of that spectral coach and four. As children we loved that beautiful white house with its spacious garden. However, for one member of the family it also held a supernatural secret that she kept until long after we had all grown up.

One day in the mid 1950s, my mother was cleaning in the lounge when she saw the bearded figure of an old man sitting watching her. Moments later, the apparition had melted away. I remained blissfully unaware of any supernatural presence at the house until over 30 years later when she finally told me about it. My mother has never liked to frighten children, bless her.

That concern prompted her not to react with any alarm when she discovered that my brother Henry had seen a ghost outside some neighbouring cottages.

'Mum, I thought you told me old Mrs Greene had died,' he said angrily.

'That's right, dear,' she replied. 'I did.'

'Well I've just seen her waiting for her son Jimmy at the front door of her cottage.'

Henry has always maintained that he saw Mrs Greene on that day three months after her death. Whilst there may be reasonable doubt about the phantom coach, neither my brother nor mother has any doubts about what they saw at Potter Row.

Lyn Drew is equally certain about her two paranormal experiences in this area of The Chilterns. A close friend of Sylvia James, Lyn does not readily talk of her paranormal experiences, particularly in company, so it took some time to organise an interview with her. What she told me follows next.

THE WOMAN IN BLACK

Lyn Drew's First Story

It was a golden autumn when Lyn Drew 'tied the knot' in 1969 and the Chiltern woodlands were splashed with the gorgeous greens, browns and reds of the changing leaves. It was as if the countryside was putting on a special show for her marriage.

After their honeymoon, she and her husband moved into an old cottage in the Oxfordshire village of Chinnor. Lying beneath the ancient Icknield Way just below the Chiltern Escarpment, it is now more of a town than a village, with rows of new houses spreading in all directions and the tall chimney of the local cement works dominating the whole place.

Before they bought it, the cottage had been occupied for many years by an old countrywoman who had done little or nothing to the place. So Lyn and her husband had plenty of decorating to do when they returned from work in the evenings. Storing all their painting materials in the spare room overlooking the garden, they set to work brightening the cottage up.

Early one evening, when they had just begun painting, Lyn went up to fetch a tin of paint from the bedroom. As she opened the door, she saw the figure of an old woman standing by the window. Since she and her husband were the only occupants of the house, the sight of someone else in the bedroom was a considerable shock to Lyn. For several seconds, she was rooted to the spot. During those brief moments the old lady turned and looked at Lyn as if enquiring why she had barged in on her privacy.

The fear that she felt burned a very clear impression of the woman on Lyn's memory. Nearly 30 years later, she remembers the figure's long black Victorian dress, the way her hair was tied in a bun and the fact that she had a large mole on her right cheek.

'I didn't really stay there but just dropped the tin I was holding and ran downstairs,' Lyn said. 'I was so shocked at seeing someone in there when we were the only ones in the house.'

After telling her husband what she had seen, they both went upstairs to confront the stranger, but the bedroom was completely empty. Glancing at his wife sceptically, Rick walked down the stairs slowly shaking his head. However, Lyn knew that the old lady had been neither a vision nor a dream. Unfortunately, her family were also disbelieving and treated the incident as a big joke. As a result Lyn rarely spoke about her experience again and shoved the whole incident to the back of her mind.

Some years later, there was a strange sequel to this story. At the time it was fashionable for friends to gather in each others' houses for an evening of 'playing' the Ouija board. To some, trying to communicate with the dead by this means may be a harmless bit of fun, but many others feel that it is playing with fire.

'I don't think that I would do it now,' Lyn said. 'But at the time there was a group of us who used to dabble with the Ouija.'

On one particular night, her group were playing the board at her Chinnor cottage when she decided to ask it who the old lady had been. The glass slid across the board and spelled out the name 'Alice Colville'.

'Will I ever see her again?' Lyn asked the board.

'Yes,' the glass replied as it slid from letter to letter.

'In actual fact I never saw the old woman again,' Lyn recalled. 'But that may have been because I left the house in Chinnor soon after that.'

Like many other people, Lyn Drew had always been sceptical about ghosts, but her encounter with the woman in black changed all that.

THE SIGHING DOG

Lyn Drew's Second Experience

The close friendship that exists between dogs and humans is as old as time. Prehistoric hunters kept dogs and the Ancient Greeks ennobled them in their art and poetry, as did the Romans. In fact, one of the earliest 'Beware of the Dog' signs was a mosaic showing a dog and the legend *'Cave Canem!'* excavated from the doomed city of Pompeii. Since then, every western society, right up to our own, has kept them as hunters, watchdogs and pets. Looking at police dogs working, the co-ordination of sheepdogs rounding up a flock or even a family pet retrieving a ball, it is not difficult to see why this relationship has been so enduring. Dogs possess a unique mix of intelligence, loyalty and perception that make them Man's ideal companion.

Lyn Drew, who has always been a great animal lover understands this relationship as well as anybody. Having lived all her life in the rich farming country on the Oxfordshire–Buckinghamshire border, she has formed many strong bonds with not only her own dogs, but also those of friends and neighbours. One such dog was a golden retriever called Conrad, who lived at a neighbouring farm where Lyn worked for many years.

During that time, Lyn built up such a close relationship with Conrad that he rarely left her side when she was at the farm. Even without looking, Lyn would know that Conrad was nearby because of the way he would flop down with a characteristic sigh or brush past her legs while she was cleaning the stairs. As time went on, the sigh became more weary and the old dog less and less active. Like all country people, Lyn is very realistic about life and death. She knows that every living

136

thing, whether it is a plant, animal or human, has an allotted span on this earth, but that did not stop her grieving for Conrad when he finally died.

After his passing, even though there were other pets and animals about the place, the farm seemed unnaturally quiet and empty as if Conrad had left a gap in the atmosphere. As time went on, Lyn eventually became used to the retriever no longer being around, but she never forgot him. Then, three years after he died, she was cleaning the farmhouse stairs when she distinctly heard Conrad flop down with the familiar world weary sigh. It was so close, so real, that she turned and called his name before remembering that it could not be him. Sure enough, the hall just behind her was completely empty. *I must be imagining things*, she told herself.

If she heard the dog on that one occasion, she might have written it off as just that, but she began to hear him regularly as she worked around the farm. Moreover, she would feel his fur as he brushed against her in that reassuringly affectionate way dogs have. Some people would have been frightened by this, but not Lyn; far from it, for she now knew that even death could not destroy their companionship.

A Centre of Dissent

For some reason, the Chilterns are a part of England that has always thrown up dissidents like John Hampden who were prepared to challenge the established order. In fact, Amersham, one of the oldest towns in the area, proved its pro-Parliamentarian credentials during the Civil War by playing host to none other than Oliver Cromwell's wife.

Such an act of hospitality would not have been undertaken lightly, in view of the likely fate of the town fathers had Amersham ever fallen into Royalist hands. With King Charles's headquarters at Oxford, less than 30 miles away, the threat of being caught and executed as traitors to the Crown this must have been a constant worry to them. They certainly would not have been the first from that town to pay the supreme penalty for defying their King. In the sixteenth century, there were those from the Amersham district who died for their religious beliefs in the most horrible way possible and who also form the tragic centrepiece of the next story

MARTYRS

Roy Baldwin's Story

On a blisteringly hot day in July 1940, two young boys wandered down to catch tadpoles in the River Misbourne, which flows through the ancient Buckinghamshire town of Amersham. The boys had been firm friends ever since Roy Baldwin had been sent to stay with his cousin Peter's family in the relative safety of the Home Counties. away from the bombing of the large towns and cities. In fact, they were inseparable, going everywhere together and that day's little expedition was no exception.

'Cor! Look at that, Roy!' Peter shouted, pointing upwards.

High above them to the south-east, the steel-blue sky was criss-crossed by a lacework of vapour trails marking another desperate battle between RAF and Luftwaffe fighters. Tadpoles forgotten, the boys sat down on the river bank to watch Spitfires and Messerschmitts engage in deadly combat.

Not that the boys saw it quite like that, of course. Like most children at the time, the full horror and danger of the war was lost on them. As far as they were concerned, the daily dog-fights were a spectacle to be enjoyed in much the same way as the weekly trip to the Saturday morning pictures. Neither of them realised that what they were actually witnessing on that scorching summer's day was the one of the most famous and decisive events of the Second World War, the Battle of Britain.

Lying on his back for a better view, Roy saw one of the fighters tumble earthwards, trailing an ugly smear of black smoke. Seconds later, a dot detached itself from the stricken plane, blossoming into a parachute as the pilot successfully baled out. While death reaped its grim harvest in the sky, life

138

carried on as usual on the earth below. Seemingly oblivious of the aerial battle, an olive-green truck followed by an ancient black taxi struggled up the road known as Station Hill which ran along the edge of the meadow where the boys were sitting.

For no better reason perhaps than what happened next, Roy remembered those two vehicles with crystal clarity. As he lay there, he felt a rhythm pulsating through the ground in a regular and sinister beat like the striking of a drum.

'What's that funny noise?' he asked Peter.

'What noise?' the other boy replied.

At that moment, Roy became enveloped in total silence. Baffled and not a little frightened, he looked around to see that everything – the truck, the taxi and even the planes in the sky – was frozen in time like a single frame of cine film. Frantically, he tried to attract his cousin's attention, but Peter was staring silently down at the river as unresponsive as a marble statue.

Then, to his left, Roy became aware of movement. Turning his head, he saw a group of about 17 people walking slowly up the field from an easterly direction. At the front of this crowd were four or five women, their heads bare and arms bound with rope. Behind them, about a dozen or so people, mainly women in old-fashioned mob caps, voluminous blouses and long dresses followed, shouting angrily. The few men in the group, also dressed in peasant's garb from an earlier age, walked directly behind the bound women, prodding them with staves and shouting: 'Burn them! Burn them!'

Even 50 years after the event, Roy vividly remembered that the chant coincided directly with the pulsating rhythm and his heartbeat. As they passed beyond the periphery of his vision, the group faded away and the normal world rushed back in a tidal wave of sound.

'What noise?' his cousin was asking in a baffled tone as the fighters continued to shoot each other out of the sky.

'Didn't you see those strange people?' Roy asked him. When his cousin shook his head, he described what he had seen.

139

'Ah, you must have fallen asleep, Roy,' the other boy said dismissively.

But Roy knew his sighting of those bound women and their tormentors had not been a dream, although he had no idea who they were. However, four or five years later, when he walked to the top of that same hill above the Misbourne, pieces of this paranormal jigsaw began to fall into place. Quite by chance, he came across a simple memorial consisting of a grey plinth on top of a stone platform. On it was the following inscription: *'In a hollow a short distance below this monument the following citizens of Amersham were burned for pursuing their faith, their children being forced to light the fire.'*

The monument was to the Amersham Martyrs, followers of John Wyclif and known at the time as Lollards. Their only crime was to want the Bible to be translated from Latin into common English, thereby making it accessible to ordinary people. A harmless even laudable aim by today's standards, but in the sixteenth century, when the church was an all-powerful arm of the state, such nonconformity usually meant a painful and terrible death. The fate of the Amersham Martyrs is probably best summed up in an excellent play that my mother wrote called simply *The Amersham Church Pageant*: *'On the hill overlooking the town, six died for their beliefs. There is a tradition that where they met their deaths, the corn will not flourish.'*

There are a number of interesting facts that surround this case. Firstly, from his description, the clothes closely match those worn by ordinary people in the sixteenth century. Secondly, the route the mob was taking is the most likely one it would have used when taking heretics to the stake. We know this because records show that the Amersham Martyrs were held in The Chequers on the night prior to their burning. It still exists as a pub in its original position slightly to the east of Station Hill. It is hardly surprising that it is reputed to be haunted, although neither the current landlord nor his family has ever experienced anything remotely paranormal. However, some years ago, a medium called Molly Moncrieff visited The Chequers and claimed to have contacted an unhappy

140

spirit of a dead man. He was, she said, one of the martyrs' executioners and was tormented by the guilt of what he had done.

After the war, Roy emigrated to Australia, where he became a successful character actor appearing not only on the stage but in popular TV programmes such as *Neighbours.* Until his death in September 1995, he lived in Melbourne and, like anybody else who has had a similar experience, impatiently dismissed such prosaic and mundane explanations that he had a dream or his eyes were playing tricks.

'In 1989 when I returned to the UK for a visit, I spoke to my cousin Peter about what happened on that day,' Roy told me recently before he died. 'He simply said: "You must have been dreaming." But I know I wasn't. I believe I saw ghosts.'

And there his case rests.

A Taboo Subject

Over the years, many hotels and pubs in Britain and abroad have been subject to paranormal incidents. Guests, staff and managers have all experienced supernatural events in numerous hostelries. Yet when the subject of ghosts is mentioned in the head offices of various hotel chains, the matter is summarily dismissed or 'swept under the carpet,' as one industry insider put it to me. The problem is that many companies know they have haunted hotels on their books, but they suppress this information because they are afraid it will frighten away business.

However, the hospitality industry *does* take the question of the supernatural seriously even if, publicly, it treats it as a taboo subject. For example, many hotels do not have any guest rooms with the number 13 on their doors, whilst others go as far as having no thirteenth floor. This was certainly the case of a Durban hotel I stayed in some years back. Fortunately, some people have been prepared to talk of their experiences in pubs and hotels. What happened at The Crown in Amersham is typical of the sort of incident that can occur in such places. I am very grateful to Vic Savage, a friend of over 40 years' standing, for this next story.

GUESTS AT THE CROWN

Vic Savage's Experience

Today, the High Street in Old Amersham looks very much as it would have done 2 or even 300 years ago. It is very wide and has as its centrepiece a magnificent Georgian town hall with large leaded windows and walls patterned with rustic red and glazed bricks. Directly opposite this building is The Crown, one of Amersham's many historic hotels. The original structure of this building certainly pre-dates the town hall and records show that it has been a hostelry and coaching inn for nearly 400 years. With an arched gateway leading into a cobbled courtyard, The Crown has been used as a location for films such as *Four Weddings and a Funeral* and one of the 'Miss Marple' films starring Margaret Rutherford.

Whilst I have no idea whether any of those involved in these films experienced anything strange at The Crown, others certainly have. In the early 1970s I remember being told by one of the managers about a room in the hotel that appeared to be the focus of paranormal activity. On one occasion the door of this bedroom was locked from the inside, even though it was empty and unlet at the time. On another, it was subjected to an inexplicable flood of water. Then there was the case of a guest in this room who thought he was going out of his mind.

The man, who was staying at The Crown during a sales trip, had woken up in the middle of the night to see the figures of a man and woman sitting at the end of his bed. Dressed in strangely old-fashioned clothes, they remained there for some minutes before disappearing. He was so shaken by this experience that he feared for his sanity and said nothing to the hotel staff at the time. It was only when his wife rang up some weeks later that the manager realised what had happened.

'Tell me,' the woman demanded, 'is your hotel haunted?'

This is not an easy question for a hotelier to answer since an admission that a pub or hotel is haunted could easily frighten away guests and harm business. However, the woman on the phone sounded so desperate that the manager decided on the truth.

'Yes,' he replied. 'We're pretty sure we have a ghost.'

'Thank God for that!' the woman said, and related her husband's experience. 'Ever since it happened he thought he was going out of his mind.'

At about the time of this incident, Vic Savage was also staying at The Crown. His room was in an annexe to the main building on the left-hand side of the entrance. One night, he woke up to find the bedroom unnaturally cold. He also sensed that he was not alone and that there was an unseen yet hostile presence in the room. Moments later, his blankets were pulled off the bed. When Vic grabbed hold of them, he found himself involved in a tug-of-war with the spectral intruder. After some minutes, the supernatural presence left and the room temperature gradually returned to normal. Vic has no explanation for this incident, but believes it could well have some connection with Amersham's dark and violent past.

By contrast, the next ghost story from the Chilterns is a very modern one indeed. Also, like many of the other cases in this book, it involves someone whom I have known for many years and who has always struck me as an extremely down-to-earth and practical person. Katharine Matthews is, in fact, the widow of my cousin Tim and, whilst she has an open mind about the paranormal, she is at a total loss to explain what happened to her in the winter of 1994.

A CLOSE CALL

Katharine Matthews' Story

Oak Lane is a narrow road that winds through the rich Chiltern farming country around Cholesbury in Buckinghamshire. Twisting and turning past verdant fields and ancient beechwoods, it is a very pretty route to take if you are not in a hurry. However, the sharp bends that make Oak Lane so attractive also mean that it is a potential death trap for unwary or careless drivers. Nobody knows this better than Katharine Matthews, a farmer's wife who has travelled down Oak Lane every day for the past 30 years. Just before Christmas in 1994 both her sons 'took to the scenery' whilst travelling down the road in icy weather.

Because of this, Katharine has always treated the road with great respect when making the daily journey between the farm and the family brickworks less than 2 miles away. On Tuesday 24 January 1995, she travelled along Oak Lane with even greater care since the road surface had been soaked by a recent rainstorm.

As she approached the S-bend where her sons had come to grief, she slowed right down, which was good because, coming in the opposite direction was a cream and red 'Hopper Stopper' minibus. Since the vehicle was well over to her side of the road, she braced herself for the inevitable head-on smash. Strangely, she felt no fear as she waited for terrible impact.

However, instead of crashing into the front of her car, the bus travelled through it and Katharine had the weird sensation of speeding down the centre aisle of the vehicle. Seconds later, the only signs of the bus were its tyre marks on the wet tarmac. Relief at being unhurt lasted for the next 60 seconds until she reached the entrance to her farm.

Then, as she pulled into the long drive to the farm, she became aware that something very strange had just happened to her:

'*Wait a minute*, she thought. 'By rights, that bus should have

144

hit me head-on and I should be dead! But it didn't, it went straight through me!'

Now a host of other disturbing thoughts began flooding into her mind. For example, why had she not felt the least bit frightened when she knew an accident was about to occur? Why had she seen no driver or passengers?

'I came to the conclusion that perhaps it wasn't my time to go,' she told me a few days later in the beamed lounge of Dundridge Manor, the Matthews family's fifteenth-century farmhouse.

'Perhaps it was a warning,' I replied, then added: 'I think the first thing to do is to check if there were any buses on Oak Lane at that particular time.'

Over the following week, I spoke to a very patient lady at the Luton & District Bus Company who must initially have wondered why I had such an all-consuming interest in one of their more obscure country routes. Finally, I came clean.

'Look, I don't know quite how to put this,' I said, 'but I am actually a paranormal investigator and I have spoken to a lady who claims to have seen one of your buses that, well, just vanished.'

At this stage I did not think it wise to tell the whole story in case she wrote me off as a nutter and slammed the phone down. In the event, I need not have worried. By her reply you would have thought they had enquiries about ghost buses every week.

'I see,' she said carefully. 'What you're saying is that one of our buses was where it shouldn't have been.'

'Yes, and I simply want to get to the bottom of things,' I replied.

The company actually calls at Cholesbury three times every weekday as part of their run between the towns of Aylesbury and Chesham. Their buses stop in the village at 8.05 a.m., 10.31 a.m., and 2.02 p.m. In addition, there is also a bus that travels around Cholesbury between 12.30 p.m. and 12.38 p.m. Initially, I thought that this must have been the bus that Katharine had seen – until I spoke to Neil Roughton.

Based in Luton, Neil is the Service and Planning Manager

145

of Luton & District. Once again, instead of giving me short shrift when I told him one of his buses had 'passed through' someone's car, he was kindness itself.

'I used to drive buses down that route myself,' he said. 'And if you are going to see anything anywhere, I would put my money on that area. As it is, none of our buses would have been in Oak Lane at 12.40 and there is nothing in the incident book to indicate they would have been on twenty-fourth.'

To this day, Oak Lane's phantom bus is a mystery with no apparent meaning, except to drive carefully.

A HAUNTING DILEMMA

Jos Winnen's Story

To most people travelling from Aylesbury to Milton Keynes, the village of Wing is little more than a double bend with a few shops. In fact, it is an attractive north Buckinghamshire village with a fine old Saxon church. It was this and reasonable property prices that attracted Jos Winnen and his wife Lynn to the place in the mid 1970s. As a builder, Jos was not afraid of buying somewhere that needed renovation. With this in mind, they picked a 300-year-old cottage in the High Street which was obviously in dire need of attention.

At the end of the day, the whole of the inside of the cottage had to be virtually gutted and rebuilt. Keen to move into their newly acquired home, Jos worked night and day on the building. Wherever he went, his pet dog would also follow, sitting or standing by his master as he drilled, cut and sawed. One morning, when the building work was well under way, Jos began work on the upstairs. Suddenly, his dog began barking and growling, the hackles on his back rising up stiffly.

'What is it, boy?' Jos asked.

Then he saw what was upsetting the dog so much. The misty shape of a man had appeared on the landing and walked straight through a wall.

146

'By this time the dog was going absolutely mad!' Jos recalled. However, before Jos could come to terms with what he had seen, the figure walked back through the wall and vanished.

'I really don't know what I saw that day,' Jos said, over a pint in my local pub. 'But I can tell you that I did see something and so did that dog. The trouble is, I don't believe in ghosts, never have done and never will.'

After that unnerving incident, the Winnens moved into the cottage and lived there for some years without experiencing any more paranormal manifestations. However, they were left with a permanent reminder of the strange figure. During the building work, Lynn took a photograph of Jos standing proudly in front of some of his handiwork in the cottage. When the film was processed, there, standing beside Jos, was the misty figure that had so excited his dog. Unfortunately, the photograph has since disappeared during the Winnen's many moves.

Jos, the most down-to-earth of all men, still insists that he does not believe in the supernatural – even though he saw what can only have been a ghost.

Postscript to a Haunting Dilemma

On a beautiful day in October 1997, I visited Wing to take a photograph of the Winnen's old cottage. Now painted light yellow, it is situated down a narrow street adjacent to the ancient church.

'It's right next door to the local garage,' Jos told me before I went. Then he added: 'Ask John at the garage about the whiskey.'

He was referring to the fact that if he ever left a bottle of whiskey on the sideboard in the cottage, it always mysteriously disappeared. I had left this out of the original story because, frankly, I was sure there was a natural rather than supernatural explanation for this phenomenon. However, after speaking to John I changed my mind.

He was clearing some rusting metal with a forklift truck

when I met him at the garage. A bespectacled man of indeterminate age, he was initially a little suspicious of me.

'Does a man called John still work here?' I asked.

'He might do, who wants to know,' the man on the forklift countered warily.

After I explained why I was there, he relaxed and admitted that yes, he was the John I had been looking for.

'I don't know anything about any ghosts in that cottage,' he said leaning back and lighting a cigarette. 'Some close relatives of mine lived there for some years and they never saw anything.'

'Jos suggested that I ask you about the whiskey,' I prompted.

'Oh there was plenty of whiskey drunk in that cottage,' John said. 'In fact that's what destroyed the old man's business. He used to ride to Aylesbury market every Tuesday and the horse would bring him home in the evening.'

'But Jos said you also knew about his whiskey disappearing for no reason,' I persisted.

'I don't know anything about that,' John replied. 'But I am sure too much whiskey killed the old boy.'

Many years previously he went on to explain, the cottage had belonged to the local miller whose business had stood where the garage was now. Sadly, his weakness for whiskey finally caused the miller to slip into bankruptcy. The mill's new owners also bought the cottage but allowed the old couple to live there until they both died. This certainly provided a possible supernatural explanation for the vanishing whiskey.

For as Jos Winnen had found out to his cost, it seemed even in death the Miller of Wing could not resist his favourite tipple.

The ancient city of Oxford, about 30 miles to the east of Wing, is justifiably world-famous for its university and many gracious buildings such as the Bodleian Library. However, there is a great deal more to the city than that. Originally founded by the Romans, it has been witness to the many turbulent and changing tides of British history. In AD 906, Edward, King of Wessex, used it as one of his main centres of occupation whilst fighting the marauding hordes of Danes.

Burned to the ground by the Danes in 1009, it again fell into their less than gentle hands three years later. On that particular occasion, the good citizens avoided bloodshed and destruction by rapidly surrendering and giving hostages. In 1141, a beleaguered King Stephen gave the city to Matilda, with whom he found himself at war for the possession of England. However, like most gestures designed to buy peace, it failed.

In the seventeenth century Oxford became the headquarters of yet another king when Charles I garrisoned his army there. Finally, because it had become one of the centres of the British automotive industry in the 1930s, it was the target of yet another would be invader in the last war. Fortunately, the university and old part of the city escaped destruction by German bombs. Today they remain, whilst Dane, Norman, Royalist and even the British Motor Corporation have long since become ghosts of history.

Indeed, one would expect a place with such a long and colourful past to possess whole legions of ghosts. In fact, the city has yielded only one story for this book, with absolutely no connection to any Viking or Cavalier, for it is firmly rooted in the twentieth century. Like many other people in this book, Caroline Woodley, who was kind enough to relate it to me, is a friend and a former work colleague. Balancing the time between her demanding job and a young family, she has a practical no-nonsense approach to life. In short, the last person you would expect to have seen a ghost, which makes her experience all the more interesting . . .

WHEN TIME STOOD STILL

Caroline Woodley's Story

Caroline looked out of the bedroom window and wondered, not for the first time, quite what she was doing living in the cramped room of the mean little terraced house. The view was nothing to write home about either. On one side, there was the main Oxford to London railway line and on the other, a graveyard, its grey headstones etched against the surrounding drabness by a hard frost.

When she had agreed to live with her boyfriend in Oxford, it seemed like the ideal way to assert her independence. However, Mill Street, where she stayed, is hardly the Oxford that poets thought of when they eulogised about 'dreaming spires'. Close to the city's station, it is a long row of terraced houses that could have been in any of Britain's many cities from Glasgow to London. Also, the reality of living in a single room with hostile landlords and shared cooking facilities was very different to what she imagined living away from home would be. If the discomfort of staying in one cold room was not bad enough, there were other, much more disturbing factors to take into account.

The first couple of weeks after Caroline and her boyfriend moved into Mill Street in October 1989 were totally uneventful. Then one night she was awakened by the unnerving sound of the electric alarm clock dying on her. As the power drained out of it with a mournful wail, Caroline checked the time. *Surely not seven o'clock already!* she thought.

In fact it was a few minutes past two in the morning.

'I didn't think too much of it at the time,' Caroline explained. 'I just thought the alarm clock had gone up the chute and I bought another one.'

However, when she set the new alarm on her bedside table it also stubbornly refused to work. This was both unsettling and infuriating. How on earth would she be able to wake up for work without an alarm clock? There and then, she

150

decided to take the clock back to be replaced by the shop that sold it to her. As she left the room, Caroline noticed that it started to tick again and the second hand was moving round the dial.

Typical, she thought, re-entering the room. *Take anything faulty back and it could always be guaranteed to work perfectly.* Except the clock had now ceased to work again.

Feeling a tingle of fear, she carried the clock out of the room a second time. Sure enough, as soon as she was on the landing, it started to work. Then she checked her wristwatch, only to find that it too would work anywhere but in the bedroom.

'In fact, no watches or clocks would work in that room,' she recalled. 'But outside, everything functioned perfectly.'

Still searching for a logical answer to the mystery of the clocks, Caroline persuaded herself that it was probably to do with her boyfriend. Just after they moved in, she had bought him a watch, which had not worked when he put it on. Somehow, it must have affected the other timepieces. This comforting solution was soon swept away by a terrifying incident. One night in the cold, dark hours before dawn, she was awakened by her boyfriend frantically shaking her arm.

'Look over there by the fireplace,' he said in a terrified whisper.

She looked and saw the ghostly figure of an old man in Victorian dress standing watching them. It was all too much, and Caroline buried her head under the sheets, willing the apparition to leave them alone. When she looked again a short while later, the man had vanished.

The last straw came a few days later when the young couple had 'a bit of an episode' with some tea bags. After going downstairs to make a light meal, they returned to discover that a box of tea bags had been scattered all over the room. Not only that, but each bag had been ripped open and the grains emptied onto the worn carpet. Strangely, the couple who owned the house raised no objections to their request that they move into a less disturbing room.

'I think they knew that there was something strange about the room,' Caroline recalled. 'But they had been in the house for quite a while and it didn't seem to bother them.'

After six weeks, Caroline Woodley realised that this was not the life she wanted and left both her boyfriend and the house where time stood still, for ever.

6

Hauntings in The Heart of England

Less than an hour's drive northwards from Oxford takes you into the very heart of England, covered by the counties of Warwickshire and Leicestershire. No less beautiful than their southern counterparts, these two counties of Middle England have their own distinctive character with countryside that appears less crowded, more rugged and not quite so managed as the Chilterns. For example, whereas many of the fields in Buckinghamshire and Oxfordshire are vast prairies denuded of ancient boundaries such as stone walls or hedges, Middle England is an interesting patchwork of fields divided by hedgerows planted hundreds of years ago. Here, dark stone farmhouses and manors preside over a countryside of sheep and cattle scattered across rounded hills. Crowned by ancient, brooding woods, this is a land of quiet villages, overgrown graveyards and distinctive Norman churches.

Nowadays, most people pass through Warwickshire and Leicestershire without even realising it, for they are hurrying northwards to Birmingham, Manchester or Leeds on one of the motorways that now slash through these counties. If only they would take time out and pull off the M40 or M1 for an hour or so; then they would find a beautiful part of England where some of the most dramatic events in her history have occurred and continue to occur as spectral echoes. Take the interesting case of the Battle of Edgehill, for example.

Fought in 1642, it was the first major engagement of the Civil War and one of the bloodiest, with an exceptionally high casualty rate for what was an indecisive result. Fought across the hilly Warwickshire countryside by tired, hungry and largely inexperienced troops on a very cold October day, it was typical

153

of many seventeenth-century battles – bloody and confused. By the end of it, many of the participants were either grievously injured or lay dead on the muddy field of battle whilst their commanding officers squabbled about who was to blame for the debacle.

Two months later, on Christmas Day to be precise, a local vicar and a magistrate were confronted by a group of frightened shepherds with a truly fantastic tale. Not only had they heard the sounds of the recent conflict being re-fought, but they had seen phantom armies clashing in the sky. On the following nights the battle was witnessed not only by the vicar and magistrate but also six officers despatched by no lesser personage than King Charles. The Edgehill haunting is probably the most famous example of a paranormal event occurring at the scene of a massive trauma such as a battle or a massacre, but it is certainly not the only one.

For example, there was the case of Anna and Maria Martens, who lived in Belgium near the French border. Late one night in 1956 they both found themselves awake after suffering from an unaccountable bout of insomnia. Whilst they were making themselves a drink, they heard the sound of marching in the street outside their cottage. Looking out of the window, they saw a long. ghostly column of tired and injured troops retreating from a First World War battle which had been fought and lost 40 years earlier. The veracity of the two respectable spinsters, one of whom was also a schoolteacher, was beyond doubt – especially after research by a Dr Laporte discovered that what the sisters described they had seen tallied in every detail with the French retreat from the Battle of Mons. Both of these incidents are typical of the imprints of history where great and terrible events leave an impression on the ether to be picked up by the psychic antennae of future generations.

This appears to be the case of Geoff Smith whilst pursuing his favourite hobby of speed walking in Leicestershire one weekend. I am actually very grateful to him, for it was the chance discovery of his paranormal experience and his willingness to talk openly about it which originally triggered off the idea for this book. It happened this way:

I have known Geoff and his first wife Jean since my wife and I joined the same theatre group in Whitchurch in the mid 1970s. We spent a great deal of time with the Smiths because of our involvement in plays, and at many parties. However, it was not until 1991 that a remark by my ex-wife Diana alerted me to the fact that Geoff had a story to tell. Apparently, the subject of paranormal experiences had cropped up at a dinner party or some similar social gathering to which both Jean and Diana had been invited.

As is often the case, stories were swapped and Jean told the gathering of Geoff's spectral encounter. Knowing my interest in the subject, Di mentioned the story to me. At that time I only had a vague intention to write this book, but something, my intuition I suppose, prompted me to speak to Geoff about it. A few days later, on a bitterly cold winter's evening, he told me his story in front of a roaring fire in his Berkshire cottage. I remember the occasion well, the bearded and athletic Geoff recounting an event which he still has difficulty in coming to terms with since he does not actually believe in ghosts. Here is his story.

RICHARD'S PIKEMEN

Geoff Smith's Story

Geoff was very annoyed, he would have won that race if it had not been for all those ridiculous soldiers streaming across the road in front of him. They had cost him at least five minutes, definitely destroying any chance of an outright win.

'He was very upset,' Jean, his ex-wife, explained to me recently. 'But, right from the beginning, I knew there was definitely something more to this than simply a group of soldiers marching carelessly across the road. For a start, it was two o'clock in the morning and then there was also the strange fact that they were carrying pikes.'

Prior to this race in 1985, Geoff had been a keen competitive speed walker for more than 20 years, taking part, and often winning, events up and down the length and breadth of the UK. And, wherever the competitions took Geoff, Jean would also go to provide sustenance in the form of sandwiches and a flask of tea. Often this meant standing around sheltering under some isolated hedgerow in all types of weather waiting for the tall figure of Geoff to appear out of the pre-dawn darkness. On this occasion in the summer of 1985, the speed walk followed a route through rural Leicestershire and, being a 24-hour event, involved quite a bit of night walking. The section where Geoff encountered his particular traffic problem was in a narrow lane lined by high hedgerows that wound through cow pastures near the town of Market Bosworth.

The incident with the soldiers bothered Jean, so she decided to investigate further. What she discovered was that the course of the race had traced the perimeter of the ancient battlefield of Bosworth, where Richard III lost his crown and his life in 1485.

'I had no idea at the time that the road skirted a battlefield,' Geoff commented, then he added, 'I don't believe in ghosts, but I know what I saw and I was not dreaming. However, the strange thing was, when I arrived at the point where the soldiers turned off the road, there was nothing but a hedgerow.'

I asked Geoff to indicate where the incident happened, then matched it up with a plan of the actual battle. Where Geoff saw the pikemen would have been less than a mile from Richard's headquarters on the top of Ambion Hill. Further investigation revealed that amongst the knights and foot soldiers on Richard's side were 2,000 pikemen.

Geoff still does not believe in ghosts, but neither is he dismissing the possibility that what he saw on that August night were the images of some of the combatants marching off to decide the fate of England's throne 400 years previously.

*

Today, the site of the Battle of Bosworth is well worth a visit. Not only is there a very good visitors' centre where you can see a short explanatory documentary, but the actual field of conflict has been laid out in a most imaginative way. The positions of the opposing armies are marked by huge banners fluttering from tall flagpoles and strategically placed signs give a brief resumé of what happened at particular points during the battle. On the day that I visited, I was lucky enough to tag onto a group of schoolchildren in the care of a very knowledgeable official guide. However, when I asked if he knew of any similar incidents to Geoff Smith's, he laughed in disbelief. Small wonder that some people keep their experiences to themselves for fear of ridicule.

Both Geoff and another good friend who had lived in the immediate area of the battle thought that such an experience was not a 'one off' and that other people had seen similar manifestations. Unfortunately, they did not have any names or addresses of those involved, so I decided to enlist the help of the local newspaper, the *Leicester Mercury*. They were kind enough to devote a diary piece on my book and, whilst it did not uncover any more Bosworth experiences, it provided me with the next fascinating incident.

AN ARMY FROM THE DARK AGES

*Sylvia Orvile's Story

Staggering away from their shattering defeat by the ferocious Norsemen, the Saxons hurriedly buried their dead on the hill overlooking the boggy marshland running along the River Sence. So that they should not go hungry or short in the afterlife, they surrounded the bodies of the slain warriors with their swords, pottery, cooking utensils and bridles . . .

Less than half an hour's drive from Bosworth, there is the town of Wigston lying on the southern fringe of the city of

Leicester. Although many might consider it to be just another suburb of the city, that is not how the people of Wigston see it. As far as they are concerned, theirs is a town in its own right with a history of a thousand years to back it up. Sylvia Orvile and her husband lived on a tidy estate situated close to the A50 trunk road. Like many people, they did not pay much attention to ancient history, or the supernatural for that matter, in their day-to-day lives. On a bright, sunny morning in 1991 an incident occurred that would change all that.

At approximately 10.30 on the morning in question Sylvia was at the kitchen sink finishing the washing-up. As she glanced out of the window, the familiar view of the front garden and the drive leading onto the housing estate disappeared. It was replaced by a barren and boggy landscape devoid of all life except a column of soldiers moving towards the house from the east. With their spears, pointed helmets and skirts of rough sacking, they looked as if had stepped straight out of the Dark Ages and were quite unlike any fighting men she had ever seen. Sylvia knew they must have come from a hard-fought battle for they all looked extremely tired and some, supported by their comrades, were crying out in pain from their wounds. Then, as suddenly as it appeared, the vision melted away, leaving Sylvia staring out at the housing estate once more.

Try as she might, she could not make her husband believe that what she had seen was not simply a daydream or a figment of her imagination. Then, one day about a year later, he brought her a copy of the local newspaper and showed her an article. It described how a woman who had been forced to spend the night in a lay-by close to their house had also seen some ancient soldiers. In fact, the article was about a book dealing with hauntings in Leicestershire.

The incident it described had actually taken place in August 1981, ten years earlier. The facts of the case are these. The woman concerned had been towing her caravan from Nottingham to Basingstoke when her car broke down on the A50 trunk road. While it was being repaired, she and her son stayed in her caravan in a lay-by opposite the Wigston Magna graveyard for two nights. After the first night, she fell into conversation with Peter Wilford, a prominent local historian who was in the area searching for buried artefacts.

'This is an evil spot,' she told him. 'I hear shouts, shrieks, groans and the clashing of metal just as if a battle is being fought.'

As he left her that evening, he expressed the hope that she would have a more peaceful night, whilst making a mental note to revisit her the next day. When he called back, he discovered that her rest was, if anything, even more disturbed than on the first occasion. She told Peter how, in the frigid hours of a misty dawn, she was awakened by the pale figure of a youth in a white robe shouting: 'Get up! Get up!'

At first she thought it was her son, but one glance told her that he was actually fast asleep in his own bunk.

'I can't wait to get away from here quickly enough. It is evil here,' she said as her freshly repaired car arrived.

Watching the caravan disappear southwards down the A50, Peter Wilford wondered if he had been right not to tell the lady of the area's dark and bloody past. In recent years, Ted Robinson, Wigston's gravedigger, and his son Roland had uncovered a broken sword, smashed skulls, bits of harness and armour whilst excavating deep graves in the cemetery. These had been surrounded by pieces of broken pottery and strange shaped stones.

'It was just as if a battle has taken place up here,' he remarked later. His comment was perhaps more accurate than he realised at the time. Probably because it occupied the strategic middle ground of central England, everyone from Romans to Royalists has left the bloody imprint of conflict on Leicestershire and the neighbouring counties. In fact, Leicester itself served as a launch pad for Viking raiding parties to ravage the surrounding countryside, as this telling passage from the *Anglo Saxon Chronicle* shows: '*In this year [914], the host [Vikings] rode out from Northampton and Leicester and broke the peace, slaying many men at Hook Norton and thereabout.*'

Wigston, however, had the dubious distinction of suffering

the malign attentions of the Norsemen even earlier when, in 876, they sacked and burned it to the ground.

'Where the caravan was parked is in a direct line approximately half to three-quarters of a mile from our house, ' Mr O explained to me. 'She was also parked close an old Saxon burial ground. Indeed, if one was to see an imprint of history, it would be difficult to find a more appropriate candidate than Wigston Magna.

With heads bowed, the Saxons moved away into the dawn from the burial ground, their collective grief and pain imprinting itself on the atmosphere.

7

Northern Hauntings

To most people who have never been there, Manchester is a cold grey industrial city which is the home of *Coronation Street*, Britain's most famous and enduring TV soap opera. However, as someone who has visited the area regularly since 1988, I know that this is a totally erroneous image. Not only is it a city of many fine buildings and an excellent Metro system, but it also has a vibrant cultural life. This is the home of the world-famous Hallé Orchestra and the Royal Exchange Theatre, a boldly modern structure built totally within a fine old Victorian building in the city centre.

The recent influx of immigrants from all over the world, particularly Asia, has also meant that the Manchester area has some of the best 'ethnic' restaurants in Britain. I remember coming across a truly global treat for the palate at one road junction in the city. On one corner there was Balti and Chinese cuisine, with Greek, Italian and Thai on the others. More traditionally, the pubs and the beer are also excellent with fast, friendly service and very reasonable prices.

Such hospitality has a long and honourable tradition in this part of the country, stretching back many hundreds of years. Some of the pubs here are of a similar age with spectral echoes from the past embedded in their fabric and atmosphere. The Godley Hall Inn, which is the subject of the next story, is a very good example of this. Like many of the encounters in this book, it came to my notice thanks to a chance mention by a good friend who knew the owners well. I am indeed grateful to Sue Lord, who took the trouble to sit down and tell me their story during a very busy Sunday lunchtime.

THE HAUNTED RESTROOM

Sue and Phil Lord's Story

The pub was packed as usual and Sue had her hands full, serving and cooking food for the customers whilst her husband Phil worked behind the bar. Then a strange little incident occurred. As she put several dishes down on one of the tables, Sue felt someone take hold of her hand. Startled, she looked down to see it was a very serene, middle-aged woman.

'Why are you so worried?' she asked Sue.

'Because we've just taken this place on as our first business,' Sue replied. 'And, to be frank, the financial commitment is a big worry.'

'Well, *don't* worry,' the woman said calmly. 'With you and your husband here, this business will grow and grow.' Then nodding towards the ladies' toilet, she added: 'He's happy that you're here as well.'

At the time, Sue did not think to ask how this woman could possibly see into the future or who the *he* was in the ladies' toilet, but the incident lodged itself in her mind. As it turned out, the customer's prediction proved totally correct. Today the Godley Hall Inn has become one of the most popular pubs in the Hyde area of Cheshire. It is not difficult to see why either. Fresh flowers always grace the highly polished tables where the customers of the attractive eighteenth-century pub drink excellent northern beer. This welcoming atmosphere is further enhanced by the appetising smell of home cooking.

Sue and Phil are the sort of people who would make a go of any pub, so the prediction could easily have been a lucky guess. However, she now has reason to believe that this was more than that. Many people must have doubted the couple's sanity when they took over the pub in 1993. Hidden behind a pie factory, it was devoid of customers and nearly derelict at the time. Restoring the Godley Hall to its former glory seemed to many an impossible task, except Phil and Sue, of course. Ignoring the Job's comforters, they worked for many hard and rubble-strewn months renovating the interior before reopening for business.

Most of this work was done by Phil, a quiet former rugby player certainly not given to flights of psychic fancy. However, as he worked on the building, he sensed that someone was watching him. Sue also began to feel some sort of presence in the pub. For example, on one occasion, she was about to throw an old chair out of the rest-room of the ladies' toilet, when something or someone, she does not know what, told her to leave it in place. The chair remains to this day.

There were rumours that the pub was haunted, then a series of incidents occurred that led Sue to believe that these were more than folk stories. The first involved the mysterious woman and her heartening prediction. Sue learned that she was actually a medium from South Wales who came up to Cheshire regularly to visit her son, who was a customer in the pub. One day she asked Sue if she realised the place was haunted.

'Well, the old regulars have always said it was,' Sue replied. 'Although I've not personally seen anything. Why do you ask?'

'Because I've just been talking to your resident ghost in the ladies,' the psychic replied.

'His name's Thomas Bennett and he's looking for his wife Mary and their children.'

She then described the man's appearance in detail. He was dressed in dark clothes with a wide white collar in the Puritan tradition and had long hair, balding at the front. During two subsequent visits to the pub, the Welsh medium has again spoken to Thomas Bennett as he sat in his favourite chair in the toilet. This is the same chair Sue nearly threw out and Mr Bennett is the presence the psychic originally referred to. It appears he is both a benign and observant ghost, as the medium discovered during her last visit. Thomas pointed out that she had lost an earring. Looking in the mirror, she discovered that one was indeed missing.

However, not all the pub's customers are quite as relaxed about Thomas Bennett as the Celtic lady. One evening a

163

woman came to the bar and asked the staff if there was a ghost. When they replied in the affirmative, she said: 'I thought so, I felt him in that area right by me.'

Eventually she asked to be moved to the other side of the bar to escape the ghost's frigid presence. Another flatly refused to enter the pub at all, saying that she felt a ghostly presence which frightened her.

Becoming a pub in the mid-1800s, the Godley Hall was originally farm buildings constructed at the turn of the eighteenth century. At the front of the building, there is a clumsily bricked up door. Over it, the year *1718* has been carved in stone. It is through this old entrance that Thomas Bennett passes before sitting and waiting for his family in his favourite chair. He is obviously someone who knew when he was well off, for there must be many worse places to spend eternity than the Godley Hall Inn.

In the next story, the trauma of the Civil War is a possible cause of a haunting. This time, it was not a complete battle that was witnessed, as in the case of Edgehill, but the lost spirit of a more private tragedy which happened 300 years ago at Stockport, just outside Manchester.

A GHOST AT THE QUEEN'S HEAD

The Harrises' Story

One night in the mid-sixteenth century, a soldier sat pondering his fate in a locked bedroom at the Queen's Head, a Stockport coaching inn. Dressed only in breeches and shirtsleeves, he no longer possessed any weapon or helmet for he was awaiting trial by court martial. Three hundred and fifty years later we can only speculate on his likely state of mind or indeed his crime. One thing was certain, though, if it was serious enough to warrant a court martial, there was only one likely outcome: death by hanging. The soldier also knew this, which is no

164

doubt why he decided to forestall the inevitable result of his trial. The next morning his guards found him hanging from a beam, his face a contorted mask of death.

In the early 1990s the brewery decided that the Queen's Head needed a facelift and spent thousands of pounds refurbishing the place. It was during these operations that the builders complained of a presence in one of the rooms they were working on. Bricks and trowels would suddenly take flight of their own accord. After the work was completed, someone in the brewery decided to paint a sign on the door of the room in question saying: *'The Haunted Room'*. Then in 1993, Dave and Paula Harris took over the tenancy of the Queen's Head. They were well pleased with landing such a busy pub near the centre of Stockport and knew nothing of the hauntings at that stage.

'To be honest, I really don't believe that the room the builders complained about was haunted,' Paula explained to me recently. 'But I've definitely seen something on numerous occasions and so have the staff.'

Her first inkling that there was a supernatural presence in the place came only a couple of weeks after they had moved into the pub. She was decorating the flat at the back of the pub, where they were living. Suddenly she felt a cold wind rush through her body like a ghostly express train. It was an experience that left Paula nauseous and frightened for some minutes. Fortunately, it has not happened again for she would not want a repeat performance.

'It was as if I had disturbed someone or something by my decorating,' she said.

Then she and her husband began to hear whispering late at night. Always indistinct, it had a desperate and troubled air about it as if someone was trying to offload a huge burden of guilt from it's conscience.

After that a figure started to appear. It always came as they cleared up after closing time, a blurred grey form moving furtively from one room to the next. When Dave went down into the cellar to change the barrels, he would often catch sight of the same luminescent form. In fact, some of their staff

165

now refuse to go down into the cellar, swearing that they saw a pair of feet in old-fashioned boots standing at the bottom of the stairs.

'We had a really butch manager looking after the place recently,' Liz Evenden, a member of staff, recalled. 'And he refused to go down into the cellar. He said there was something down there. It certainly feels icy cold down there and something does keep messing around with the gas taps attached to the barrels. You know, switching them on and off.'

Even if it did not possess a ghost, the Queen's Head is certainly a very interesting and atmospheric pub. The small, friendly bars are devoid of modern tat such as jukeboxes and fruit machines. Instead there is a beautiful Victorian fireplace and old photographs lining the tastefully papered walls. It is also obvious that many alterations have occurred during its long history. For example, just behind the main bar there is a door that is at least 5 feet off the modern floor. To visit the gents' toilet, you have to climb a long flight of stone steps. On the way, you pass another strange door that is not more than 2 or 3 feet wide. On it is the legend: '*For Thin Gentlemen Only*', written in old English lettering. A little further up the stairs is the door with the sign '*The Haunted Room*'.

The manifestations have continued, but the Harrises and their staff treat it as all part of being custodians of one of Stockport's most historic and unusual pubs.

(*N.B. the Harrises' have now moved from The Queen's Head*)

A Touch of Evil

Whilst many ghosts are harmless, there is a reverse side to this particular coin that I call the Spectral Underworld. It is a world inhabited by much more malign forces, whose hauntings range from unpleasantly mischievous to downright harmful. At one end of the scale, a manifestation might simply be an awful smell, such as rotting flesh. At the other end, it can be a physical attack causing actual bodily injury, as in the case of the woman who suffered a broken tooth. Fortunately, I do not know of any cases where the injuries were severe enough to end in hospitalisation or death. Nevertheless, they are extremely frightening for those involved.

The reasons for these incidents can vary. Sometimes an angry and malign entity will attack someone simply because they are in the wrong house at the wrong time. For example, the spirit of a dead murderer may be trying to re-create his earthly crime by attacking someone who enters a house or building that he haunts. Old habits die hard. On other occasions they seem to occur for no better reason than pure devilment and mischief.

The following experience of Neil M. involves just such a malign force who used its powers to gain entry where it had no business at all.

FORCED ENTRY

*Neil M.'s First Manchester Experience

This is the experience of someone who may well have been the unwitting accomplice of a hostile ghost. In 1992, Neil M. helped his friend Rene move flats in the Manchester suburb of Levenshulme. Built in the late 1930s, there was nothing particularly remarkable about the exterior of the building, but inside it was a different story.

'The day she moved in I felt that there was something in the flat,' he said. 'But I didn't want to suggest it, knowing what Rene was like and that probably she had felt the same thing. Then a week later I just had this feeling that I should go round and see her. It was quite odd because I felt as though someone had called me, that I *should* go round.'

Worried without knowing quite why, Neil called at Rene's flat. He knocked at the door and waited, but nobody came. Then, as he knocked again, he had the sensation that someone was behind him. Turning, he saw a large aggressive man walking purposefully towards him. He did a double take and looked again, but the man had vanished. However, in that moment of looking away and then back again, Neil had the sensation that somebody had walked through him and into the locked flat.

'It was as though I had been used as a way of getting into the flat,' Neil recalled.

Still feeling very unsettled, he went home, but made a point of phoning Rene later. To his immense relief, she sounded fine. However, he was reluctant to leave it at that, so he visited her the next day.

'Tell me, has anything odd happened to you?' he asked, after the initial pleasantries.

'You could say that,' Rene replied. 'Last night I woke up and, well, saw this really tall man with cropped hair just looking at me. I didn't exactly feel threatened by him, but I was very aware that he'd been there.'

Although she never saw the aggressive man again, from then on, Rene had plenty of spectral visitors to her flat. Every time she woke up in the night, she would see a constant stream of people moving past her open door in the hallway outside. On some nights she would just lie there and watch people walking to and fro. That in itself did not frighten her, but the flat had also developed a dank coldness that no amount of heating would dispel. Accompanying this was an overriding atmosphere of unfriendliness about the place.

However, what finally drove Rene from the flat was not its supernatural occupants, but a mundane domestic disaster. Returning home from work one night, she flicked the light switch on with the back of her hand. A massive bolt of electricity knocked her into the room, which was about 3 inches deep in water. Looking up in the gloom, she could just see water pouring through the light fittings and down the walls. It later transpired that the occupant of the flat above hers had gone out and left his washing machine on. A pipe on it had then ruptured, leaving water to pump out unhindered, flooding his and Rene's flat.

It was very lucky that she had not switched on the light in the normal way because the result would almost certainly have been electrocution. But was it just luck or some sort of warning? Coming on the heels of the aggressive man and the spectral crowds, it was too much for Rene and within two days she had moved out, never to return.

A GHOST WITH A SENSE OF HUMOUR

*Neil M.'s Second Manchester Experience

Fortunately, not all of Neil's supernatural experiences have been hostile. On one occasion, he encountered a good-humoured ghost. In 1990, he moved back into a Victorian house in Levenshulme that he had previously shared with some friends.

Neil found that the house certainly had a spectral atmosphere and that everyone who lived there had experienced one sort of manifestation or another. However, unlike the dank coldness of Rene's flat nearby, the atmosphere in this house was warm and friendly. 'This presence certainly wasn't malevolent or evil in any way, it was just interested,' he recalled.

Even when he was alone in the house, Neil always felt that somebody else was there with him. It was not threatening in any way, more like a friendly person looking for company. On more than one occasion, the ghost also showed that it had a talent for practical jokes.

The first prank occurred when Neil had first moved into the house. At that time a friend of his called Janine had the room at the top of the house which was the focus of the haunting. Returning home one night, she discovered that all the mirrors had been taken off the walls and one of her drawers had been filled with water, soaking her clothes.

'Nobody had been in the house at the time and it certainly wasn't our cats because there was absolutely no smell,' he said.

Shortly after that incident, Neil moved away from Manchester for six months. When he returned, he was given the haunted room on the top floor. During the first two nights he stayed in it, he heard someone come up the stairs and then knock on his door, but, when he opened it, there was nobody there. He asked Janine about this and she confirmed that everyone who stayed in that room, including herself, had the same experience. Neil also recalled that when Rene had stayed there for a night, the ghost had not only knocked on her door but also opened it.

'It just seemed as if the ghost was interested in seeing who was there, getting to know them and then going about its own business,' Neil said.

The ghost seemed to have a particular liking for Neil. On many occasions, he sensed that the spirit was watching him and chuckling good-humouredly. Often, he would also feel someone sitting on his bed all night. 'If I woke up, I wouldn't be able to move my legs because it felt as if somebody was occupying that particular space.'

Although the spirit was entirely benevolent, it still could not resist the odd practical joke. First it had been Janine's turn and now it was Neil's. One night, after searching high and low for his nail clippers, he finally gave up and switched the light out. Within ten seconds, there was a dull thud. Switching the light back on, Neil saw the nail clippers in the middle of the floor.

'Obviously they weren't there before or I would have noticed them,' he explained. 'I just felt that someone was having a good laugh at my expense.'

Nobody ever discovered who the phantom practical joker was and, for all Neil knows, it is still making its good-humoured presence known in the house at Levenshulme.

A PHANTOM HAND

Tony Kvetaras's Story

Anybody who thinks that all there is to a decent golf course is a bit of grass care should talk to Tony Kvetaras. He will point out that a mower for a heavily used green is likely to cost £11,000 or to renovate one hole in a course will not leave the owner any change out of £10,000. For Tony is a greenkeeper by profession. Now in his early thirties, he has looked after golf courses in Switzerland, Los Angeles and the north of England, where he now lives.

Tony is a very down-to-earth sort of bloke who has rarely given the subject of ghosts or the paranormal a second thought. He did remember his Austrian mother telling him of an encounter with a dead soldier when she was playing the Ouija board, but that was over 30 years earlier. As far as Tony was concerned, ghosts and the paranormal were for the films, newspapers and old houses. They were experiences that happened to other people, not him. But that was before his encounter with the unknown.

It was 1980 and he was living in a block of flats in the Lancashire town of Rochdale at the time. Built in the 1960s, there was nothing remotely weird or eerie about the place, which made his experience all the more frightening and unexpected.

He did not know what awoke him on the night in question. It may have been the fact that the room was deathly cold or perhaps it was the terrible fear he was feeling. All Tony knew was that there was something directly behind him and that if he turned his head, he would be killed. As he lay facing the wall, too petrified to move, he felt a hand grab him round the back of the neck. In reality, the experience probably lasted a few seconds, but, to him, it seemed like a lifetime before the entity released its grip and the room gradually warmed up.

'I have no idea what it was or why it picked on me,' Tony said recently. 'All I know is that I felt a very bad presence that would have killed or seriously harmed me if I moved in any way.'

What happened in Rochdale was Tony Kveteras's one and only experience of the paranormal, but he fervently hopes it was his last.

My close friend Hilary Wilding is employed at one of the Manchester area's larger hospitals. Working on the assumption that such places abound with paranormal stories, she had the very good idea of putting up a card on the noticeboard asking

171

people to share their experiences with us for inclusion in this book. Much to my disappointment, there was absolutely no response to the notice for the next few weeks. Then it was as if the floodgates opened as people came and told us of their strange and often unsettling experiences. What surprised both Hilary and myself was the number of her work colleagues who had interesting paranormal encounters which they rarely if ever spoke about. A good example of this was *Joan Talbot, who had her experience at a neighbouring hospital. For the sake of everyone involved she has asked for real identities and locations not to be published.

THE CONFESSION

*Joan Talbot's Story

Sometimes, not often perhaps, we learn things in this life that we wish had remained unlearned. On rare occasions these can be dark and terrible secrets that present us with acute moral dilemmas. Little did Joan Talbot realise that this was to be the case when she went on night duty for the first time in a Greater Manchester hospital. It was midsummer in 1984 and she was a young and rather naive trainee nurse.

The ward she was in was known in the business as a 'Nightingale' with a high ceiling and beds down each side of its length. At one end there were three separate rooms with glass windows, where patients who needed special attention were kept. In this case there were two men recovering from cardiac complaints and a third called Fred, who was terminally ill. It was Joan's job to sit at the desk close to these rooms and watch the patients' cardiac monitors. If there was any sign of abnormality, she had to call one of her two more senior colleagues. This was especially important for the gravely ill patient in the third room. Joan felt very sorry for this 50-year-old man, who was suffering congestive cardiac failure or, as she put it with brutal simplicity: 'Basically, after two previous attacks, his heart was knackered.'

The job of the nurses in this case was to make the poor man's days as comfortable and painless as possible. This was easier said than done since one of the effects of this condition was oedema, the retention of excessive fluid in the body. Twice a day the patient had to have new dressings and was given morphine to alleviate the pain of the massive blisters that sprouted like obscene growths all over his body.

At eleven o'clock on this warm June night Joan was sitting at her desk a few feet from the three rooms when the red call light above Fred's door went on.

'Hiya, Fred, how are you feeling?' she asked cheerily as she entered his room.

'Terrible,' he replied. 'I want my dressings done, I'm really uncomfortable.'

Normally Rita, a more senior nurse than herself, would dress Fred's bandages, but she was at the far end of the ward fetching the drugs trolley at the time. Wishing to be helpful, Joan decided to have a go at changing Fred's bandages. To do this, she helped him gently into the armchair beside his bed. Unfortunately, the experiment was not a success and Fred became very agitated, demanding that the more experienced nurse finish the job.

'I'm really sorry, Rita, I tried my best to dress his bandages right but I think I hurt him,' Joan said in a voice quivering with distress.

'That's all right, love, it could happen to anyone,' Rita said kindly. 'I'll see to him.' With that, she left Joan to help the chief nurse to organise the drugs for the other patients on the ward.

When Rita entered Fred's room she found him sitting in the armchair, his face creased with pain. However, as she moved to help him he motioned for her to sit on the bed. Uncertainly, she sat down, not quite knowing what to expect.

'I haven't got long, Rita, I know that and so do you,' he said simply. 'But before I die, I need to tell someone about something terrible I did when I was younger. It was so dreadful I haven't told anyone about it, not even my wife.'

'Why do you want me to know then?' Rita asked.

'Because you have a face that will tell me what you honestly think, that you believe me.' he said. 'It's very important that you believe me.'

With an effort Fred swung the anglepoise lamp just above the bed so that it shone directly in Rita's face. The brightness hurt, causing her to avert her eyes.

'Look at me, girl!' he commanded. 'Don't you understand, I must see your face so that I can see whether or not you believe the story I'm going to tell you!'

Squinting in the blinding light, the nurse looked up at Fred and he told his story. 'Twenty years ago I went potholing in North Wales with a young lad who wasn't more than eighteen. Well, during that weekend I murdered him and shoved his body down one of the deepest holes I could find. Nobody's ever discovered him or accused me of his killing, but now, at the end of my life I've got to tell *someone honest.*'

When she emerged from the room 20 minutes later Rita was so pale and shaken that Joan and another nurse, a senior sister, took her downstairs to the staffroom for a coffee. It was there that she recounted Fred's dark secret.

'What do we do?' she asked the others.

'Well, we're bound by rules of confidentiality,' the senior sister replied. 'Besides, the man'll be dead in a couple of days, so why not let sleeping dog's lie?'

'Because he's still alive and has admitted to murder,' Joan said.

'But if we tell the police it won't bring that lad back to life,' the senior nurse said. 'I think we are bound to keep this between ourselves.'

Reluctantly the others agreed and spent the remainder of the shift uneasily examining their consciences.

At nine the next morning Fred passed away in his sleep. His room was thoroughly cleaned, the sheets removed and the lamp was moved from the rather strange angle the orderlies found it. According to hospital rules it was then locked.

Twelve hours later Joan and Rita met at the bottom of the stairs to the ward.

'How are you feeling?' Joan asked her colleague.

'Rotten, I didn't sleep a wink all day thinking about Fred's confession,' she replied.

'I didn't either,' Joan said. 'Still, maybe it was the morphine.'

'No, I'm sure it wasn't that,' Rita said. 'I just know he was telling me the truth. God, it's cold in here, don't you think?'

'Yes it is,' Joan agreed, rubbing her arms.

Indeed, they both found the atmosphere heavy and chilly. Moreover, Joan felt queasy and nervous as if her stomach was full of butterflies. When the duty nurse handed over to them she mentioned all the patients except Fred. When asked about him, she told them of his death. Not knowing whether this actually simplified matters or not, the nurses went about their duties.

At eleven o'clock that night Joan suddenly became aware of a red call light flashing above the door of one of the rooms. When she looked up, she realised that it was Fred's room and hurried to see what the problem was. It was only when she reached the locked door she remembered that he was dead and the room was empty. Looking through the window she could see the bed devoid of sheets in the light of the anglepoise lamp. Not only was it switched on but it was back in the position Fred had put it in when he confessed to murder.

But how can that happen? she asked herself. *The room's locked. Nobody's been in there since he died.*

In the intervening years since that incident Joan has encountered other strange occurrences that have convinced her that the lights in the locked room were caused by a force that lay outside the normal bounds of nature. For example, there was the time when she was caring for a ward of old ladies. One of them told her how a beautiful lady had held her hand for nearly the whole night. It had, the old woman said, made her feel so well and peaceful. The following day that patient died.

'When you work in as many hospitals as I have, you learn that there are certain things that can't easily be explained,' she told me. 'Sceptics might say that those lights in Fred's room had something to do with the wiring. If that were the case, why didn't the other lights play up? After all, they were on the same circuit.'

Although she comes from a cultural background that has always set its face against the supernatural, Joan believes that the lights in the locked and empty room were an urgent signal for forgiveness from beyond the grave.

Janet Steward who now works in a secretarial capacity at a large Manchester hospital. has had a series of experiences that had begun when she was very young and are still continuing. Janet, who is now in her thirties, is certain that this is due to the fact that she is very psychically aware. Like Joan Talbot, her experiences are not a subject that she often talks about. Like many other people with similar gifts, she treats her experiences very much as part and parcel of everyday life as you will see in her story:

A FOND FAREWELL

Janet Steward's Story

When she was a little girl of six, Janet Steward was terrified of the dark. Every night she wished her mother would stay in her room instead of kissing her goodnight and leaving her to the unknown terrors of the dark. But she knew that this was not possible since her mum like all grown-ups always had more important things to do once they had switched off your light. Then something happened that helped Janet conquer her fear of the dark.

One night, a kind and gentle stranger drifted into her bedroom and sat with her, singing nursery rhymes in a soft voice that helped her drift off to sleep. Thirty years later she still clearly remembers the kind woman dressed in modern clothes who paid her many nocturnal visits.

'I remember that she was in her thirties,' Janet recalled, 'and was a very ordinary yet kindly person.'

However, there was one aspect of these visits which certainly was not normal. For she actually came through the closed door without opening it. Strangely, this did not frighten the little girl, who simply accepted the manifestation as someone who had come to comfort her. When she tried to tell her mother about the 'nice lady' it was dismissed as a figment of her childish imagination, an explanation which as an adult Janet still does not accept.

'Even at that age you know whether you're dreaming or not, and that lady was real enough,' Janet told me recently.

The spectral nursery rhyme singer was to be the first of a series of paranormal experiences Janet Steward has had throughout her life. She describes herself as a 'do-it-yourself spiritualist', I prefer the term psychic savant, someone with highly developed occult powers. Probably the most vivid and unsettling of these incidents happened many years later in the Summer of 1985 at a large hospital in the Manchester area which can not be named for reasons of confidentiality.

At the time, she was employed as an auxiliary nurse in this particular hospital. At the end of the ward where she worked there was a room used for very ill patients which Janet always disliked entering. The reason for this was that she and a number of her colleagues had often witnessed the lights in this room switching themselves on and off as well as the door opening of its own accord. Moreover, the room always had an intensely chilly feel about it.

'It was always cold, no matter how much heating you had on in there or how hot it was elsewhere,' she recalled recently. 'and this was not a normal cold either but one that made you shiver inside with the hairs on your neck standing on end.'

As is often the case in hauntings, this frigid atmosphere proved to be the precursor of more intense spectral incidents over the next few months. For Janet these began in the early summer of 1985 with a vivid and unsettling experience immediately after she returned from a week's sick leave.

At the time her task was to replace the drinking water in the various wards and rooms in the hospital. When she entered the 'Frigid' room, she saw Annie, an elderly patient sitting up

177

in the bed smiling at her. It is not unusual for nursing staff to develop strong bonds of friendship with the patients in their charge and this was the case with Annie and Janet. So she was delighted that the old lady was one of the first people to welcome her back to work. However, her pleasure at seeing Annie was mixed with concern since the patient appeared to be frail and unwell.

'Hello Annie you look a bit peaky,' Janet said placing a tumbler of water on the table beside the bed. 'I think I'll get someone to come and look at you.'

With that, the she hurried off to arrange this at the nursing desk. But when she arrived there, her request was greeted by mystified stares.

'Annie died last week Janet,' the nurse explained with a baffled expression on her face.

'Oh,' was all Janet felt able to manage as a reply. Then, feeling as if she had been punched in the stomach, she hurried back to the room only to find it cold and empty, the bed unruffled and unoccupied. Of Annie, there was absolutely no sign.

'I had no idea at the time of the incident that she was dead,' Janet said reflectively. 'You see, you don't get told who has died at the time of the handover and I had only been working for about half an hour. She looked totally solid, as real as you and me, not like a ghost at all.'

Three months later, the room again became the focus of paranormal activity when Janet was on duty. At the time her task was to stock up the rooms for the weekend. Quite simply this entailed changing the towels and soap as well as making up the beds and closing the curtains.

'It was three o'clock one Friday Afternoon,' she recalled. 'and because we didn't have any clinics then, everyone else had gone home leaving me to work in the ward on my own. Anyway, I was going round the rooms, stocking them up and closing them down for the weekend when I came to the "Frigid" Room.'

After making up the bed, she closed the curtains, switched out the light and shut the door. A few minutes later, she passed the room again only to find the light on, the door wide open, the curtains drawn and the covers at the foot of the unmade bed. Telling herself that this was some sort of a practical joke, Janet remade the bed, closed the curtains and switching off the light, shut the door once more. She then continued to work at the other end of the ward, but always in sight of the 'Frigid' Room.

'I passed this room a few minutes later and exactly the same thing had happened,' she said. 'The door and curtains were open, the light was on and the covers were folded at the bottom of the bed. The room was always in my sight. Anyway it had a noisy lino floor so there was no way anyone could have got in there and done all that without me hearing them.'

This was the last incident that Janet Steward experienced before she left the hospital. As to the reason for the hauntings, she feels that the staff may have unwittingly contributed to the room's paranormal atmosphere. Because it was so cold, it tended not be used except for patients who were actually dying.

'I think that because a lot of terminal patients were put in that room, many spirits of the dead remained to make their presence felt to the living,' she told me. 'As for Annie, well, I think she wanted to say goodbye and show me that she was now better off than in the living world she had left behind.'

Janet has lived in the village of Timperley just outside Manchester for the whole of her life and it is here that she has had all her other paranormal experiences. Some are prolonged and involve contact with dead relatives whilst others are very brief. The majority feature sightings of ghosts in one form or another. This may seem far-fetched to many, but I believe that she sees what has been denied to the bulk of the population by the dead hand of materialism. This is a parallel world of spirits and ghosts that exists alongside that of the living.

The way Janet sums it up is typically succinct:

'I see a lot of ghosts because I'm actually psychic,' she explained to me in a calm Northern voice as matter of factly as if she were discussing some minor allergy. 'For example, there was the old man I saw near the cemetery.'

179

This was one of her shorter sightings, but nevertheless has stayed clearly in her mind to this day. She was cycling home form work at nearby Sale one summer's evening. Part of her route home was a road that passed between two cemeteries with railings on either side. As she cycled up the incline, she saw an elderly man in a smart, rather old-fashioned tweed suit walking along the edge of the cemetery. Janet looked away momentarily to change into a lower gear, but when she glanced up again, the old man had vanished. I have seen this road, it runs for at least a quarter of a mile up hill with the cemeteries at a slightly lower level behind an unbroken barrier of railings. It has no turnings, exits or entrances that anyone could turn into and it is very unlikely that a rather infirm old man would have suddenly leapt over the fence.

Such a paranormal experience is by no means unique as Carol Voice would testify (See *Out of His Time*). There is also the case of Rushna Khan, a work colleague of mine who also runs a general provisions store with her husband near Reading. In the summer of 1995, she was behind the counter in the shop when an old lady walked swiftly into the back of the shop. When she had not emerged after some minutes, Rushna went to look for her only to discover that the shop was empty. The only other exit at the rear was locked and barred. The noise of trying to open this door would surely have alerted Rushna. Like the old man at the cemetery, the woman had vanished into thin air.

Perhaps the experiences that have brought the most comfort to Janet, are the contacts she has had with her much loved grandparents. These started with a premonitory dream about her grandmother's death two days before she passed away in September 1986

In this dream, Janet found herself in a garden filled with beautiful trees and flowers that were totally real and solid but also bathed in a brilliant and clean white light. In the middle of this garden, Janet saw her grandmother lying in bed. As she walked up to her, the old lady began to float upwards with a thin, golden thread linking her body to the bed. As she rose higher, the thread snapped causing Janet to grab at it.

'It felt warm in my hand but simply slipped away and I found I couldn't hold it,' she told me in a quiet voice.

Two days later Janet's Nana, as she still affectionately called her, died quite suddenly of a heart attack. Janet also remembers a time when she left her body and visited her grandfather in a similar, celestially brilliant garden. She has also had several visits from both her grandmother and grandfather.

'They usually come when I am in some sort of trouble,' she told me. 'Like when my fiancee left me or my car was stolen recently.'

The visitations always occur in broad daylight and when Janet is wide awake. On the first occasion, her grandmother seemed very concerned that she had frightened her. She has had more visits from her grandmother than grandfather. She puts this down to the fact that her grandfather probably sees this business of visiting to keep watch on and comforting close relatives is 'woman's work.' Even in death, it seems, old fashioned chauvinism can hold sway.

The most recent visitation by her grandmother was in the late winter of 1995. Janet was particularly upset because her prized Van Den Plas Maestro had been stolen and wrecked.

'I was sitting in my room feeling rather sorry for myself,' she recalled. 'When suddenly my grandmother was there. She made me understand that I should feel sorry for those people who had stolen and wrecked my car.'

Had that been the case? I asked her. After a pause she said, yes it had.

The majority of people would look askance at someone like Janet who has regular conversations with dead relatives. The conclusion many would doubtlessly come to is that they were, to put it mildly, a little odd. But as far as Janet Steward is concerned, they can go hang, in the nicest possible sense of course. She knows what she has experienced and nothing will shake her from that. End of story.

Anne Evans works at the Wythenshawe Hospital as a midwife. Although she and Hilary are acquainted, we only heard of her supernatural experience by chance. In fact, it was during my interview with Joan Talbot. She mentioned that a friend she worked with had actually seen a dead patient. I was naturally very interested because it seemed to have some strong similarities with other hospital hauntings that I was investigating. This was confirmed when I spoke to Anne herself in January 1996.

A CASE OF MISTAKEN IDENTITY

Anne Evans's Story

In the early 1980s Anne Evans worked as a newly qualified staff nurse in a male medical ward at Bury Hospital near Manchester. It was a particularly challenging assignment since a number of the patients were curmudgeonly and uncooperative old men in their seventies and eighties. One of these patients, whom we shall call Cyril, proved to be particularly troublesome.

Although Bury is quite an old hospital, this particular ward was not a long 'Nightingale' with a nurse sitting at one end, such as feature in films and TV series with monotonous regularity. It was in fact square and quite compact with the nurses' station situated in the middle. To one side, there was an annexe of three rooms and opposite there was a sluice room.

'Cyril was in one of these rooms,' Anne said. 'As luck would have it, we had to measure his urine at very regular intervals but he was quite difficult to handle and we could not get over to him how important it was to get these samples. He'd tip them down the sink or throw them around the place.'

Because of this, the nurses had to keep a special watch on this particular patient. At two o'clock one morning Anne really thought Cyril was going to give her trouble. She was on her own at the time, writing at her desk. Suddenly, she saw a movement in the corner of her eye. Looking up, she saw a figure she took to be Cyril walking rapidly towards the sluice, bedpan in hand.

What's the old devil up to now? she thought in exasperation as she hurried after him. However, when Anne entered the tiny sluice area, it was completely empty. Thinking that he must have slipped past her, she went to his room in the annexe. There she found Cyril fast asleep.

'There was no way a seventy-year-old man could have hopped out of bed that nimbly in the short space of time that had taken me to cross the ward,' Anne said. 'But I knew that I had definitely seen someone.'

It was at this time that Anne noticed two very strange phenomena. Firstly, the annexe was deathly cold, like a deep-freeze. Secondly, the ward seemed unnaturally quiet at the time of the incident. There was no sound at all, with not even the constant bleep of the heart monitors to be heard. Turning the incident over in her mind, she also remembered that the old man padding silently across the ward was wearing odd pyjamas. Cyril's pair, on the other hand, were a perfect match. Before she could dwell on the incident much longer, the other duty nurses returned from their meal break.

'Do you know, I've just seen the weirdest thing,' Anne said, and told them about the mysterious patient.

'Yes, a lot of people have seen him,' one of the nurses said. 'And when they went to look in the sluice there was never anyone there.'

Then other nurses began recalling other strange incidents in the ward, such as call lights going on in empty rooms.

Unlike many devout Christians, Anne does not have a problem with belief in the supernatural. However, she simply does not know what to make of her one and only paranormal experience.

'I definitely saw that old man,' she said emphatically. 'But I have no idea who or what he may have been.'

The Pendle, that ruggedly beautiful moorland area of Lancashire lying to the north of Manchester, has long been associated with the occult and the supernatural. This is largely due to two infamous seventeenth-century witchcraft trials. For it was here that a group of women and at least one man were accused of causing the death by witchcraft of one Robert Nutter, an itinerant peddler.

Their trial in 1612 bore all the quality hallmarks of seventeenth-century justice: false confessions, rigged witnesses and mob justice – nothing, it seemed, was too good for the defendants. A flavour of this heady yet poisonous brew of prejudice can be gained from an extract of the indictment against Mrs Ann Whittle aka 'Old Chattox':

> *For that she feloniously had practised, used and exercised divers wicked and devilish acts called witchcraft, enchantments, charms and sorceries in and upon one Robert Nutter of Greenhead in The Forest of Pendle in The County of Lancashire, and by the force of the same witchcraft feloniously had killed the said Robert Nutter.*

As was usual in witchcraft trials, the authorities were determined to obtain a verdict of Guilty. For example, when Anne Redfearne was found Not Guilty of bewitching Robert Nutter to death, the angry and dangerous reaction of the courtroom crowd prompted the judge to take corrective action. Without further ado, she was accused of bewitching the tinker's father to death. This time, the court got it right and she was one of the ten accused to be hanged.

In 1633, there was another outbreak of witch hysteria in Pendle. This time, 17 people were accused and convicted of witchcraft on the false evidence of a young boy. Ironically, one of those accused was Elizabeth Device, who, as a nine-year-old witness at the previous trial, sent her own mother to the gallows. Fortunately for those arraigned on this occasion, the boy's evidence was proved to be fraudulent. However, it took nothing less than a pardon by the King himself to save the defendants from the gallows.

Whether those unfortunate victims of seventeenth-century justice were actually witches is still a matter of considerable speculation. What is beyond question is that there are still witches practising in this part of Lancashire in the latter part of the twentieth century. But these are not practitioners of the black arts – far from it. They would no more use their powers to harm anyone than they would stop breathing. For these are white witches, people who believe that they can help others and alleviate suffering by tapping the hidden inner power of the mind and nature itself. *Kathy Heath is just such a witch. The next story involves her and Lynn Whitlock, a close relative, who actually told me what happened.

Once again, this was an experience that I learned of quite by chance. Lynn and I were working in an office where a complete smoking ban existed. To make this more acceptable for the employees who smoked, a room had been set aside for them to worship the deadly weed at set times. It was during such a break from work that she told us of her experience.

I forget quite how the subject of ghosts arose, but it did, and Lynn, a very likeable and outgoing girl whom I had worked with for a couple of years, volunteered her story. It certainly was a conversation stopper.

THE PENDLE PHANTASM

Lynn Whitlock's Story

The occult was the very last thing on Lynn Whitlock's mind when she arranged to baby-sit for her aunt Kathy in August 1981. Sure, the vivacious 18-year-old knew that her aunt had a reputation for being a powerful white witch. She also knew that some of her family would not enter Kathy Heath's house in Accrington. But this did not worry Lynn, who had always enjoyed an excellent rapport with her aunt. Anyway, she did not believe in the supernatural or witchcraft.

185

'She's actually a very gregarious person,' Lynn explained. 'Of course, as a white witch, she has had a number of very strange experiences. But I never felt it wise to enquire about them too closely.'

By ten o'clock that night, Kathy's two children were in bed and Lynn settled down to watch television whilst the remnants of the warm summer's day melted into dusk. Apart from the odd car driving past and a dog barking in the distance, it was a deceptively peaceful evening with no inkling of what would happen next.

Suddenly, the lights dimmed and the picture on the TV broke up into a mosaic of waving lines and snow. Then, to her horror, Lynn saw a foot-wide band of incandescent yellow light appear diagonally across the lounge floor. A split second later, a blob of white mist shot down the line of light and both vanished.

'It didn't really have any substance at all, ' Lynn explained. 'It was like a fuzzy mist with slightly dulled edges. Needless to say, I was still absolutely terrified when my aunt returned a little later.'

Many people would pour scorn on such a story, but Kathy Heath knew better than that. She knew exactly what had happened in front of her petrified niece. A ley line, one of the bands of natural energy, ran diagonally through her house. What Lynn had seen, she explained, was the spirit of a person who had recently died. For some reason it had been trapped in the ley line and was unable to pass into what Kathy called the Other World.

To this day Lynn does not know what to make of either the incident or her aunt's explanation. But one thing is for sure, she is no longer the sceptic she once was about the paranormal.

'My nan always said you shouldn't laugh at the supernatural, now I know she's right.'

Because of Lynn's story and my interest in history and the occult, I had long wanted to see this area of England. However, there never seemed to be time as I rushed northwards on visits to Scotland or Hadrian's Wall. Then on an autumn day in 1995, an opportunity finally arose to visit the Forest of Pendle. Unfortunately, the weather chose to celebrate the occasion by being absolutely filthy

In fact, this actually enhanced the atmosphere of my visit. You see, to fully appreciate the mystical quality of the Pendle 'Witch Country' it is necessary to do as I did and go to the area on just such a grey, drizzle-laden day. Travelling up into the moorlands, my close friend Hilary Wilding and I were always conscious of the huge mass of Pendle Hill brooding under a swirling mantle of cloud. It dominates the surrounding landscape of hill farm and village like some primeval god of the earth. Its very presence seems to separate this area from the rest of Lancashire. Indeed, even in this age of satellite TV and the two-car family, the Pendle villages of Fence, Whalley, Roughlee and Newchurch have an isolated feel about them. Faced with a harsh life of subsistence farming, it is not difficult to see why the women of these parishes might have sought the vicarious pleasures of witchcraft. A little bit of satanism must have proved a welcome relief from the drab Puritanism of seventeenth-century England.

I could not have chosen a better companion to visit the area than Hilary. Having often stayed with relatives who lived in the surrounding area, she knew exactly where to find many of the places most closely associated with the Lancashire witches. We visited Roughlee Hall, the former residence of Alice Nutter, one of the accused, and Newchurch, where Alice and many other members of the Nutter family are buried. Her grave, marked by a fading inscription and *Memento Mori* skull and crossbones motif is in the shadow of the church wall. Such consecrated ground is indeed a strange place to bury a convicted witch.

Ancient and tiny, the Church of St Mary's is easily missed as you drive down the winding main street of Newchurch. Apart from its connections with the notorious Lancashire Witch Trials, it is worth visiting for its sheer history and beauty. However, on the tower, there is a strange and unnerv-

187

ing symbol that I have never seen on any other religious building, let alone a church. A dark circle surrounded by a white oval, it is known as 'The Eye of God'. Without doubt this was placed for all to see, whether Christians or witches, that no deed however small escapes the attention of the Almighty.

According to local historian John Hope, the Newchurch area also has its fair share of ghosts. In his fascinating book *In Pendle's Shadow*, he tells of a phantom witch gathering herbs in a local barrow and the forlorn figure of a girl waiting out eternity for the lover who jilted her. He also mentions the legend of a piper appearing in Newchurch graveyard. On the face of it, this last seems the most incongruous manifestation of all. Why on earth should a Scots piper haunt a Lancashire graveyard? The answer could lie in the Jacobite rising of 1745, when Bonnie Prince Charlie's army came as far south as Derby before finally retreating to Scotland.

The solitary piper could be the spirit of one who fell in battle and, for some reason, found an anonymous grave in this Pendle village. However, the most interesting account was of two young girls who saw a phantom detachment of Civil War troop and horse returning from a nearby battle. By all accounts it was a classic 'battlefield' manifestation, with the girls describing the dress of the soldiers in uncanny detail. It would be fascinating to know if there have been any similar sightings in the area.

As we drove down twisting lanes lined with drystone walls, their surfaces patterned by fallen leaves, Hilary told me of the strange finds she, her brother and cousin made when playing in the area.

'We used to play up on Pendle Hill,' she reminisced. 'And I remember coming across these strange little shelters. I suppose they were for the shepherds looking after the sheep. Anyway, in one of these I found a sort of sheep's horn with an unpleasant red wax inside it.'

Such an item is always used in pagan and witchcraft ceremonies. To me, her recollection provided further anecdotal evidence that witchcraft had not died with those wretched women who were hanged in Lancaster 350 years previously.

A Trigger Mechanism

Deliberate actions of the living have often been known to trigger a supernatural visitation. The most common and dangerous example of this is the use of the Ouija board. All too often this is done by people looking for a bit of excitement. Since it is often followed by periods of severe and hostile supernatural disturbance, the participants usually get much more 'excitement' than they bargained for.

> *It was a big glass ashtray yet it lifted by itself and smashed on the carpet.*

> *They tried to raise this dead boy by using the Ouija and a terrible wind came from nowhere and ripped the curtains off their runners.*

> *One of the girls used the board to raise the Devil. She's been in an asylum ever since.*

These are just three incidents that occurred during sessions with the Ouija. As many people around the world will testify, they are certainly not unique. I personally believe that there is something inherently powerful and dangerous about this device that very few people really understand. As far as I am concerned, 'playing' the Ouija board is the paranormal equivalent of messing with nuclear fission, and about as sensible.

Neil M. would not go along with this since he has used the Ouija board many times without apparent ill effect. However, this was not always the case, as the next story from the northeast of England illustrates.

A BAD NIGHT IN GATESHEAD

*Neil M.'s Story

Neil's next paranormal experiences did not occur until he was well into adulthood. When he was 24 he and the girl he was living with were introduced to the mysteries of the Ouija board by a friend. Although the word has a mystical, eastern ring about it, Ouija is simply the French and German words for Yes run together, forming a single name. Usually consisting of a board with a moveable pointer or a glass and letters of the alphabet on it, the Ouija is reputed to give its users the power to receive messages from dead spirits. This is done by the participants placing their fingers on the pointer and then asking questions. The pointer or glass will then answer by spelling out words by moving from one letter to the next.

Many theologians, specialists in the occult and paranormal investigators advise strongly against having anything to do with the Ouija or its derivatives. They believe that, particularly in the hands of novices, such devices can unlock potentially dangerous psychic forces. However, Neil believes that he and his girlfriend used their board without any ill effect for six months. In fact, it became a party trick to amuse friends and visitors.

'It became a bit of a cult thing and anyone who came around would have to perform their Ouija board experience,' Neil explained.

He still believes that the dangerous power of the board is greatly overrated. Be that as it may, he did have at least one very bad paranormal encounter via the Ouija. This time it occurred when he went to stay with friends in the northern town of Gateshead near Newcastle in July 1987. He had travelled up with a friend called Sue, whose parents owned the house. Outwardly, there was nothing unusual about the building, which dated back to the turn of the century. However, as soon as he set foot inside the front door, Neil sensed that there was a supernatural presence in the place.

190

'I felt an immediate coldness,' he recalled. 'I walked into one of the rooms that was obviously the focus for whatever was there because the drop in temperature was quite dramatic.'

Strangely, none of the people who actually lived in the house were aware of the coldness. Although he felt very uncomfortable about the house's atmosphere, Neil did not mention it to the family for fear of embarrassing them.

The next day, Rene and Sue, two of Neil's other friends, arrived. They had all known each other for some years, so they had an enjoyable day catching up on news, exploring the area and visiting the local pubs. Then one of the girls came up with a suggestion that would round the evening off nicely.

'I know, let's have a session with the Ouija,' she said.

Readily agreeing, the two girls called Sue went off to find a mirror and glass that would substitute for a Ouija board. But, for the first time in his life, Neil felt strangely reluctant to become involved in a Ouija session. Perhaps it was because they were in the room that was the focus of the house's paranormal presence – he simply did not know. While the others were out of the room, he quietly confided his reservations to Rene.

'I really don't like this idea, Rene. What do you think?'

'I agree,' she replied. 'It's not that I'm scared, just apprehensive about where it will lead.'

When the girls returned, Neil told them they would have to play on their own. This made them quite angry.

'Oh come on, Neil, you know very well you can't play the Ouija with only two people, chided one of the girls.

'That's right,' the other joined in. 'Play with two and you raise the Devil.'

'I don't care,' Rene said categorically. 'Neil can do what he likes but I'm not having any part of this.'

Eventually, after a great deal of wheedling and persuasion, Neil agreed to take part. However, immediately after they started the session, he knew that this was a big mistake. The glass began to slide around the mirror in fast, angry movements that became so violent it flew onto the floor on two occasions. He was certain that they had managed to raise a malevolent force.

'Bastard! Bugger! Fuck! Fuck!'

As the glass spelled out obscenity after irate obscenity for over an hour, a palpable sense of fear built up in the now frigid room. Rene crouched in a corner pleading with them to stop. But, although they were frightened, the two girls insisted on continuing. They wanted to get to the bottom of it all. However, the only answer the presence gave to their questions was a string of swear words. As always, time passed very quickly during the Ouija session, and, before they realised, it was four in the morning.

'I'm sick of this,' Neil said, stretching his tired arms. 'I'm going out to watch the sunrise.'

'OK, but let's try the Ouija once more,' said one of the girls. 'Perhaps this time we'll get a message.'

Which is exactly what happened. It was the same evil presence, but instead of curses, it had a chilling command:

'Don't leave the house! Don't leave the house!'

The message was repeated again and again as the room temperature dropped to an arctic coldness. Then it was replaced by an even more urgent command:

'Death! Death! Fire! Death! Death within one mile! Don't leave the house! Don't leave the house! Lock all doors now! Danger! Danger! Danger!'

'I don't think we should go out,' someone said quietly. 'Let's go to bed.'

This time there was total agreement, but there was one little job to be done first. They had to ask the spirit on the Ouija to go. At first it refused, but then departed with a huge release of pressure, like air escaping from a balloon. Whilst it was there, the feeling of oppression had been so great everyone had been hunched close to the ground.

Immediately the session finished, there was the unmistakable sound of tenders leaving a nearby fire station. Their sirens faded slightly as they sped down the road, then the sound continued at one level for a long time, as if they had already reached the fire or accident to which they had been called.

192

Neil estimated the incident could not have been more than a mile from the house.

'We decided it was not a good idea to go and see what had happened,' he said. 'And we ended up all sleeping in the same bed, like modern adults.'

The next day, nobody felt like discussing the events of the previous night. In fact, it was not until Neil and Rene returned home to Manchester that they felt able to raise the subject. Then both of them agreed they felt that the malevolent presence did not want them in the house or using the Ouija board.

'In fact, I had another bad experience in Sue's house,' Rene told him.

Apparently, on a previous visit, she had also felt a deep coldness, an oppressive fear and a sense of rage at her very presence. This was manifested in very concrete terms when she went to the downstairs toilet. Because of her unease, she did not even lock the door. But, when she tried to leave, the door was jammed tightly shut, as if someone was leaning against it and holding the handle. After Sue and her parents tried unsuccessfully to open it from the other side, Rene had to climb out of the window and re-enter the house by the front door. Immediately, she tried the toilet door and it swung open with no trouble at all. Not surprisingly, Rene cut her visit very short, not returning again until the fateful Ouija session.

Neil's feelings about the Ouija board are mixed.

'Having done Ouija sessions every night for six months with different people, I think it is telekinesis. I mean, eighty per cent of our brain is working without us being aware of what it does. So when a circle of people all concentrate hard on one particular object, they must be able to focus some mental power to actually move that object. At the beginning, all our messages were from dead relatives, and I think that was serving an emotional function for us all. But, on occasions like the Gateshead experience, the glass moved so violently, so fast and erratically, that, perhaps there is something more to it than mere telekinesis. I'm not really too sure.'

8

Supernatural Scotland

Rather than take the direct route from Gateshead to Scotland, it is well worth detouring via Hadrian's Wall. An excellent Roman road runs parallel to the wall itself, allowing easy access to its many points of interest such as the Roman fort and museum at Vindolanda. For my money though, the most fascinating place on the wall is the Temple of Mithras, which owes its existence to an eastern culture far older than the Romans'.

Not many people realise that the legions who guarded this northerly part of the empire were not actually from Italy. In fact, by the time the Romans pulled out of Britain in about AD 410, Hadrian's Wall was manned almost entirely by Romano–British troops to whom Rome must have seemed as distant as the moon.

Initially, however, the legions who came here to hold the line against the warlike northern tribes were Persians and Syrians. They were worshippers of Mithras, the sun god, and erected a temple to him at a fort they called Broccolitia, which means 'A Place Infested with Badgers'. What these troops made of this dangerous and desolate country can only be imagined, although on many a dark winter's night they must have thought their god had abandoned them to the local pagan deities.

Generally speaking, the Romans disliked these gods of the indigenous tribes and sought to stamp them out wherever they could. This was mainly because their rituals involved human sacrifice. which they felt was barbaric. However, the power of such beliefs outlived Rome and pagan religions still exist in Britain today, albeit in a more benign form and without

194

sacrifices. Nevertheless, the dark forces of those early pagans can occasionally reach across the centuries. Take the frightening case of the Hexham Heads, for example.

THE STRANGE CASE OF THE HEXHAM HEADS

The Robson and the Dodd Families' Experiences

In 1971, two strange effigies thought to be of Celtic origin were unearthed in the garden of a council house in Rede Avenue, Hexham, close to Hadrian's Wall. Their discovery sparked off a controversy as well as claims of very disturbing paranormal incidents.

It was a bright Saturday in May of that year when Jenny Robson sent her two bored sons out into the garden of her house to play. She was fed up with them squabbling around the house and she hoped that playing in the fresh spring air would tire them out. Colin, the elder boy, climbed under a privet hedge that ran by the side of the house and started to dig. After a while he ran to his mother in great excitement and showed her what he had found. In his hand was what appeared to be a carved stone head about the size of a tennis ball. Jenny took an instant dislike to 'the evil, spiteful little thing'. Then her other son came to her crying. If Colin had a head, he wanted one too, he wailed.

'Then you'll just have to go and dig for one yourself,' his mother said.

Sure enough, another head of similar shape and size emerged and the two boys ran off to show their finds to the Dodd boys next door. At this time, nobody connected the heads with the Celts. In fact, one of the grown-ups thought they might be corbals of Roman origin and they took them to one of the Anglican priests at Hexham Abbey. From there, they were sent for examination and analysis by Dr David Smith, Keeper of the Museum of Antiquities attached to Newcastle University. At this stage, Dr Smith was by no means sure about the heads, but thought that they might be of Celtic origin.

In the days that followed, the Dodd family began experiencing some strange and inexplicable occurrences.

'About two nights after the heads were sent away we heard Nellie Dodd screaming away all night,' Mrs Robson recalled recently.

When she asked her neighbour what had happened, Mrs Dodd told her a truly fantastic and unnerving tale. It seemed that the children of the house had seen a strange dark form half man and half beast. If this manifestation was not unnerving enough, Nellie had felt the creature brush against her as it rushed out of the house, its feet making a heavy padding sound as it ran.

'Nellie was absolutely terrified,' Jenny Robson told me. 'And they kept on having these experiences.'

Meanwhile, the heads themselves were on the move. After examination and analysis in Newcastle, they were sent to Dr Anne Ross, a prominent Celtic scholar at Southampton University, for a second opinion. She had examined hundreds of similar effigies, but these would prove to be very different. Almost immediately after the heads arrived, the Ross household was haunted by a cold and malevolent presence remarkably similar to the one that had frightened the family in Hexham. From the night the heads arrived at their house, Dr Ross and her daughters were to see and feel a threatening half human form on many occasions. At this time, Dr Ross did not know of the Hexham incidents and it was only after a period of time that she connected the manifestations to the heads.

Don Robins, a friend of Anne Ross, who was also an inorganic chemist, had the heads analysed and found that they contained a high content of quarz. After several inexplicable experiences whilst the heads were in his possession, Don thankfully returned them to Anne Ross, who sent them back to Dr Smith in Newcastle.

This time, the heads resided in the Robsons' house, where they had originally been found. This also coincided with some very strange incidents. The heads themselves were placed on a high shelf in the kitchen. Strangely, whenever they were left facing into the kitchen, the following morning the heads would be turned back towards the garden. Mrs Robson wondered if this was because the ground on which the houses were built was on an old Celtic burial ground. She was sure Dr Smith had expressed this opinion during one of his visits to the house.

On another occasion, Mr and Mrs Robson awoke to find their bed showered in glass from the frame of a family photograph hanging on the wall. On another occasion, the couple heard the sound of a large animal padding down the stairs.

The atmosphere in the Robsons' house also seemed to change at this time. Not only had it become permanently cold, but their was a general air of aggression. To complete this cocktail of unpleasantness, Mr Robson also lost his job as a scaffolder. Next door in the Dodd household, matters had gone even further. Following the severe disturbances experienced by the family, they had been rehoused by the council elsewhere in Hexham.

The strange story of the Hexham Heads, as they became known, had also attracted the attention of the media. Reports about them appeared firstly in the local press and television and then were picked up nationally. This interest continues and the story has appeared in numerous books about the paranormal including *No Common Task* by Peter Underwood and *English Folklore Myths and Legends*, published by the *Reader's Digest*. I also understand from Jenny Robson that Arthur C. Clarke has been investigating the story.

On the face of it this is indeed a disturbing case because it challenges the bedrock of logic upon which our society is based. What was this horrible creature that haunted Dr Ross and the people in Northumberland? Could the two heads have unleashed the spirit of some Celtic god whose followers had a particularly nasty reputation as headhunters? I decided to look more closely at these incidents to find out. As is often the case in such stories, what I discovered left me with more questions than answers.

One aspect of the affair that has not always been covered very thoroughly is the question of the origin of the heads. Had they actually been crafted by the Celts a thousand years previously? Approximately 2,000 such heads have been discovered, particularly in the north of Britain. Hexham is in the heart of the old Celtic Kingdom of Brigantia so it seemed more than likely that this was the case. However, Dr Smith was now sure that the Hexham Heads were certainly not of Celtic origin.

'He was never very happy about those heads,' his successor, Lindsay Allison-Jones recalled recently. 'For a start, they were too small. Celtic heads normally measure about ten inches by ten inches and these were only about four inches across. Dr Smith also had them analysed and found them to have made of concrete and only a few years old.'

Ms Allison-Jones had worked with Dr Smith at the time and recalled the case of The Hexham Heads very clearly. She was also quite sure that Dr Smith, whom she described as 'a very careful and cautious' researcher, would not have said that the houses in Rede Avenue were built on a Celtic burial ground. In fact, to her knowledge there were no such burial grounds in Hexham.

Someone else who was somewhat taken aback by all the fuss about the heads was Desmond Craigie. He had lived in the house where the heads were found, before the Robsons. In 1956, he worked at a firm that made artificial stone monuments and garden ornaments. One day his young daughter asked him about his job, and to show her what he did, he made three small heads, one of which was lost fairly quickly. His daughter played with the other two for some time, putting silver paper in the eye sockets. Eventually Mr Craigie threw the heads out after the little girl tired of playing with them. When he saw the heads that the Robson boys had discovered under the privet hedge 15 years later, he was certain they were the same ones.

However, Mr Craigie's and Dr Smith's sides of the story have often been omitted in the retelling of the case. When it covered the story, *Unexplained* magazine did give Desmond's side of the story, showing a photograph of him holding the actual heads. In his autobiography *No Common Task* (published by Harrap in 1983), Peter Underwood also refers briefly to his claim that he made the heads, without mentioning him by name.

It is also very curious that while the archaeologists at Newcastle think the Hexham Heads were modern and not Celtic, apparently Dr Ross holds the opposite view. Since hardened concrete is a conglomorate of cement particles, sand and aggregates, it is unlikely that any chemist would mistake it for solid stone. Unfortunately, the heads themselves have subsequently vanished, so no further examination is possible. Whatever the answer, everybody involved in the case is sticking to their respective stories.

The next story tells of the Gallacher family's experiences, which began in Glasgow during the 1980s. Then, certain incidents occurred in Tony and Caroline Gallacher's house that convinced them it was haunted. However, when they moved south to Reading a few years later, the ghost was not left behind as they had expected. Instead, the hauntings continued.

I first met Tony when I started work for him at BT in the spring of 1991. Although he was the manager of my department, he never liked anyone referring to him as the boss. 'I'm a work colleague not your boss,' he would tell me.

Tony tends to be driven by an intense energy when he is working, but his wide range of interests and salty Glaswegian sense of humour ensure that he is good company at any time of the day or night. Because of this, he and I have always found many common points of interest to talk about, including the paranormal. It was during such a discussion that a chance remark of his introduced me to the story his family's supernatural experiences. However, pinning him down for a detailed account of what happened and is still happening was another matter entirely.

Whenever I asked him for that promised interview, he was always too busy, but next week or the one after perhaps ... For a time I began to fear, quite wrongly as it turned out, that he had had second thoughts about the inclusion of his story in my book. Finally, we sat down in a quiet office with winter rain spattering the windows. I switched on my cassette recorder, Tony lit up a cigarette and began to talk. This is what he told me.

A GHOST IN THE FAMILY

Tony and Caroline Gallacher's Story

Caroline sat bolt upright in bed, her heart beating unnaturally fast, a feeling of apprehension deep in the pit of her stomach. Something very bad was about to happen, quite what, she did not know. Instinctively, she thought of her newly born daughter and hurried through to the baby's room. Once there, she saw with relief that the little girl was sleeping soundly. But the room was absolutely frigid. She turned the heating up to full before returning to her own bed.

When Tony and Caroline Gallacher moved to Reading from Scotland in 1987, they mistakenly thought that harsh winters would be a thing of the past. How wrong they were! It seemed that in southern England, the frosts could be every bit as hard and the nights every bit as cold as they were in Glasgow. The night when Caroline hurried through to her daughter's room was no exception.

Proof, were it needed, came in the form of a report in next day's local newspaper. Apparently, at least four cot deaths had occurred in the previous 24 hours and it was thought that the extreme cold was to blame. If Caroline had not turned the heating up, her daughter could well have added to those tragic statistics.

Caroline's incident would normally be put down either to chance or a mother's intuition. However, the Gallachers knew better than that. In 1986, they were living on an estate in the Glasgow suburb of Toll Cross. Their son Kieran had been born three months before and he was already proving to be quite a handful. One blessing about having such a lively baby was the fact that, by early evening, he was more than ready

200

for his bed. Invariably, the little boy slept soundly through to the next morning.

Like many other caring parents, Tony and Caroline had bought a baby alarm so that they would know immediately if there was anything amiss with their son. Placing the transmitter in the baby's room, they fixed the receiver in their bedroom about 5 yards away. A few nights later Caroline looked at her husband, a worried frown on her face.

'Tony, I know this sounds daft, but I've been hearing voices on the baby alarm.'

'Ah, it's probably just the local taxis,' he replied reassuringly.

'Yes, perhaps,' Caroline said uncertainly. But the voices continued and Tony still said he thought they were taxis.

Then, a few nights later, an incident occurred that would finally and frighteningly put paid to Tony's taxi theory. The couple were suddenly awakened by the sound of a man talking over the baby alarm.

'There's a good boy, Kieran,' he was saying. 'You're doing well and growing up to be a good wee lad.'

Shaking with fear, Caroline forced Tony out of the room and down the short passage to their son's room. As they approached the closed door, they could hear Kieran giggling with pleasure. However, when they entered the nursery, the baby was sleeping peacefully with no sign of the supernatural visitor. In fact, everything was totally normal except that the room was icy-cold.

Over the next weeks and months, the voices continued. Caroline and Tony coped with this by making the disturbances a joke between the two of them. But this was not the sort of joke they shared with another living soul. Then, a few weeks later, Tony was at work when he had a frantic phone call from his wife which caused him to return home immediately.

Caroline had been talking to one of her neighbours whilst ironing in the living room. The early spring sun shone through the windows, making the house feel warm, comfortable and safe. It was then that they heard a man's voice at the top of the stairs, apparently talking to Kieran. For once, natural fear overcame maternal instinct and the two women ran into the street, only going back into the house five minutes later. They hurried up to the baby's room, but once again, he was fast asleep with no sign of the mysterious intruder.

Such paranormal visits occurred infrequently over the next 18 months and, although they still held back from discussing them with anybody else, they now had their neighbour as an independent witness. By this time, Kieran was a highly mobile toddler with a limited but growing vocabulary. It was then that he began asking his parents some disturbing questions.

'He started to speak to us about the man who came to visit him in his room,' Tony explained. 'He didn't know him or have a name for the man, but he said that he was friendly and used his name.'

This was when Tony and Caroline decided to ask the advice from someone else in the family, so they plucked up courage to speak to Tony's father.

'He's quite a closed person,' Tony said. 'He doesn't open up, really. For example, he never expands on what he did in the RAF or in the '56 Suez Crisis.'

To their surprise, Mr Gallacher was very forthcoming when they told him about Kieran's supernatural friend . Perhaps this was because he has seen not one, but two ghosts, those of his dead parents. He remembered meeting his dead mother with particular clarity.

It was the day he went to join the RAF in the early 1950s. He awoke to see his mother sitting on an easy chair in the corner of his bedroom. She pleaded with him not to go. But, although the apparition greatly unnerved him, he went anyway, returning unharmed eight years later.

Working from Kieran's rather patchy description of the ghost and from Mr Gallacher's own experiences, the couple realised that it must have been Tony's grandfather.

'From what we gather the ghost closely resembled my dad, who looked very much like my grandfather, so think it must have been him,' Tony recalled.

Shortly after their meeting with Tony's father, the Gallachers moved south to Reading in Berkshire and for two years, they experienced nothing unusual. Then, just after their daughter Natalie was born, they began to feel that there was someone else in the house watching them.

'You've probably had it yourself,' Tony said. 'You can feel that somebody's there and you turn around and, sure enough, there they are.'

However, whenever they turned round, expecting to see one of the children or a friend, nobody was ever there. Tony and Caroline began to think that their supernatural visitor had travelled south with them.

It is often said that ghosts do not like being ignored and perhaps this is the explanation for what happened next. One Sunday, Caroline started the task of cleaning out one of her kitchen cupboards. It really was an awful muddle, she thought, as she stacked tins of beans and jars of marmalade on top of the refrigerator. Suddenly, one of the jam pots took off and flew across the room. Glancing off the opposite wall, it smashed on the floor with great force. Was 'Ghostie', their phantom friend, making a mischievous bid for attention?

Although this was an isolated incident of destruction, other manifestations have continued. Unlike many Scots, Tony and Caroline have never been keen on making a huge celebration of Hogmanay, and New Year's Eve 1993 was no exception to this rule. Just before midnight, when they both preparing to see the new year in with a quiet drink, they both clearly heard a female voice.

'Was that the kids?' Tony asked. His wife slowly shook her head.

Three days later, on 3 January 1994, they both felt a definite presence in their bedroom and simultaneously they both said: 'It's back.'

Perhaps they should have said 'They're here!' for the latest ghost appeared to be female. So, had Tony's grandfather been joined by another phantom watcher? Later, Caroline remembered that 3 January was the birthday of her much loved grandmother, who had died three years earlier. When this happened, she had the unmistakable feeling that the old lady had joined her in the kitchen. Minutes later, the telephone rang. It was her father with the sad news that her grandmother had passed away.

The Gallachers' continuing experiences are a paranormal mosaic. When looked at in isolation, individual pieces have little apparent meaning. But place them all together and a definite picture emerges. There is also the matter of other witnesses, such as Caroline's friend in Glasgow and, more recently, one of their neighbours in Reading.

True to their northern roots, the Gallachers have always been very hospitable, encouraging friends and neighbours to visit any time they wished. So it was no surprise when Jane, who lived next door, called round for a cup of coffee and a chat in January 1994. Suddenly, she broke off from their casual conversation. There was a quizzical and uneasy expression on her face.

'I know this is going to sound daft,' she said. 'But I feel as if there's somebody at the top of the stairs. Someone or something is moving about up there.'

Whoever Jane heard, it was not any of the four humans in the house at the time, for they were all in the living room with her.

At the time of writing, the family are still experiencing paranormal happenings at their Reading house. In the summer of 1994, when the Gallachers invested in a new fitted kitchen, Caroline decided this was the most appropriate place for a photograph of her late grandmother. After all, it was where she had made the farewell visit to her granddaughter at the time of her death in 1991. So she stuck the small photograph of the old lady on the inside of one of the new cupboard doors. But when she tried to close the door it would simply open again. Annoyed at the thought of the new kitchen being shoddily made, she called Tony. However, when he checked the door, it was perfectly sound, with all the screws in place. Nevertheless, the door which holds the photograph has remained stubbornly ajar ever since. Once or twice, when the photograph has become unstuck and fallen off, the door will then shut perfectly.

Then there is the case of the trail of slime that keeps

appearing across the middle of their dining room carpet. At first, Tony and Caroline thought it was a snail that had somehow crawled in from outside. However, after checking the house thoroughly, they could find no trace of any insect. Even stranger was the fact that it would not start at the edge of the carpet, but near the middle. Equally baffling is the fact that although the residue appears in some quantity, it will then disappear completely, leaving no damage to the carpet.

'We've chatted about it and have decided that it might well be paranormal,' Tony told me recently.

The latest incident occurred on 16 November 1994. Tony was at home typing some business letters on his computer. With Caroline out shopping and the children at school, the house was completely quiet except for the clicking of the keyboard as Tony typed out a quotation for one of his customers. Suddenly, the screen went dead as the power in the house failed momentarily. Before Tony could utter the customary expletive for such occasions, the electricity was restored, only to fail yet again for a few seconds. Although he had not lost the letter he was typing, the power cut had left all the clocks flashing inanely and he had to break off and reset them. Before going back to his work, he decided to check with his neighbours to see how extensive the failure had been. But when he asked about a power cut, he was met with blank looks. It seemed that the Gallacher house had been singled out for special treatment.

Two hours later, Tony was disturbed yet again when his pager went off. Walking over to the mantelpiece, where he had left it, he realised there had been something strange about the sound it had made. Instead of the usual melodic beeping gradually increasing in intensity, there had been just three long harshly electronic squeaks. Picking the pager up, he discovered something even odder. It was not even switched on.

'What do you think?' he asked Caroline as she offloaded armfuls of groceries onto the kitchen table.

'I really don't know, love, but it's strange about the date,' she replied.

'How do you mean?'

'Oh really, Tony, don't tell me you've forgotten,' she cajoled.

'What have I forgotten?' he asked in frustration.

'It's the sixteenth, isn't it?' she said. 'It's Granddad's birthday, God rest his soul.'

So, how do people deal with resident ghosts? In the case of the Gallacher family, the simple answer is they become used to them.

'We now accept it as part and parcel of our normal living,' Tony concluded.

Besides, it is hard to feel afraid if your ephemeral visitors are all in the family.

The problem is simple, you are a tutor on the first day of a sales course and in front of you is a group of people who have not met you or each other before. Everyone is feeling awkward and tongue-tied. So how do you bring your students out of themselves and interact? The answer is equally simple, you get your class to talk about themselves – nothing lengthy, just their names, where they are from and what their hobbies are. I have been on many such courses and it always works. It also provided me with a bonus on one occasion.

I was on a course at Milton Keynes and when the tutor came to me, I told everyone who I was and also about my 'ghost book', as it became known.

'Well, there you are,' the tutor said. 'If any of you have had supernatural experiences, you know who to talk to.'

He had hardly stopped speaking before a blonde girl in her twenties called Jean Mearns had her hand up. She certainly had a strange story to tell, as I found out after the day's work had finished. Like Tony Gallacher, Jean was born and brought up in Glasgow, which is where her encounters with the supernatural occurred:

VOICES ON THE WIND

Jean Mearns' Story

Jean Purdie and her friend Natalie Devlin loved to play at shops in the backyard of the flats where they lived. The buildings were situated in the suburb of Cadder, close to the bustling heart of Glasgow's Maryhill. However, when the two ten-year-olds played at grocers, they could have been a million miles away. What they liked best about playing there were all those lovely flat grey stones. They made really good shelves for the shops, even though they did have names and numbers carved on them, like '*John, Beloved Son of...*' and '*Depart ... Life on ... 1836*', that sort of thing. To the two girls, they were just names and letters on pieces of granite, nothing more.

When it was too cold to play outside, they used to take their games indoors. On these occasions, Jean liked playing in Natalie's room because she had a proper 'press', which was a special cupboard for all her toys. Natalie, however, was not always so keen.

'There's something in my room,' she said to Jean one day.

'What?' Jean asked.

'I dunno, something – a ghost. It keeps opening my toy press,' Natalie replied.

Then, as if on cue, the doors of the press opened, causing Natalie to gasp in fright.

'They must have just opened,' Jean said nonchalantly as she closed them. Then, no sooner had she sat down again, than the doors on the toy cupboard opened.

'Let's go down to my flat and play,' Jean said, trying to keep the nervousness out of her voice and, without further ado, the two friends ran out of the room and down the stairs. The girls played happily enough for a while. Then Natalie paused, a pensive look on her face. 'Do you think the ghost'll get us here, Jean?' she asked quietly.

'No, we're safe from it here,' her friend replied with a confidence she secretly did not feel. Immediately after she spoke, three small china animals sitting on a toy record player took on a life of their own, jumping in the air and landing on the floor. This was too much for the two girls, who fled out of the room in terror.

For 20 years after that day in 1974, Jean and Natalie experienced a succession of strange occurrences in the flats at Cadder. Furniture and ornaments apparently moved about the rooms on their own and Jean would often wake in the middle of the night convinced that there was a hostile, non-human presence watching her.

Then there was the way her three black-and-white cats would stare intently at some invisible presence, their heads moving in unison as they watched it move across the room. Whilst two of the cats would simply watch, the third, more outgoing one, called Sadie, would run out of the room miaowing in a friendly fashion, as if being called by somebody.

'Her tail would go up as if she was greeting someone who was standing there,' Jean explained. 'It was quite frightening to watch because she was definitely going to greet somebody.'

However, the cats were not the only pets to 'see' something in the flats. Between the ages of ten and thirteen, Jean had a terrier–collie cross-breed called Blackie. Normally a very friendly and rather lethargic dog, she would often undergo a startling change of character for no apparent reason. Suddenly, her hackles would rise and she would start growling whilst following something round the room with her eyes. Then after a minute or two, she would return to her normal, lazy self.

When she was 15, Jean began to have even more unnerving experiences. On alternate nights she would hear her name being called by a strange and distant voice. *'Jean, Jean, Jean!'* came the faint cry on the breeze and the frightened girl would close the window to shut it out.

There were many rumours that this area of Cadder had actually been built on part of a huge neighbouring cemetery. Rejoicing in the truly gothic name of The Western Necropolis, the graveyard had been the last resting place of Glaswegians for at least two centuries. Try as she might, Jean could not dispel the idea from her mind that the disturbances were all connected with this. Now she came to think of it, those stones that she and Natalie had played with when they were children had looked awfully like smashed gravestones. When she tried to discuss these fears with her parents, they would have none of it. Ghosts did not exist but hysterical daughters certainly did. End of story.

Whilst that might have been the end of the matter for Mr and Mrs Purdie, Jean continued to hear the mysterious voices. Moreover, when confiding in Natalie about it, she discovered her friend had also heard somebody calling her name. After two years the voices simply ceased, becoming just a scary memory. Then Jean met up with an old friend called Pauline Innis. She was 18 at the time and had not seen Pauline or her sister Mary since they had moved from Cadder some years previously.

'I bet you really miss the old place, Pauline,' Jean said jovially.

'You must be joking,' Pauline said seriously. 'I have never been so glad to move away from a house in all my life!'

It was then that Jean learned she and Natalie were not the only ones to hear phantom voices calling them. The two Innis sisters had also heard dismembered voices calling their names. They were so upset by the experiences that the local priest was called in for an exorcism. When this appeared not to work, the whole family took the drastic step of moving out of the area completely.

'Until that time, I had no idea they had also heard voices,' Jean explained. 'What Pauline said really shocked me.'

By the winter of 1994, Jean had become Mrs Mearns and had a baby daughter. When she married, her parents had obligingly moved to a house nearby since they felt the flat in Cadder was an ideal first home for the young couple. Although the Mearns were reasonably happy, Jean decided in the November of that year the time had come to move.

'I didn't sell the flat because I disliked it,' she explained. 'But I always had the feeling that something else might happen. I've got a one-year-old daughter now and the thought that *something* might happen to her when she's older began to prey on my mind. You see, I really do believe there was some sort of ghost or spirit in those flats that was either trying to contact or frighten us. Anyway, it definitely wasn't human and it certainly wasn't very friendly.'

Less than 40 miles apart, Glasgow and Edinburgh are directly opposite one another at the narrow pinch point which separates Scotland's east and west coasts. At one time, they would have been connected by the Antonine Wall built by the Romans after Hadrian. Now, the two cities reach out unlovingly towards one another down a motorway that would have made the Roman civil engineers green with envy.

Historically, the two cities have always been very different. Glasgow is gritty yet industrious whilst Edinburgh is genteel and cultured. Like all stereotypes there is a great deal of truth and falsity in both generalisations. Glasgow has now changed drastically from the industrial centre of Scotland. Gone are the shipyards and in their place is a vibrant city with new businesses with a lively cultural soul. Edinburgh, on the other hand, still retains the image of Scotland's ancient capital, with beautiful historical buildings and a world-famous festival. However, in recent years, the city has seen a darker side develop with the growth of crime in some areas most people would prefer to stay out of at night.

The suburb of Leith, near the city's docklands, has always had a rather rough reputation, with strippers inside the pubs and drugs and prostitution outside. However, it is also an area with a long history. Many of the tenements which now serve as small flats and bedsits are 2 to 300 years old. Over the centuries, they have silently witnessed many dramas and tragedies similar to the one that apparently sparked the next haunting:

A HAUNTING IN EDINBURGH

Pam McKay's Story

'I suppose you would call me an agnostic verging on atheism,' Pam said as we talked at the bar of The Greyhound, our local pub. 'I certainly don't believe in the afterlife, but I definitely believe I once saw a ghost.'

Pam McKay is an attractive and petite girl with a penchant for dark-rimmed glasses and has jet-black hair that tumbles down to her shoulders. Working in the flinty world of finance, she is certainly not given to flights of fancy about ghosts or the paranormal. Perhaps this is why her voice still tremors slightly when she talks about her experience in an old building in Edinburgh.

It was in the early winter of 1987 when she and her then husband Ron went to stay with friends in a flat in Leith. The building itself was typically late eighteenth century, with tall windows and high ceilings. At the time of the incident, Pam was getting ready to go out and was running a dryer over her recently washed hair. Although she was alone in the bedroom, she suddenly caught sight of a figure in the mirror looking directly at her.

Switching the hairdryer off, she studied the figure standing by the tall windows. It was a woman in an old-fashioned white dress with frills and her hair pulled back tightly into a bun. Pam turned to take a closer look and she could see tears staining the woman's cheeks. To Pam, the apparition's face seemed to be awash with grief. At the time, she was also struck by several other factors. Firstly, the tears on the woman's cheeks seemed to be reflecting the glow of a fire. This was strange because the gas heater in the fireplace was not lit at the time. The room had also grown noticeably colder, as if it had been invaded by the leaden presence of midwinter. Secondly, the modern double glazing seemed to have been replaced by much older windows, the sort that must have been in the flat a hundred years previously.

211

Pam has no clear idea of how long the manifestation lasted before the sad image faded into nothingness. However, as she picked up her hairdryer again, she realised it was cold, indicating that the haunting must have lasted some minutes at the very least. A few moments after the tragic woman faded away, Ron came into the bedroom.

'My God, Pam, you look pale. Whatever's happened?' he exclaimed.

'Was that you standing over by the window?' Pam asked him as she brushed her hair.

'No of course it wasn't, I've just come into the room,' he answered.

'Yes, of course,' Pam replied. 'Silly of me.'

A day or so later, she plucked up courage to mention it to her friend the owner of the flat.

'Oh yes,' he said. 'Perhaps I should have warned you. A woman killed herself in that room about a hundred years ago. Flung herself from that window. Don't know who she was, though.'

These days, Pam does not talk about the apparition, partly because she does not want to invite ridicule, but also because it still disturbs her to think about the phantom and what exactly it meant. It is worth noting that when she told me of her experience, she had not even shared it with Pete, her partner. She opened her heart to me only because she knew of my interest in the paranormal.

'I know two things for sure about that incident,' she said as we stepped into the sharp autumn sunlight. 'Firstly, I didn't imagine it and secondly, that woman definitely looked at me. I'll never forget the look of sadness on that face. It was pure tragedy.'

NEMESIS AT NECHTANSMERE

About a hundred miles to the north-east of Glasgow, there is a pleasant little town in the county of Angus called Letham. On the face of it, there is nothing unusual about the place except for two remarkable events which occurred 1,300 years apart.

Early in AD 685, the warlike and acquisitive Northumbrian King Ecgfrith embarked on an ill-judged foreign venture. Leading his troops northwards, he swept beyond Hadrian's Wall to capture and lay waste the lands of the Picts. Initially, the invasion was successful and his forces had soon captured a large part of south-eastern Scotland. However, Ecgfrith had not reckoned on the sheer cunning and ferocity of the Picts whose lands he had raped. In reality, the Pictish leader Brude Mac Beli was drawing the Northumbrians into a well-laid trap. One Saturday in May 685, deep in the Sidlaw Hills, Mac Beli's trap finally snapped shut.

It happened when the two adversaries met for battle near a loch known as Nechtansmere. At first, the battle seemed to be going the Northumbrians' way. Then, as afternoon turned to dusk, there was a dramatic change of fortune. The Northumbrians charged, confidently expecting to beat their enemy yet again. Sure enough the Pictish line wavered and then broke, to be chased by the triumphantly bellowing Northumbrians. However, not all was what it seemed. The retreat was simply a clever ruse and all too late Ecgfrith found himself the victim of an ambush from which there was no escape. Victorious pursuit now turned into a bloody rout as he and his men were driven down to be slaughtered on the shores of the loch. Ecgfrith, his bodyguards and the bulk of his army all perished that day, hacked down by the Picts in a welter of merciless revenge. A lucky few Northumbrians survived by running faster than the Picts, but Ecgfrith had met his nemesis. By the early hours of the following morning, all that remained for the victors was to search for their dead comrades on the field of slaughter.

It is said that St Cuthbert, who had advised strongly against the venture, had a vision of the defeat whilst in the north of England some hundreds of miles away. Another bishop had also dreamed of Ecgfrith being carried to hell by two demons. Whatever the truth about these visions, few seemed to have shed many tears for the dead king. Even the writers of *The*

Anglo-Saxon Chronicle gave the wretched man short shrift: '*In the same year [685] Ecgfrith was killed by the Northern Sea and a great host with him, on May 20th; he had been king for fifteen years.*'

On a bitterly cold January night in 1950 a spinster in her late fifties left a cocktail party thrown by some friends at Brechin. Although she did not relish the 10-mile drive back to her home at Letham, she comforted herself with the thought that at least she had the company of her small dog. Unfortunately, driving conditions were worse than she thought and after only a couple of miles she had skidded on the packed snow and put her car into a ditch. Shaken but uninjured, she began the 8-mile walk to her home in Letham, carrying her pet dog.

It was two o'clock in the morning by the time she reached the outskirts of the town and she was frozen, but then something extraordinary happened that made her forget her plight. Her dog started to growl nervously, then she saw why. A large group of men carrying long torches burning with a deep red glow were approaching. Curiously, although they were walking over fairly level terrain, they approached in a curve as if they were skirting some sort of barrier. As she walked down the road, the woman was able to see the men in much greater detail, Their dress consisted of a strange brown garment that covered their whole body and had 'a sort of roll collar' at the neck. Their headgear was roughly similar to the hats worn by old-fashioned butcher's boys. She also noted that they had no boots on their feet. Even though her dog continued to growl, nobody took the slightest notice of them. In fact, it was as if they were not there at all. As she continued to walk towards the safety and comfort of her home the woman noticed more details.

The nearest figure, who was about 50 yards away, seemed to be searching for fallen comrades amongst the many bodies she could see lying on the ground. Moving from one corpse to the next, he turned them over and 'if he didn't like the look of them' put them face down again. In all the incident lasted about 12 minutes before the figures and their torches faded into the dark night. Such is the nature of these things, it was only the next morning that the woman awoke to the realisation that her nocturnal experience had been something very strange indeed.

In 1971, Dr James McHargh, MD, heard of the story from mutual acquaintance of the lady whom he only refers to as Miss S. As an active member of the Society for Psychical Research, he decided to investigate the incident in greater detail. After initially meeting Miss S., who was then in her seventies, he returned for a longer taped interview. Although she now suffered from failing eyesight, Miss S. was very alert, having lost none of her mental faculties. Besides Dr McHargh and Miss S., a clinical psychologist and tape technician were present at the interview, which took place on 22 September 1971.

In the event, Miss S. had total recall of the whole incident, which Dr McHargh estimated must have lasted approximately 12 minutes. This is an unusually long time for a paranormal manifestation, whose duration can often be measured in seconds rather than minutes. At the end of the interview, Dr McHargh was satisfied that there was a very strong likelihood that Miss S. had in fact seen a paranormal manifestation and had not dreamed or hallucinated the incident. However, he did not leave his investigation there. What followed next is a textbook example of paranormal detective work.

Not only did Dr McHargh visit the battle site on numerous occasions, including the anniversary of the event, but he also researched the background of life in Scotland at the time. It often surprises people to learn that a great deal of documentary evidence survives from earlier times. Although it is not always in a medium that we would readily recognise, it is often in a more enduring form than either video or CD-ROM. For example, Miss S had given a very clear description of the warriors' clothes. So, to check its accuracy, Dr McHargh found and examined a stone carving of a Pictish warrior from Golspie on the north east coast of Scotland. The detail on the carving matched Miss S.'s description very closely, right down to the fact that the stone soldier had no footwear.

Then there was the question of those long torches that had burnt with such a strong red glow.

'They were carrying very long torches in their left hands,' Miss S. had said during the interview. 'The torches were *very* red. I wondered what on earth they had been made of, tar I suppose. Was there tar in those days?'

The answer to that is that tar certainly did not exist in ancient Scotland but a ready source of material for torches certainly did. When Dr McHargh consulted a leading specialist on ancient Scottish life, he discovered a very interesting fact. The resinous roots of the Scottish fir were commonly used as torches for thousands of years. Moreover, the root has a distinctive red colour.

Sceptics will doubtlessly argue that the Nechtansmere Haunting is simply a case of fraud or information subconsciously retained in the far recesses of Miss S.'s memory. In his article, in the SPR's journal in 1977, Dr McHargh deals with both these possibilities and still comes down on the side of an actual manifestation. In common with so many other sightings throughout the world, it is the body of accurate yet obscure detail that makes Miss S.'s Nechtansmere sighting so fascinating.

Today, all trace of that momentous battle which secured Pictish independence for hundreds of years has vanished. The loch where the slaughter took place has long since been replaced by fields and hedges. The name Nechtansmere does not even appear on any maps. In its place, there is the tell-tale symbol of crossed swords with the year '685' printed directly above it. This and the ghosts who haunt the battlefield are the only epitaph for a greedy king and his hapless army.

A Strange Postscript

On 2 September 1996, Hilary Wilding and I were travelling through the little village of Meigle to visit Glamis Castle a few miles up the road. As we passed through the village, I spotted a sign saying '*Pictish Stones*' and, having plenty of time on our hands, we decided to investigate further. It was a typical spur-of-the-moment holiday decision and yet it was to lead us into a fascinating adventure which still leaves many unanswered questions in our minds.

We did not have to travel very far to find the stones since they were situated in what looked like an old church hall in one of Meigle's back streets. As we parked, another couple pulled up behind us in a blue Ford Mondeo. There was a charge of £1.20 to go in and see the stones, a factor which nearly put us off.

'Ah, to hell with it,' I said. 'Let's go and have a look. After all, We are on holiday.'

Until we entered that old wooden building, I am ashamed to say that I had never thought very deeply about the Picts as a people. All I knew about them really was that they were woad-painted warriors who usually gave anyone who crossed them a pretty nasty time. What we saw in that sun-splashed hall would change all that, for here was one of the most extraordinary displays of ancient artistry that either Hilary or I had ever seen. Ranged around the room were 20 or so warm-red stones varying in size from about 3 feet to 8 feet. Many were standing, whilst others had been laid on low platforms. However, these were not simply relics of a long-dead culture, but a vibrant record of one of the most remarkable nations ever to have inhabited the British Isles. Each stone was a mass of elaborate and often surrealistic carvings showing Pictish warriors, dragons, mermaids, cattle and even a delightful cat-like creature. On the reverse side of the standing stones were crosses decorated with interlaced patterns. Although the Picts (From the Latin *Picti* – Painted Ones) did not have a written history, these stones told as much about them as any ancient chronicle.

Whilst we were admiring the stones, the couple who had parked right behind us entered the hall. They were indeed a strange pair. She was large lady with close-cropped greying hair and eyes that seemed to be permanently half closed. The little she said was with a transatlantic accent. The man, who was in his late fifties, had a high domed balding head fringed with curly ginger hair. His pale blue eyes sparkled with enthusiasm behind rimless glasses and his face was lit by an enthusiastic grin accentuated by huge white teeth. Both of them were carrying a set of divining rods.

The man stepped up to one of the stones lying by the door and held the rods over it. Immediately they crossed over. He then walked over to the main standing stone on display and extended one of the rods towards it. When the end was about half an inch from the surface, the rod swung away as if pushed by an invisible force. In fact, he was able to walk right around the stone and trace its contours in this way.

'All these stones have energy trapped inside,' he explained, and to show that this was no freak, he allowed all of us, including the curator, to hold the divining rods close to the stones. To see simple rods of metal behaving in this way and swaying from side to side whilst I held them in my hands was an extraordinary experience. However, I was both worried and curious. Perhaps it was all simply caused by the involuntary movement of our arms. After all, even when you hold your arms completely still, there is always movement there.

That night, I made my own pair of divining rods from a coat hanger kindly donated by our hosts and spent an hour or so crashing around the undergrowth in their garden to see how good I was at dowsing. Sure enough, when I reached an identifiable water source such as the river and tributary streams that ran through their garden, the rods would cross over. Hilary's experience was the same. Nevertheless, we were still not completely satisfied and decided to try divining Meigle's Pictish stones once more – but this time on our own.

As it happened, our hosts Roger and Rene actually had a set of divining rods which they had purchased in Guernsey and they kindly lent them to us. On the following day we revisited the display of stones. Initially, I tried the largest one on which the diviner had enjoyed the most success the day before. Holding my arm out, I extended the rod towards the stone, only to see it touch the surface without reacting in any way. I was disappointed but not surprised at this. I then realised that the portion of the stone I had tried was in fact concrete, since a middle section had been destroyed at some time in the past. I pointed the rod at the stone again, but this time at the upper section. About half an inch from the surface the rod began to react, swinging around as if it was being pushed away by some unseen force. Then we tried the rods over the recumbent stones that the diviner had tried on the previous day. Once again they crossed over.

Perhaps the most dramatic incident occurred when I held one of the rods between two of the stones. Even though I kept my arm completely still, the rod began to rotate like a helicopter blade.

Hilary pointed out that the rods with their plastic handles tended to swing rather too easily. Perhaps it was all down to arm movement after all. However, when I held the rods in my hands at the site of the Battle of Nechtansmere some time later, they did not move at all. There is also a fibreglass replica of a Pictish stone at that battlefield, but when I held the rod close to it, there was no movement or reaction at all.

Later in the day, we tried the rods at Aberlemno, a small village about 4 miles to the north of Nechtansmere. Once again, the rods reacted strongly to all three Pictish stones at that location. This was especially so with the biggest stone in the churchyard. This has particular significance in Pictish culture since the figures on its reverse side are thought to depict their decisive victory over the Northumbrians at Nechtansmere. When held close to the stones, the rods swung away and began to rotate as they had done at Meigle. However, when they were held near to the stones in the church wall or on the graves, there would again be no reaction. Our experience with the Pictish stones in the pretty little village of Fowlis Wester, which lies between Perth and Crieff, was broadly speaking the same.

What do these experiences with the divining rods actually mean? Many dowsers will discount the possibility that their craft has anything to do with the paranormal. They would argue that the rods were merely reacting to the many force fields in the earth. Nevertheless, our experiences with the

Pictish stones in north-eastern Scotland indicate that they have in some way been imbued with an energy that does not exist in stones without that remarkable visual history carved on them.

9

Foreign Bodies

Some years ago, long before this book was thought of, I was at a party near Reading when the subject of the supernatural came up in conversation.

'Ah, we know all about you English and your ghosts!' a Dutch lady said with a dismissive smile.

It was quite clear she felt that the supernatural had no place in such a tidy and matter-of-fact country as Holland. According to her, ghosts did not exist there or anywhere else in mainland Europe because people simply did not believe in them. In retrospect, I am surprised that she did not quote some Common Market directive banning the paranormal completely. The thrust of her argument was that supernatural occurrences were simply a figment of the collective British imagination. Ironically, this was all said in the presence of at least five of the people whose experiences are recounted in this book. Her theory might have pleased the hardened sceptic, but in fact it was as erroneous as it was superficial.

The truth is that ghosts have been seen for thousands of years in many different parts of the world including southern Africa, the Middle and Far East, Germany and America, to people from all walks of life. To illustrate this point, here are a selection of five paranormal experiences from around the world, starting with a story from Ireland.

THE FIELDS OF ATHENRY

Diane Allum's Story

They had wanted to do something special for their twenty-ninth wedding anniversary, something they would remember for the rest of their lives. Finally, Diane and Danny Allum decided upon a week's 'fly–drive' holiday in the Republic of Ireland. It was a place they had both wanted to visit for many years. Besides, there were many long-standing invitations from Irish friends. In the event, it proved to be exactly the right choice and they had a near perfect holiday, apart from one bizarre incident.

This occurred about three days after they left Dublin to travel west. Although it was already late September in 1992, the weather generally behaved itself, but now, as they travelled through the barren and rocky landscape of County Galway, it suddenly changed. Grey, driving rain wiped out the blue sky in a premature and stormy dusk.

'I wouldn't like to be a farmer in this!' Danny commented as they looked out at the rain-lashed hills.

'I don't think it's going to get any better tonight,' Diane said. 'Let's stop in the next town.'

This turned out to be Athenry, a sad and ancient place well past its prime. Diane and Danny drove slowly through the rain-soaked streets looking for a small hotel or bed and breakfast, but everywhere seemed closed and deserted. Then, just as they had decided to press on to Galway city, they came upon a house with a white *Bed and Breakfast* sign swinging in the wind.

The house, which was about 150 years old, had obviously been two adjoining dwellings at one time. Not only did it have two identical front doors, but also two sets of stairs. To complete this rather strange appearance, it had also been decorated in the style of the 1820s by the American owner. Everywhere, there were chintz curtains, simulated gas lights and old furniture.

222

Although the owner was not there, her daughter, a polite but solemn girl, showed them the bedroom. Once again, the immaculately clean room was decorated in the period style, with a high bed standing on spidery iron legs. Diane and Danny decided that they could not do better and agreed to stay the night.

When they returned to the room with their cases, they both smelt an alien and unpleasant smell that was quite unlike anything they had experienced before. Diane remembers it as being 'like gas, but not like gas'. Although they opened the windows to air the place, the odour persisted for the whole of their stay in the room. In addition to this, Diane had begun to feel distinctly uneasy about the house. Their room seemed to have an atmosphere that was heavy with sadness and foreboding and she began to wish that they had not decided to stop there.

Since no supper was provided at the house, they went in search of a meal at the local hotel. Unfortunately, when they arrived at the hotel, Athenry continued to live up to its original dire expectations:

'Sorry, we've no food available, you see our cooker's blown up.'

Eventually, they were forced to settle for some very unappetising fish and chips from an establishment of very questionable cleanliness before returning to the bed and breakfast. When they went to their room, the unpleasant odour persisted in spite of the open window. Diane had already decided that never would be too soon to return to this half-horse town. The bad atmosphere, awful smell and what happened later that night certainly helped to crystallise that decision.

The following incident was probably connected in some way with Athenry's tragic and violent past. For many centuries, the town was the seat of two great Irish families, the De Burghs and the Berminghams. In 1316, they found it necessary to defend their domain from a predatory chieftan. Phelin O'Connor, King of Connacht, had cast covetous eyes on the town and mounted a bloody but ultimately unsuccessful attack on Athenry that left many dead.

For the next 280 years, the town remained intact despite periodic clan wars. Then in 1596 Hugh Roc O'Donnell reduced it to a smouldering shell inside its shattered walls. Although the surviving townspeople rebuilt their homes, Athenry remained a shadow of its former greatness. Like the rest of Ireland, subsequent starvation and de-population reduced it further and cast a shroud of tragedy over the town, as is told in a famous Irish folk song called 'The Fields of Athenry'.

Diane Allum knew little of all this, of course, but she was well aware of the unhappy atmosphere, and it was only some time after Danny was snoring peacefully that she finally fell into a fitful slumber. Much later, she was awakened by an unnerving sound, which, at first, she had difficulty in identifying. Then she realised that it was the grief-stricken crying of a woman in one of the adjoining rooms. Although there were other guests in the place, Di instinctively knew that this pathetic yet alarming sound was not from any of them. Something about the crying told her that this was the spectral signal of some dreadful tragedy echoing down the centuries. With a shiver, she pulled the blankets over her head and willed the awful sound to stop. Half an hour later, it finally ceased and she slipped back into an uneasy sleep filled with ill-defined images of deprivation and sorrow.

The next day they met the owner briefly at breakfast. The woman apologised for not being there when they arrived and asked if they slept well. Diane nearly asked the woman about the smell and the crying but, for some reason, she held her peace. Then, in sparkling sunshine, they drove out of Athenry, leaving the town to its ghosts and dark past.

The next experience happened to someone I have known for a number of years and would never have judged to be susceptible to any supernatural forces. Dudley Singleton is the very essence of matter-of-fact countryman, given to wearing tweeds and owning dogs. As he explains in this next story, he would always go to great lengths to find a natural explanation for any strange occurrence. However, what happened in France has left him frightened and baffled to this day.

TERROR AT FORT VAROIS

Dudley Singleton's Story

Mediaeval France was a turbulent and bloody land. Warring fiefdoms such as Normandy and Aquitaine were continually at each other's throats in the life-and-death struggle for power. The wretched peasantry, who comprised the bulk of the population, often found themselves caught between opposing armies, suffering injury, death or starvation as a consequence. Unless, of course, they were fortunate enough to have the protection of a fortified town or castle.

Varois et Chaignot is a typical castle from that period. Strategically situated just outside the Burgundian town of Dijon, it commands the junction of what were two important routes in and out of the region in the Middle Ages. Hundreds of years later, it was again put to use by the Gestapo during the Second World War. However, this time it was a place of torture and imprisonment not refuge. All too often, the ancient cells of Fort Varois would echo with the tortured screams of captured Resistance fighters. When liberation finally came, the local population broke into the old fort. Anything remotely valuable was stripped from the building, including the cell lights and copper wiring.

Long after the war, Fort Varois was put to another, more pacific use as a youth hostel. It was here that Dudley Singleton, an 18-year-old English student, came to stay in 1962. Like most students, he was chronically short of money. So, after enrolling for a language course at the University of Dijon, Dudley went in search of the cheapest, most reasonable accommodation he could find. The hostel at Varois et Chaignot suited both his pocket and temperament.

Dudley was able to do a deal with the concierge. He would

225

live at the fort for a preferential rate, provided he kept the hostel open in the winter months. It was an arrangement that was ideal for both parties. The hostel proved to be an excellent base from which to explore the surrounding area and Dudley spent the first five months happily acquainting himself with the cafés, bistros and population of Dijon.

However, Fort Varois was certainly not a place to stay if you were nervous or faint-hearted. Dudley remembers that returning at night, he had to cross the drawbridge spanning the dark waters of the moat to enter the actual building by a Judas gate in the huge studded main doors. Since there was only one light at the entrance, he then had to feel his way up dark passages to his dormitory. Fortunately, Dudley was not easily frightened either by the dark or anything supposedly supernatural.

'I was born and brought up in the country,' he explained. 'And believed anything that "goes bump in the night" was either a rat, a foraging badger or an old fox killing a chicken. So I've never been bothered by things of that sort.'

Then, certain events at that ancient French fort on a cold autumn night altered this down-to-earth perception of the unknown for ever. The bedrooms in the hostel lay off a wide corridor that ran right the way round the outer wall of the castle. The original purpose of these rooms had been to house the knights or officers of the garrison. Across the corridor were the large dormitories of the 'other ranks', the common foot soldiers and servants. These rooms had arched entrances and, with no doors, were open to the elements. With no heating, they were bitterly cold during winter. The lot of the common foot soldier in mediaeval France was not a particularly happy or comfortable one.

This did not suit the Gestapo, who weather-proofed the high archways with glazing and panelling with small doors.

'I actually had a bed on the left hand side of one of these dormitories,' Dudley recalled. 'It was right by the door, for convenience as much as anything. I was unlikely to be disturbed since there were very few people around besides the concierge and myself.'

226

Nothing appeared unusual or out of place as he groped his way to his room on that chilly autumn night. Drawing the blankets around him, he soon fell asleep. Much later, he was awakened by an overwhelming sensation of great fear. Every muscle in his body was paralysed as he was covered in a shroud of terror. Dudley lay transfixed for what seemed like hours but may only have been a few minutes. Finally, he managed to overcome his fear sufficiently to reach for the knife he always kept by him. As he grasped the handle with fingers aching from the extreme tension, he saw that there were lights running at regular intervals down the corridor.

'You couldn't see them properly because of the dust on the glass, but you could see their outline,' he said. 'I remember seeing those lights vividly.'

Suddenly, all the lights went out, plunging the castle into total darkness. Clutching the knife and clad only in pyjamas, Dudley sprang out of bed and ran like a man possessed. He did not stop until he was well clear of the fort and in the surrounding countryside. Although it was bitterly cold, he could no more return to the warmth of his bed than stop breathing. Instead, he endured the discomfort of a draughty barn until the sky became coloured by the dawn. It was only then that the terror drained away and he plucked up enough courage to re-enter Fort Varois.

As he walked over the drawbridge and through the massive gates, he felt no aura of evil or terror. Once again Varois was just an old building filled with the many objects that had become so familiar over the past five months, a heavy wooden chair here, an old desk there. The only signs of that traumatic night were his bedclothes strewn on the floor and the knife, dropped as he fled the bedroom. Kneeling down, he picked it up. Then he glanced upwards at the ceiling of the corridor and he realised that something was missing. That was it! The lights! He distinctly remembered seeing a row of lights running down the length of the passage. But now there was nothing but bare plaster.

Later, he hesitantly broached the subject with the concierge, who confirmed that there had indeed been lights in the corridor when the Germans occupied the building. However, he also said that there had been none since they were stolen during the liberation.

'I have never been able to explain that incident,' Dudley concluded. 'It was quite obviously something paranormal. A ghost? What do you think?'

The next experience which happened in the wreckage and desolation of post war Germany is fantastic by any standards. However, what makes it especially remarkable is that it happened to one of the most down-to-earth and sceptical of my friends. Like many of those who have told me their experiences, she is someone I have known and trusted for many years.

THE CHEMNITZ REAPER

Gisa Uhlig's Story

I had always imagined East Germany in 1948 as a drab and fearful place with as little hope in the air as there was food for the populace. Everywhere, I thought, there must have been the scars of war, bombed out buildings, hastily dug graves in cemeteries and long queues for everything. However, whilst life was undoubtedly hard, I was surprised to discover that my friend Gisa remembers her East German childhood during this period with considerable warmth and fondness. Perhaps this was partly due to the fact that her family (the Uhligs) had remained in the same comfortable apartment in the industrial town of Chemnitz since 1938. For although accommodation was at a premium, there were many similar families who were still living in the homes they had occupied since before the war. To Gisa the apartment was an oasis of comfort from the grey world outside. Apart from a cosy lounge which the family tended to use for special occasions such as Christmas, there was also a comfortable kitchen complete with settee.

Instead of a bath with taps, there was a metal tub which

stood against the wall of a bedroom. Once a week, there would be bath night with the Uhlig children bathing in the tub filled nearly to the brim with many pots of hot water.

Ten-year-old Gisa, the eldest Uhlig child, was a particularly sensitive little girl who had already seen enough war to last her a lifetime. This made her an insomniac and she would often lie awake long after her brothers and sisters were asleep, listening to the murmur of her parents' conversation.

One particularly cold night in the Winter of 1948, she was lying in bed, unable to sleep, when the bedroom door swung open. In the gloom she could see the outline of the bath leaning against the bedroom wall. Suddenly, the tub began to move on its own and, to her horror, Gisa realised that there was something behind it. The next moment, a skeleton with an ancient lamp emerged from the bath tub and walked towards the door. Gisa froze, terrified that she might draw the spectre's attention. She screamed and screamed until her mother hurried through from the kitchen to comfort her.

A great deal has happened to Gisa since that winter's night in early post-war Germany. As a young woman she defected to the West, subsequently moving to Italy and then South Africa. It was there that I met her some twenty years ago. Over the intervening years, we have become sufficiently close friends for me to trust her implicitly. Agnostic and highly intelligent are both words that would fit her perfectly. She is certainly not the type of person who could be accused of imagining visions of spectres.

'I just wish somebody could explain what I saw that night,' Gisa said to me recently in her Derby home. 'I was not asleep and I certainly did not dream up that horrible thing.'

For thousands of years Death has stalked the land we now call Germany. First it was the warring tribes, then the Thirty Years War, The Black Death, and finally The First and Second World Wars. The blood spilled on that beautiful country would no doubt fill a very large lake. Perhaps that little German girl, who herself had been close to death on more than one occcasion, managed to tap into a folk memory of violence and evil that had imprinted itself on the ether. Who knows?

An Arabic Taboo

The supernatural is not very fashionable in the Middle East these days. This is mainly because Islam, the major religion in the area, frowns upon such ideas. According to the Koran, when you die, you either go to paradise or hell, depending on the way you have led your life. As far as devout Muslims are concerned, the spirits of the dead certainly do not inhabit some spectral other world.

Another reason why Arabs do not readily admit to a belief in ghosts is because they fear this will open them to ridicule as superstitious peasants. I remember discussing this very subject with a Christian Lebanese friend of mine in 1987. I explained that I was interested in compiling a book of Arabic ghost stories.

'Nick, you will never get these people to talk about such things,' he said, smiling and spreading his hands wide, 'because Arabs would not like anybody to think they believed in such matters for fear of appearing stupid.'

He then told me of an incident that occurred to one of his uncles in Beirut during the 1960s. This was before the country was racked by civil war and still had a democratic parliament of sorts. The uncle was running for election to this parliament at the time, but was very worried by the possible result. He remembered waking up late one night to see his dead mother standing over his bed. She assured him that everything would be all right and he would be elected, as indeed he was. Although this is a third-hand account, there have been many similar instances throughout the world. In itself, such a story does not amount to evidence of ghosts existing in the Middle East, but nor should it be summarily dismissed as rubbish.

In fact, I was presented with compelling evidence of an Arab ghost very recently. It took the form of a series of paranormal incidents that happened in one of the oldest cities in the Middle East. They occurred in Cairo, the teeming capital of Egypt, in the late spring of 1995 and, ironically, were experienced by a 'sophisticated' Westerner and not an

Arab. The person involved was Chris Ingram, my ex-brother-in-law, who has been a friend of mine for nearly 25 years.

The natural ability to communicate and get along with people from all walks of life has equipped Chris well to pursue his chosen career in hotel and catering management. During his professional life he has worked in such diverse environments as Southern Africa, the US, Scotland, and the Middle East. Having led such a varied life has also meant that he has had many strange and amusing experiences. However, none was more bizarre than his frightening encounter with the Egyptian ghost who took umbrage with him in May 1995.

A CAIRENE POLTERGEIST

Chris Ingram's Story

Mohandoseen is one of the better suburbs of Cairo. Far from the crowds and the choking traffic of the central city, it is much favoured by foreign and expatriate visitors. Meaning 'Area of Engineers' in English, it is a district of spacious apartments surrounded by luxuriant gardens. It was here that Chris Ingram's Egyptian employers found him a large flat when he came to work for them in Cairo in the winter of 1993. Because the job of managing their chain of restaurants would be very demanding, they reasoned that he would need somewhere comfortable to spend his few leisure hours. So Mohandoseen was the natural choice.

When he first saw the flat Chris was frankly amazed. Large enough to house a whole family let alone one person, it had huge rooms with marble floors and 10-foot-high ceilings. It occupied half of the first floor of an eight-storey block of flats that had been built by an affluent Egyptian businessman to provide an income for his children. He and his wife then occupied this large apartment on the first floor until he died. After that, the flat was split with the strong-willed matriach living in one half and her daughter, Lula Hussein, living in the other half with her Palestinian husband. When the mother finally died, her flat was put out to rent.

'When I first moved into the flat there was something very cold about it and I could never work out why,' Chris recalled. 'Then Madame Lula explained that this was because nobody had lived in there on a regular basis since her mother had died ten years previously. In fact, the flat had only been rented out to Saudis and Kuwaitis for each summer.'

The firm rented the apartment for an initial period of six months. However, after that time Madame Lula, a short dumpy woman, asked Chris to stay on since his presence had succeeded in making the flat warm and lived-in again. He agreed and eventually stayed there for a total of 17 months.

'I then decided it was time to move on,' he explained. 'The place really was too big for one person and I had found a smaller, more convenient apartment elsewhere.'

When he broke the news to the Husseins they were dreadfully upset and tried hard to persuade Chris to stay. It was as if his decision to leave was a poor reflection upon them. Chris explained that this was certainly not the case, but to no avail. Finally and reluctantly the couple accepted the fact that they were to lose the young Englishman whom they had come to value not only as a tenant but also a friend. However, their fatalism was not matched by the spectral presence that shared the flat with Chris.

'Madame Lula often referred to "Mummy" as if her mother was still in the flat,' Chris said. 'And, to be honest, I often felt as if somebody was in there with me.'

On more than one occasion this *somebody* proved to be quite helpful. For example, there was the case of the candles. To the world's tourists, Cairo is famous for the Pyramids, but for its 13 million inhabitants the city is best known for the monumental power cuts that occur with monotonous regularity. Because of this, every household has a supply of candles stored in a convenient place. Chris's flat was no exception and he always ensured he knew where they were. It was only during a power cut lasting 24 hours that he realised his maid

232

had tidied the candles away and he had no idea where to find them in the dark.

'I went into the kitchen not knowing where she had put them,' he recalled. 'And for some reason I went to straight to the bottom cupboard, which I only opened to get bin bags out. I certainly didn't keep any candles in there. But that night I found a candle just sitting there. This may have been a simple coincidence, but seemed very strange at the time.'

During many subsequent power cuts over the following months, Chris was always 'helped' in this way. Until his very last evening in the apartment he was never 100 per cent sure whether some invisible presence was actually there helping him or if it was all in his mind. But on that hot May night a frightening series of incidents convinced him beyond shadow of doubt that the flat was haunted.

It all started with the carpet in the hall. As he carried one of his cases down the long passageway to his bedroom, the runner that secured the carpet unstuck itself and tripped him up. Thinking this a little strange, he picked himself up and went to the bedroom to pack. On a return journey with some more items to be packed, Chris actually saw the carpet detaching itself in a different place and rippling in front of him just before he was again tripped up.

Laughing in disbelief, he went into the kitchen to pack the cutlery and utensils into two crates stacked one on top of the other. Suddenly, the crate on the floor literally moved away just as he was about to place the other crate on top of it. Going into the spare bedroom, he began to clear out the wardrobe. As he opened the door, a beach ball that his nephew Peter had left behind after his last trip to Egypt flew out of the cupboard as if it had been thrown by someone.

Telling himself that there had to be a logical explanation for these small yet unsettling incidents, Chris went into his own bedroom to pack. It was then that he was overtaken by an eerie feeling that the whole flat had rejected him and he was no longer welcome there. Although it was very hot and the air-conditioning was off, he began to shiver so much that his arms became covered in goose pimples. However, much worse was to come.

One wall of his bedroom was dominated by a huge, ornate mirror measuring 8 by 12 feet. With an elaborate gilt frame and thick glass, the mirror would have needed at least two men to lift it. Yet, as he was packing his clothes, some invisible force threw the mirror across the room and it shattered on the floor in an explosion of glass.

'I could not believe my eyes. The mirror actually detached itself from the wall, moved about nine inches into the room and was then thrown onto the floor,' he told me. 'It was the most bizarre and terrifying thing I have ever seen in my life.'

With his sense of unease now turning into outright fear, Chris felt the need for a stiff drink. Fixing himself a large whisky, he went into the bathroom to put some water into the drink. As he poured water into the tumbler it was snatched out of his hand. He managed to grab it back, only to see it snatched a second time and smashed on the tiled floor. Chris now knew that Lula's mother was in the flat and was furious at him for leaving. He also knew that he had to do something to quieten the poltergeist or else he could be the next item to be smashed on the floor. Then he remembered the advice a spiritualist had once given him: *'If you have a bad spirit in a house, you must tell it to go away because it's frightening you.'*

He had treated the advice with some scepticism at the time, never thinking he would ever have to deal with a poltergeist. Now he was very grateful for the tip. Sitting down on his bed, he spoke quietly yet firmly to the presence.

'I think that you're upset because I'm leaving here, and if that's the case I'm very sorry but I really do have to go.'

After that, there was no more spectral activity that night, although the unfriendly atmosphere remained. The next morning the cold and unwelcome air in the place persisted and Chris vacated the apartment as quickly as possible. Before finally leaving he went next door to explain about the mirror.

'I'm very sorry about all the noise last night,' he said to Mr Hussein apologetically.

234

'What noise, Chris?' the big Palestinian asked with a puzzled frown.

'Well, the big mirror was smashed, didn't you hear it?' Chris asked.

'We heard nothing,' Mr Hussein replied.

Chris found this very odd because he knew that, as their bedroom backed onto his, the couple must have heard the commotion. Even stranger was their attitude to the broken mirror. Chris knew from what had been said in the past that it was a prized family heirloom and yet they refused any payment for its destruction. In fact, they brushed the whole matter aside as if it was best forgotten. His parting words to Chris were also very peculiar.

'We're very sad you are leaving because Madame Lula's mother would have liked you to stay here for ever.'

Chris is certain that the Husseins knew the apartment in Mohandoseen was haunted but could never admit it to an outsider no matter how friendly.

As I said in my dedication, Sylvia James was a tremendous help in the writing this book. However, her support went much further than continual encouragement for she also began finding paranormal experiences for me such as this one by Marti, her manicurist.

A DEVIL IN THE CITY OF ANGELS

Marti Uriarte's Story

Usually, the only supernatural evils to come out of Los Angeles' vast urban sprawl are the creations of Hollywood. The Uriarte family tell a different and more unsettling story. In 1971, Marti, her baby son Chris and her brother Robert were living with their sister and widowed mother at the family home in the town of San Gabriel, situated on the southern part of Los Angeles County. Since space was at a premium in the house, Marti and her sister slept in one room with baby Chris, whilst 17-year-old Robert slept on a settee in the room they called the den.

Marti's encounter with the paranormal started late one night when, for no apparent reason, she found herself wide awake and very frightened. In the doorway of the bedroom, she saw a figure in white. As her eyes became more accustomed to the dark, she realised that the mysterious figure was exceptionally tall, probably not far short of 8 feet.

Paralysed by fear, she watched as the intruder bent over and dipped its hands in the nappy bag hanging on the end of her son's crib. As it did this, the figure rocked back and forth. Desperately, Marti tried to nudge her sister awake, but she stubbornly slept on. Then, as if sensing Marti was awake, the apparition looked up and she saw her face for the first time.

'It was the most awful and frightening thing I have ever seen,' she recalled with a slight tremor in her voice.

Eyes of glowing coals stared out of a cadaverous face alive with a dreadful malice. Above peaked eyebrows the creature's hair stood straight up. Suddenly its mouth split into a horrid grin as it laughed silently and beckoned to Marti with fingers topped by 6-inch-long nails. Terrified for her baby son, Marti tried to scream but no sound emerged. Finally she managed to shake her head for she had no wish to go with this ghastly spectre.

Then, mercifully, her sister woke up.

'What is it, Marti?' she asked with drowsy annoyance.

'Look over by the door!' Marti hissed in a hoarse whisper.

'What?' her sister asked.

What indeed? For the figure had vanished.

Hearing the two girls talking, Mrs Uriarte came in to see what all the commotion was about. After hearing Marti's story, the old lady, a devout Catholic, said nothing but simply crossed herself. The next day, Mrs Uriarte called Marti to one side.

'I didn't want to tell you this last night,' she whispered, 'but I've called the priest in for an exorcism. You see, Robert saw exactly the same thing a few nights back.'

Like Marti, Robert did not know why he woke up in the middle of the night. At first he thought his mother had left a work light on. However, when he turned towards the desk where the lamp was situated, he realised that the illumination he could see did not come from any of the room lights. As he looked towards the unfocused glow, he became aware of a woman's silhouette in the area of the desk. To begin with, he thought the figure was his mother, but quickly dismissed this idea when he realised it was much taller than her. Then he began to fear that it was a burglar. However, intuition told him that this visitor was no common street thief. There was something strange and terrible about it, something inhuman. The realisation it was not of the normal living world filled him with fear and foreboding.

'She was looking down. Then she must have sensed me watching her, because suddenly she looked up and smiled, her face becoming a mass of wrinkles. Even when I talk about it now, my skin comes out in goose pimples.'

Looking towards him, the grinning hag began to beckon with bony fingers out of which grew long nails like talons. Although he was almost paralysed by fear, Robert dragged a blanket over his head and began praying. After a moment or two, he plucked up enough courage to make a break for the door. As he ran towards it, the old woman vanished. The next day, after some hesitation, he told his mother about the incident. However, when she dismissed it as a bad dream, he let the matter drop. Then, two weeks later, he overheard Marti discussing her experience with their mother.

'That really made me scared,' he said. 'For her experience was exactly the same as mine and I had not told her about it.'

'When I talked to Robert, his description of what he saw matched mine exactly,' Marti said emphatically. She also discounts any ideas that her brother's sighting fed her own imagination a few nights later, since he had spoken to nobody about it except their mother. 'He only talked about what he saw after he heard of my experience,' she explained, then added: 'I don't believe in spooks or the Devil, I never have.'

Then what did she think the figure was?

'Well, my mother thought it was the Devil,' she shrugged. Then a thoughtful frown crept across her beautiful olive face. 'But I just don't know. I wasn't dreaming, though. I definitely saw that thing, and so did Robert.'

Robert, who now practises as a lawyer on the West Coast of the United States, is similarly at a loss about what he saw. However, after the priest had called and performed a short exorcism, the old woman never bothered them again.

A thousand miles to the south-west of Los Angeles, there is the Mexican city of Monterrey. It is here that Carrier, the largest air-conditioning company in the world, have a manufacturing plant. In 1974, Martin Rosenfeldt was manager of this factory. A great deal was happening in Martin's life at that time. Not only was he studying for his Ph.D. in Business Administration, but he and his wife Enid were awaiting the birth of their fourth daughter. As things turned out, the little girl decided to arrive on the Fourth of July . . .

THE PHANTOM VOICE OF MUGUERZA

Martin and Enid Rosenfeldt's Story

This is one Independence Day that we certainly won't forget, Martin Rosenfeldt thought as he ran up the steps of the Muguerza hospital. Walking into the blessed cool of the echoing corridor, he saw his mother-in-law already seated, pretending to read a magazine. However, Martin was not fooled. She may have been a grandmother several times over, but he could see she was as nervous as if this were her first. Martin checked his watch, it was five minutes to three.

His wife Enid had already driven herself to the hospital and was in the latter stages of labour. There was nothing else to do but sit down and wait. Fortunately, Martin had had the foresight to bring the papers for his Ph.D. along so that he could use this time studying for his forthcoming exams. Experience told him that this could be a long wait.

As events unfolded, Enid gave birth to the baby 15 minutes later. However, the relief and joy at the birth was clouded by a fear gnawing away at her. She could not help noticing the palpable air of tension in the delivery room. She was also worried by the way the nursing sisters hurried away with the baby before she could hold it. As the nurses and doctors huddled over the little girl at one end of the delivery room, Enid sensed that something had gone terribly wrong, threatening the very life of her newborn child.

'Please,' she said, 'I want my husband.'

Nobody replied or took any notice of her. Fearing they had not understood, she repeated the plea in Spanish, but this met with a similar lack of success. What Enid could not know at that time was that the doctors and nurses were desperately trying to save her baby's life. As sometimes happens, the umbilical cord had wrapped itself around the baby's neck, effectively strangling her as she was pushed out of the womb. Now the little girl was the ugly blue colour of strangulation as the doctors fought a rearguard action to make her breathe.

At exactly the same time, Martin Rosenfeldt worked on, totally unaware of the drama unfolding a few feet away. Then, at ten past three, his concentration was broken by an announcement on the hospital's public address system. Martin remembers that it was one of the sisters who spoke.

'A little girl's life is in grave danger,' the voice said in Spanish. 'Please pray for her.'

'Say, did you hear that?' he asked his mother-in-law.

'Here what, dear?'

'That announcement asking us to pray for a little girl.'

'I didn't hear anything,' she replied.

For no reason that he could explain, Martin had a great feeling of concern. He walked over to the nurses at the reception desk and asked them about the announcement.

'There was no announcement, *señor*,' they replied.

'Are you quite sure?' he persisted. 'I just heard it.'

239

'There was nothing, *señor*,' the nurse reiterated with equal firmness.

Fearing that they might think him unbalanced, he let the subject drop and returned to wait for the birth of his daughter. Fortunately, the baby's life was saved by the doctors in that hospital. However, neither Martin nor Enid has ever been able to explain the mysterious voice of warning that apparently came from nowhere.

This next experience was the one which prompted Jessie Heard's initial phone call and happened when she was living in the Far East.

THE SENTRY

Jessie Heard's Hong Kong Experience

For both Britain and the United States 1941 was a black year. On 7 December, the same day they attacked Pearl Harbor, the Japanese invaded the British Colony of Hong Kong. Singapore, Malaya and Burma would also fall to Hirohito's forces within 12 months. In many cases, the Allies appeared to be grievously unprepared for such an aggressive and innovative invader. The arrival in Singapore of Japanese troops on bicycles is perhaps the most famous example of their unconventional yet successful military tactics.

However, it would be wrong to paint a picture of the Allies where lack of preparation was always the order of the day. For example, in the area of Hong Kong known as Wan Chai, there was a large Admiralty telephone exchange. Prior to the Japanese invasion, it was decided to build a second, secret exchange 200 feet underground so that communications could be maintained with the defending forces in the event of an attack. When, after three weeks of bitter fighting, Hong Kong finally fell, the victorious Japanese took over the Admiralty exchange and the underground one beneath it. With the

240

arrival of peace in 1945, the exchange reverted back to its former owners. However, for a number of years it stood idle while the Admiralty exchange coped with the growing traffic in military telecommunications.

In 1954, Jessie Heard and her two children sailed out to join her husband, who was serving a three year term as a sergeant with the British Army in Hong Kong. It did not take long for the life of unaccustomed leisure to pall and Jessie was soon looking around for something more stimulating than dinner parties to occupy her time. Fortunately, her years as an operator in English GPO exchanges set her in good stead and she successfully applied for a job in the military telephone network.

Normally, she would have worked at the Admiralty exchange in Wan Chai, but it had been severely damaged by a fire, so the old underground switchboard had been pressed into service once more. Only accessible by 150 steps cut into the earth, the exchange was a maze of dimly lit corridors and was indeed a gloomy place to work. Jessie did not mind, however, for she was delighted to have found a job she really enjoyed.

Apart from Jessie, a naval officer's wife called Ethel Dann and the teenaged daughter of a sergeant, the rest of the workforce were a mixture of Chinese and Portuguese drawn from the local community.

'With one hour on and one hour off, it was a nice easy job,' she recalled. 'But once a month we had to do a night duty, each person doing a three-hour shift.'

Because Jessie is one of those people who have difficulty sleeping once they have been awakened, she would often work through the night, leaving her colleagues to slumber on undisturbed. Anyway, you could usually count the number of nocturnal phone calls on the fingers of one hand, so the night work was not especially onerous. But there was one aspect of the job that Jessie quickly learned to loathe, and that was going to the toilet. The reason for this was that the lavatories were situated a long way from the actual exchange, down the complex of dingy corridors.

241

This would not have been too bad were it not for the fact that the passages had become the home of a colony of large spiders. Since they had the unnerving habit of suddenly jumping from one wall to another, every journey to the toilet became an unpleasant ordeal.

'If you were unlucky, one of these creatures would land on your face,' Jessie remembered. 'But when you had to go, you had to go.'

Then, late one night, when she was running this arachnidan gauntlet, Jessie saw something that would take her mind off her eight-legged friends for a while. Turning the first corner, she saw a shadowy figure at the end of the next corridor. This was especially unnerving since she knew that not only were all her colleagues fast asleep, but the exchange was locked against intruders.

However, drawing on all her reserves of courage, Jessie moved forward. As she walked closer to the figure she saw that it was dressed in a Japanese Army uniform, complete with a forage cap and neck guard to protect against sunburn. There was also something strangely insubstantial about the soldier, with his legs fading into nothingness below the knees. By the time she reached the spot where the ghostly sentry had been standing it had melted away, leaving nothing but 'a cold and shivery' atmosphere.

Dreading what she might see on the return journey, Jessie ran as fast as she could, but of the phantom soldier, there was no sign. Any thoughts that the apparition might have been a figment of her imagination were dispelled during her next spell on night duty. Once again she encountered the sentry on his lonely vigil in the spider-infested passageways. It was then that she approached one of the WRAC sergeants and told her of what she had seen. To Jessie's surprise, her story was taken perfectly seriously, without a hint of the scorn and disbelief she expected.

'Look, Mrs Heard, do us all a favour will you,' the sergeant had said. 'Don't say anything about this to the others or it will only scare them. If the Chinese get to hear of it we'll have a

242

mass exodus on our hands – you know how superstitious they are.'

As it was, some of the Chinese had also seen the phantom soldier and told the sergeant about the 'dead bad man' walking in the passage. She had simply laughed at them, hoping this would dispel the matter once and for all. As for Jessie, she did not discuss the ghost with any of her colleagues except Mrs Dann, who had recently moved to another military exchange.

'No, you're not mad and you're not hallucinating,' the other woman replied. 'I've seen that Japanese soldier down there as well and wild horses would not drag me back to that exchange either day or night!'

After that, Jessie saw the sentry on his spectral duty every time she worked in the exchange at night. Strange as it might seem, he became part of the work routine and she found she no longer had to steel herself when turning that particular corner. Or was it so strange? After all, except for the initial fright, the ghost had done her no harm. In fact, there was something rather sad and pathetic about the Japanese. Perhaps sudden death had trapped him in the underground corridors for eternity. She never became used to those large spiders, though; they always scared her to death.

My family has a had a long connection with Australia. It began during the last century when Charles Stacey, my great-great-uncle, went out to seek his fortune in the goldfields. Like thousands of others, he failed to make his fortune there. However, today his descendants are still making their mark in Australia. Philippa, one of Charlie's great-granddaughters, runs a television company with her husband Jim Davern. Today, their series *A Country Practice* is watched by millions of viewers not only in Australia but also around the world. My sister Priscilla and her husband David have also made Australia their home and founded Kangaroo Press, a very busy and successful book publishing company. This next story, which involves both these families, is certainly typical of many hauntings I have encountered. As unexpected as it was brief, it happened to someone who, paradoxically, still does not believe in ghosts.

COUSIN JOAN

David Rosenberg's Experience

Wollombi is a small village in the heart of the Hunter Valley near to Australia's main wine-producing region. It was here that Jim and Philippa Davern bought a weekend retreat that had previously belonged to an artist. Tucked high above the dirt road and surrounded by gum trees, it was the perfect place to escape from the pressures of life in Sydney. Philippa's mother Joan, granddaughter of Charles Stacey, also loved the place, and she stayed there on many occasions before her death in 1988.

When they were not using the house themselves, Jim and Philippa would often lend the place out to friends such as Priscilla and David Rosenberg. One weekend in the Australian summer of 1991, Priscilla and David travelled up to Wollombi for a few days. One of the couple's favourite pastimes when they stayed there was to drive around the neighbouring vineyards. It was after arriving back from such an excursion that David had his paranormal experience. It was twilight when they arrived back at the house and David went to unlock the door whilst Priscilla unloaded the car.

As he pushed the door open, David realised that someone else was in the house. On entering the lounge, he saw Joan, Philippa's mother, walking towards him with a welcoming smile on her face. At the time, the encounter was so sudden and unexpected that he did not even think it strange to see somebody who had died three years previously. However, he did notice that Joan had a rather ephemeral and unreal air about her. David went to switch the light and when he turned back Joan had gone.

Now this may sound very strange, but David did not share his experience with Priscilla immediately. In fact, it was not

244

until some months later that he told her about the sighting of Cousin Joan, as everyone affectionately called her. Even then, he did not describe her as a ghost but simply said: 'A funny thing the other night at Wollombi, I saw Joan.'

When he told Philippa of his experience she smiled and said: 'Mum loved Wollombi, in fact her ashes are scattered there.'

Although he has been married to my sister Priscilla for over 25 years, I do not know David very well. However, on the occasions I have met him, he has always struck me as a very down-to-earth north countryman who uses words sparingly. He is certainly not somebody who is prone to 'seeing things'.

'If anyone was going to have an experience like that, you would think it would be me,' Priscilla told me on a recent visit to England. Not David, who has little or no truck with the supernatural. (She also recalled that the couple had their Rhodesian Ridgeback 'Ruff' with them at the time. The dog showed no signs of agitation, which is unusual for dogs when they are in haunted houses.)

However, as has often been shown throughout this book, that is not the way the supernatural works. Take Geoff Smith, for example, who encountered those phantom soldiers at Bosworth ('Richard's Pikemen,'), or Jos Winnen, who also saw a ghost in the Buckinghamshire cottage he was renovating ('A Haunting Dilemma,' Chapter 5). Like David, they do not believe in ghosts, but this did not stop them having vivid paranormal experiences without any explanation.

10

A Cautionary Tale

THE ADMIRAL

The Landlord's Story

It was nearly eleven o'clock and the main bar of The Roebuck pub near Reading, Berkshire, was packed with Friday night revellers. Suddenly, the landlord pointed towards one of the large picture windows that overlooked the Thames.

'Look at that figure,' he said. 'Isn't that the Admiral?'

A hush fell on the bar as everyone turned towards the window. Then people gasped in surprise and fear. Walking past the large picture windows was the silhouette of an eighteenth-century admiral. Moments later, the figure had vanished from sight.

The incident caused a sufficient sensation to make the local newspapers. The Roebuck had always had the reputation of being 'The most haunted pub in Berkshire' with little or nothing to show for it. However, now there was a confirmed sighting of the eighteenth-century admiral who had haunted the building since he fell to his death trying to rescue his dog 200 years earlier.

THE LAST WORD

A phantom Admiral seen by a pub full of people? Well, the art of good storytelling is to save the best until last and this certainly is a riveting example of the paranormal. Or is it? Sadly, this tale is not quite what it seems. In fact although this incident happened it had very little to do with the supernatural. The Admiral *was* seen in The Roebuck in 1993 and when I went to investigate, I really thought I was on to an extremely good true ghost story. I was to be disappointed.

'To tell you the truth, I don't believe in all this nonsense about ghosts,' the landlord quietly confided in me.

'What about the Admiral then?' I asked.

'I don't know who he was and neither I nor any of my family've seen him.'

'But what about all those people who saw him in the bar?'

'Oh that,' he laughed in that peculiarly rasping way heavy smokers have. 'Well, when I first arrived here last year, I got so fed up with people asking me if I'd seen the Admiral, I hired an admiral's costume from a carnival novelty shop in Reading. Then I waited until nearly closing time one Friday night and got a member of staff to walk along the scaffolding we had outside the windows, dressed up in the costume. Well, that certainly showed the punters.' Finally, he added the *coup de grâce*. 'Then this young reporter chap heard about it and came round. Well, I didn't like to disappoint him because it made such a *good* story!'

Apparently, it still is a good story. When I cycled home from work the other night, I passed The Roebuck and could not help noticing that a sign had been placed on the grass verge opposite the building. What it said on it, brought a smile to my face: 'Rooms To Let. Some Haunted!'

I have finished this book with this story not with the purpose of casting doubt on the other experiences – far from it. I merely wish to show that when investigating the paranormal and supernatural, you have to do it with an open and healthily sceptical mind. Because it is an area that seems to defy the normal laws of nature, it is often difficult to verify incidents and this makes it a minefield for the unwary. However, I firmly believe that the end result is so rewarding and fascinating that it is well worth that risk